V&R unipress

V&R unipress

Plamen K. Georgiev

The Bulgarian Political Culture

Mit 2 Abbildungen, 4 Grafiken und 17 Tabellen

V&R unipress

FSC
Mix
Produktgruppe aus vorbildlich bewirtschafteten Wäldern, kontrollierten Herkünften und Recyclingholz oder -fasern
Zert.-Nr. GFA COC 1229
www.fsc.org
© 1996 Forest Stewardship Council

„Dieses Hardcover wurde auf FSC-zertifiziertem Papier gedruckt. FSC (Forest Stewardship Council) ist eine nichtstaatliche, gemeinnützige Organisation, die sich für eine ökologische und sozialverantwortliche Nutzung der Wälder unserer Erde einsetzt."

Bibliografische Information der Deutschen Nationalbibliothek

Die Deutsche Nationalbibliothek verzeichnet diese Publikation in der Deutschen Nationalbibliografie; detaillierte bibliografische Daten sind im Internet über http://dnb.d-nb.de abrufbar.

ISBN 978-3-89971-356-5

Gedruckt auf alterungsbeständigem Papier.

Contents

Preface

»We, Bulgarians, sit not that close to God's mantel, as other nations...« – thus bitterly Prof. Marko Semov – a most penetrating connoisseur of the Bulgarian national character. Indeed, we, Bulgarians are Christians, but »still« orthodox, yet Greek and not Russian orthodox. Even though as close linked to Russia ever since our Liberation from Turkish oppression and the foundation of the new Bulgarian national state (1908). We are considered to be a »young nation«. But, we still inherit more than 1300 years of own history, as one of the oldest states here on the Balkans and in Europe. Being well aware of all this, we seem not so proud, however, as other nations. Patriotic feelings are buried deeper in the Bulgarian heart, for there is not much to be praised in our past, less even in the present.

The Bulgarian cultural spirit has been still grasped most successfully in »an optimistic theory on the Bulgarian people« (Ivan Hadjiski, 1938). And this after 5 wars lost, and 2 most devastating national catastrophes, starting from 1912 onwards! The Bulgarian political culture, however, is not just a matter of history. It has less to do with systematic political theory even. »Political cultures are learned« – so Almond and Verba, as they unveiled a most fascinating field of comparative study of political behaviors of nations decades ago. We could add from this side of the Balkans: they are suffered in an own way. But do we really »learn«? Do we utilize their immense creative potential indeed? Or, what seems more relevant, ignore and even crash them in a most resoulute, inherited »barbarian« pattern?

Political cultures appear more than ever a matter of rationale choice in a rapidly changing world and (what still count), a chance indeed (Weber). The collapse of communism in Eastern Europe has changed the old paradigms. Within the initial chaos of »transition« a new critical rationalism seems to emerge, as related to the shaping of new structures of social and political life. Nations have lost, but also gained on significance. And this occurs in a wider context that goes beyond sheer borders. Many collective identities are not relevant to their old frameworks, bounding territories, languages, or even religious beliefs. Ideologies fail to motivate significant and moreover desired societal change. We are »on the road« again, but seem less aware where we are headed to (Baumann).

Politics discovers new scopes of interests, as it faces immense new responsibilities in a world of growing uncertainty. Thus the shaping *civic cultures* in Eastern Europe, relevant to the new tasks and risks of our civilization seem in a way »in«, but in a rather »twisted« way. The »ex-socialist« brothers and sisters are not inspired by the idea to inevitably »kiss capitalism« (Giddens). At least not its repulsive shapes and forms, offered in the East. Thus the question of the shaping new political identities in many Eastern countries seems more crucial than ever. Could those cultures master the craft of not just »coping« other's experience, but make own contribution for the European integrity, from which all nations could profit? As we believe, this might well be possible. But not before a systematic, deeper fusion of mutually responsible and sharing cultures occurs. Europe is not so much some realm, but a competitive field of this new political architecture in shape. It is, as we believe, the one of a new European identity in which political cultures will have to add a new quality to societal structures of the present. For, it is the present and not so much the past, which determines our future in an interdependent, still too risky world.

This book is a contribution to the long delayed and most suffered European future of my nation. I hope that it will support scholars, politicians, or even men of art, to better grasp the Bulgarian cultural spirit. But what might give even more sense to my research efforts is the new generation both in the East and in the West, which might utilize the ideas of this book and upgrade a new Europe. One-way to reach such a capacity is *to add specific experience,* as related to the cultural diversity of Europe in the framework of its shaping new integrity.

Christianity and paganism have mixed together in most peculiar patterns and forms at this side of the Balkans. They have molded the unique conglomerate of a Bulgarian unilateral nation. The latter, as this book shows, proved to be European, long before it has fully shaped into a nation. The land where couple of religions and a variety of ethnic groups »mixed« into an amazing life style of tolerance and a sense for worthiness of others, may well be a cultural pattern worth following in our most perplexed post-modern age.

Here, at both sides of the Balkan, one will find no »Silicon Valley", but a real »Valley of the Roses«. The »Golden sands« of the Black sea offer more than generosity of Nature. So does the Rhodopi Mountain, which still hides the chants of Orpheus ...Mysticism has never ruled however over the pragmatic Bulgarian mind. One reason for this might well be his »instinctive realism«, that has prevented him from most temptations. Except the one of »big politics«, which we have always considered as a great chance, but most often paid its high price for decades on.

How come, that a small people like the Bulgarians, survived hundreds of years of oppression, different cultural dominances, most devastating wars, but still managed to keep its cultural identity? Was it our devoted Christian tradition, which protected the Bulgarian national spirit? Or. More likely, as some believe, the sharp daggers of our ancestors, who voted »like one« in April 1876 to raise against the Ottoman Empire in favor of liberty and sacred freedom?

Cynical attitude to politics and politicians of all featherings, mistrust in both government and state, corruptive style of business and politics, etc. »at this side of Europe« – shaped the fermenting »mix« of the Bulgarian political culture. Some define its present stand in terms of a *»defective« -democratic transition.* (Merkel, 2001) Still Bulgaria has dared to join the old European family, and did this with own dignity and resolution. As I shall try to illustrate, this nation has both the cultural and political capacity to undertake its new responsibility in a wider European context. Democratic values are not less »embedded« in the Bulgarian heart and mind, compared to other European nations. We still have to put order in its own yard and in a typical *ad hoc* go even beyond the trivial frameworks of sheer reforms.

As I believe, the sharp European public eye, has not just to look behind the *façade* of projected (media performed) »images« of Bulgaria. European citizens should understand better a new/old European comer. And, what counts even more, is that we have to discover together a two-way road to a new common European future. As Karl Jaspers stressed once: »we shall be Europeans in so far we learn to be human«. This is the simple message of my book, which I offer to the English speaking readers worldwide. I shall consider its mission for achieved; in so far it backs the idea of a deeper European integrity of my nation. For this is what political cultures come and go off the world stage. But not before they are lived and suffered through.

I would like to thank Prof. Klaus von Beyme, Prof. Wolfgang Merkel, Prof. M. R. Lepsius, and other dedicated friends from the University of Heidelberg, as well as the DAAD, who backed my academic efforts mid in couple of crisis and devastating wars on the Balkans. I am very much obliged to Prof. Marko Semov, who has encouraged my »nation wide« scope of research, but left us earlier to judge on it. I thank also Misha Weigl and Mariana Marinova for the translation of substantial fragments of the text into English language.

Last, but not least, I would like to thank V&R unipress Göttingen for their dedicated work and patience, needed to bring this book to the European reader

Sofia – Langgöns bei Gießen, The Author
January 2007

Introduction

Paradigms of political culture: An Eastern-European outlook

Two basic approaches determine the analysis of political cultures, grasped as typical behavioral patterns of interaction of bigger social groups (nations) with their political »objects« – institutions, systems of governance, or even cultural and religious traditions and styles, as related to power and politics. The general difference between both has been most clearly pointed out by D. Berg-Schlosser. Therefore it seems worthy to remind it here. The first one of Karl Marx – builds on the premise that it is the *structure*, grasped as an independent variable, which determines the norms, and by converting them into concrete acts, the behavior of individuals and groups, as members of society. The second one, as in the case of Max Weber claims that it is the *normative system*, or the operationally determined social and group values, which shape the individual and group behavior. This gives birth to social structures, i.e. the way capital is accumulated, is influenced, by certain values and norms of the protestant ethics.

This brief dichotomy seems still limited to us, as it sticks to some notorious idea of *»Kultur an sich selbst«*. Culture is a most complex phenomenon, bound to specific meaning, prescribed by its adherents to social facts, as Dürkheim has showed us. Thus, a clearer and more detailed vision of the existing paradigms of political culture seems in demand. At least 6 approaches to the comparative studies of political cultures have more or less clearly shaped in the last decades. Let us brief them here as to get a better notion of the specific field of study, tackled from different points of view:

- The first one is represented by some psychological attempt (Parsons, Shills) and most explicitly by Almond and Verba's, as to »compare« in a systematic framework typical (modal) political orientations of couple of nations in a post-WW II era.
- The second one is the attempt of a *»Verstehende Soziologie«* of some post-Weber inspiration, to study those orientations and behaviors, as »carried« into politics and political life – Tucker (1973), Geertz (1983).
- The third one is to be related to some post-Dürkheim tradition of *»objective study«* of political cultures, as embedded in a given society through its dominating norms and values.
- A fourth one, known as *heuristic,* uses hypothetic »ideal types« of social and cultural constructs, which tried to »explain« authoritarian, or even cynical values, as by Lipset (1960) or Bell (1964).

- A fifth one is the *linguistic* – reflecting the discourse on the meaning, which certain political objects shape in the mind of the individuals or groups (Winch, 1958).
- Last, but not least, to be mentioned here is a »dualistic« approach which uses the concept of political culture in a rather ambivalent way, grasping culture as »everything«, which often leads to ... nothing.[1]

In one way or another a systematic, complex, interpretative approach seemed most acceptable in our case, To us John Gibbin's conclusion, as related to the modern studies of political cultures, seems to a great extend still relevant to our present reality:

> »The study of political culture is thus the historical account of their emergence, a critical analysis of the political and economic forces they represent, a study of their internal character and a vigorous critique or negation of their logic and effect«.[2]

Some »libertarian« approach to the field of study has spread in the last decades as well, as we could witness. This has lead to most unrealistic, non-historical, or even »pseudo-interpretative« comparative studies of political cultures. We have ignored such formalized (or even open partisan-oriented) »contributions« to the field. What is of special interest for us here – is not so much a disputable, less even rationalist debate on the »system transition« of post-communist cultures. We are more concerned on the shaping of new social structures and forms, as related to their internal dynamics and own creative capacity. We shall try to add to this field of study, with all the risks at stake.

***

Political cultures after the fall of the Berlin wall, and beyond this symbolic act, seem to have lost on importance. At least what concerns a »dull consensus« on some ultimate »mix« of their *»parochial«, »subject«* and *»participant«* elements, as guarantee for structural stability (Almond and Verba, 1963).

The general impression is that political cultures, which operated until recently within the totalitarian regimes, rapidly lost their meaning. At the same time, as it seems to us, they followed some inertia of their conservative social nature to deviate from some initial democratic mainstream.

1 Plamen Geogiev, Balgarskata politicheska kutura (The Bulgarian political culture), K&M, Sofia, 2000, pp. 18–25.

2 Gibbins, John R. (Ed.) Politics in a Post-modern Age, Sage Publications, London, 1989, see: Preface: Contemporary Political Culture: an Introduction by John R. Gibbins.

Moreover – a variety of *quasi-political sub-cultures* seems to have shaped in Eastern Europe, which turn old theoretical frameworks and marks into less useless instruments.

Global structures and ideas in a digitalized world encouraged patterns and forms of political »inclusion« and »exclusion« of certain social groups from what was until recently regarded as »public arena« of civic cultures. As the experience of »transitions« in the last 17 years showed, the Balkans offer a most »peculiar« variety of such *»hybrid political cultures«*. They are in support of democracy and market economy, but still lean on old experienced (or even recycled ideas) and schemes of cultural protectionism. This backs a »new-old elite« and a *status quo,* where significant and desired social change is being postponed, or even redefined in less acceptable terms.

A new kind of escapism has overwhelmed the initial democratic hopes and »revolutionary« energy in Eastern Europe. The state(s) – or what is left of it, turned into intermediary between disputable »actors« of an imposed system and most uncertain governments. The »fragmented« and perplexed political culture in transition not only tolerated, but practically backed in its own way shadow schemes of criminal allocation of wealth, accumulated in the years of »real socialism«. The idea that this is just a transitory stage of some metamorphoses of capitalism with human face, which sooner or later might offer its paternalistic care to the masses, is even less persuasive. The great expectations are gone. Capitalism at this side of the Balkans, proved to be a most tasteless *»ornament of Satan«* (Weber).

More than that – the lack of political ideas and adequate managerial skills among the newborn elites in those countries has opened a real Pandora box of anti-democratic, authoritarian, or even asocial activity, revitalizing structural remnants of the passed. All this is matched with most populist notions of freedom, social justice, or even social security. The result is an ambiguous cluster of corruptive practices that have eroded the institutions, encouraged criminal »shadow economy«, ruined vital state and public sectors, as people are pushed back to historically rejected and most primitive means of production. This leads to decline of cultural traditions and even achievements of modern civilization.

The »lack of strategies«, or the voluntarism of a revolution »from above« have been often blamed for most of these misfortunes in Eastern Europe. Other arguments have stressed on the state-centered economies, dominated by ex-communist parties in Eastern Europe. That fact that most of them failed to go in pace with the demands for significant, but not less desired societal change is obvious. A third source of argumentation is the *swap of sovereignty*, or merchandizing of geo-strategic positions in favor of »better" positioning in a global world of growing uncertainty.

What we face today is deepening crises of collective and national identities in most Eastern European countries. As nationalism (whatever brand), xenophobia, religious fundamentalism etc. spread at this side, new structures that emerge seem less predictable than at the start of the transition.

It is often claimed that the grass rooting of civic cultures of a participant type, might be a savior, or give some second breath to proper democratic and social change in Eastern Europe. This approach seems to have reached its limits. There are number of reasons in favor of this. What we find out is that a new culture of abstaining from involvement into politics and political life has shaped in most Eastern European countries. The public common sense has grasped (after a decade of quasi- dissident and oppositional activity) that the values of real freedom and democracy have been swapped by the initial leaders of the »democratic revolutions« against life-long protection and/or oligarch-bound ruling status. The New Deal – more glocal (Baumann) – has ended with the biggest robbery of the XX c., the illegal »privatization« not only pauperized whole nations in transition. It has reached an extreme, as related to its incompatibility with modern forms of labor and capital accumulation.

The energy that has propelled this chaotic quasi-democratic and social change is even more frightening. Clear markers of old ideologies are out No innovative capacity seems able to give a new meaning to politics and political life. What is then to be done? The answer is – not much – but still a lot. This means that a new paradigm is in shape. As we believe, this bitter rationalization means that national identities have to change – both in the East and in the West, as they merge together. We have not so much to encourage (or offer remote control) but shape together political cultures of a new type. The latter have to contribute not so much for »keeping order«, less even support an ill functioning (and morally discredited) *status quo.* They must add new meaning to political life – as they involve citizens in the immediate political decision making processes. Europe can flourish only as a creation of sovereign participants, as it undertakes the role of arbitrary, but only if we all decide on our own destiny. Thus, as we believe, political cultures turn into priority. They are more than ever bound on their capacity to generate proper democratic structures and add new quality to a world, which is to be improved.

This could occur, however, only if the process of transition becomes mutual and sharing.

Chapter 1: Roots of the Bulgarian Traditional Political Culture

Features of Bulgarian Parochialism

It would be most fair to look for the specific features of the Bulgarian parochial culture[3] and its traditional shapes and forms, as springing out of the values of Eastern orthodoxy. The latter, as is well known, lagged behind the massive process of spiritual revival, initiated by the West European Renaissance. This approach followed most recognized Bulgarian historians such as Iv. Shishmanov, or Bojan Penev, since the beginning of the XX c. In this context the *incompatibility* of the Bulgarian traditional culture is the first significant marker to differentiate it from Western European values and social structures. This difference goes beyond the formal criteria. It springs form a deeper demarcation line between both religions and their spheres of influence.

> »Indeed the West European Renaissance had an impact only on the Catholic world – as Iv.Shishmanov, one of the most respected Bulgarian historians in the end of XIX c. This is the reason why its refreshing Spirit touched only The Check and the Polish and partially the Serb-Croats on the Adriatic Sea, out of all Slavic people. The Orthodox world, the whole South and Eastern Slavic community, together with Byzantium, stayed aside from this great cultural and historical process. Byzantium could not raise up the humanity in Eastern Europe up to a

3 The concept of »parochial culture« (in terms of Almond and Verba) is rather formalized, as relevant to the traditional type of religiously influenced patterns of political interactions in a community of people. The meaning of the world parochial is related to the Greek *»parochia«* – the smallest unit of territorially and religiously bound community. The big diversity of religions (still existing forms of paganism) and other lofestyles on the Balkans added more secular connotation to Bulgarian parochialism The latter as institution had certain control not only on the religious, but the cultural, educational and professional activity of the Bulgarian diaspora within the Ottoman Empire. This process of amalgamation and building of own cultural identity, as part of some initial political emancipation, culminated in 1861 when the Bulgarian Church has been declared for independent after over two decades of igorous religious fights. On secular aspects of »parochial« see for more details: Cambridge International Dictionary of English, Cambridge University Press, 1995, p. 1027.

> new spiritual, creative, moral and social height, as Italy did in the epoch of the Renaissance and Humanism .«[4]

The alienation of the Bulgarian parochial culture from the European one determines to a great extend the patterns of uncertainty and deeply rooted mistrust of Bulgarians towards their social surrounding. This casts a dark shadow on the intimate world of the parochial Bulgarian and hindered him from significant achievements of his social creativity for ages. A most expressive emotionality darkens the parochial Bulgarian mind, enchaining him to his introvert, internally limited world, bounding him to isolation and a kind of an enclave spiritual existence that is notorious for the Balkans. This process has even deepened after the fall of the Bulgarian kingdom under Turkish yoke. (XIV c).

To get a vivid impression on this we have to only remind some paragraphs of older writers who dared to dig deeper in the Bulgarian parochial mentality:

> »The man of the shepherds flute – as one of the most gifted scholars in the field – Galabov depicts the figure of the Bulgarian of the long passed – whose suffered spirit filled five hundred years of most humiliating slavery, was a man of an introvert nature, deeply alienated from his surrounding world, as anyone with such a destiny, living in his closed circuit of highest emotionality. The culture, which the oppressed Bulgarian managed to create spontaneously, despite the all-alien influences, was an emotional culture. The emotional man of the shepherds flute had no sense of the material culture and because of this, hardly managed to create anything significant in this respect, as he grasped too little from the aliens. The man of the shepherds flute had to exist deprived of the material culture since he was deeply alienated from the joys of the surrounding world. He lived through his emotionality, being his only chance. Left without material culture, poor and shabby, he was after all a slave of his own heart, because of his emotional attitude to the real world and the only capacity left – to observe this reality and embed it in his creativity. But by no means to confront it and put it under own creative control, as the sober Greek does this. His heart was his only destiny.«[5]

This *existential pattern* shaped for centuries the general concepts of the parochial Bulgarian, as related to power and domination, social order, or lifestyle, in other words most of the elements of the traditional political culture, placed in its universal civilization context. No doubt we could speak of a significant turn over of this »*enclave mentality*« not earlier than the new era of Bulgarian revival, crowned by the most creative work of Paisij

---

4 Ibid.

5 Konstantin Galabov, »Chovekat na kavala. Chovekat na Ribnia bukvar. Chovekat na Balkana«, Iztok 1, 1926, Nr. 15. See also: Zasto sme takiva. V tarsene na balgarskata kulturna identichnost, Sofia, 1994, p. 205–207.

Hilendarski – »History of Bulgarian Slavs« (XI c.) This unique Bulgarian cultural event, delayed as it is, had a great cultural impact and in its own way re-established the dramatically cut off cultural links of Bulgaria with the European cultural mainstream, after 500 years of Turkish oppression. This exceptional cultural act had the significance of re-adoption into the realm of the civilized world, of which a small, but heroic people, as the Bulgarians saw themselves, having been drastically cut off for more than 500 years.

As Galabov (ibid) pointed out,

> »A New age comes however, starting with Paisij and a significant change occurs in the Bulgarian spirit,« It discovered a new life phase. As he woke from the deep sleep of his emotionality, the Bulgarian sobered into the reflectivity of an adolescent. The impact of the alien factors was no doubt great, as they came from the West, to bring ideas, which he started to grasp during his revival. But one cannot explain all this only with the impact of alien and conditional factors. Such explanations, which are essentially based on the search of causes for all cultural phenomena in their environment, lack rigor and are therefore inadequate. At the center of each culture there hides a creative organizing core, whereby the life of a Spirit is first of all a manifestation and immediately after a reflection of some external stimuli...« [6]

The typology of *»the man of the shepherds flute«,* the *»one of the Fish reader«* and *»the man of the Balkan»,* even though strongly influenced by Nietzsche, reflects in a most inventive psychological way the metamorphoses of the Bulgarian national character in the transition from the old parochial mentality to the one of the New age. Pacing thresholds in his historical and cultural development, even later than other European nations, this thrive of the Bulgarian spirit impresses most observers with it's civilization courage. This adds specific meaning to the Bulgarian culture, which considered lesser, as we believe, rational »outputs« or outcomes of its spontaneous movements in one direction or other. But has always been loyal to some internal voice of our own. This culture has stayed aside from rationale rules and regulations, as conditionally required by modern civilization, but has been in constant search of an unreachable *internal sense of freedom,* which we trace to our present.

All this links Bulgarians with some *paganism* that relates us to over 1 300 years of own history. The ruthlessness and »Gods denial« of the Bulgarian go hand in hand with his incredible human feeling and warm heartedness. This penetrates; in it's own way, into his world of politics. The latter seems however pushed aside, even out of reach in his mind. The indigenous people of the Balkans are still to a great extent slaves to their own superstitions, prejudices and related belief systems. The parochial Bulgarian, as consequence of some childish instinct of self-protection, pushes him away from all that seems alien to him, even though it might be a progressive or

6 Ibid.

useful development. At the same time he is often ready to embrace any imported idea, even though as false, or totally inadequate to his reality. One could claim this to be a rather desperate attempt of his own to get rid of a most humiliating lack of original ideas, which usually has led Bulgarians into so many dead end streets. But that is hardly the case. What is more relevant is that fruitful and significant ideas have often been neglected, or even sunk without trace in this culturally enslaved realty of the Balkans.

The tragic historical and cultural development of the Bulgarian people is another constant dominance, which predetermines in its specific way the forms and shapes of the Bulgarian parochial culture. Most often this sense has crystallized a notorious *fatalism* deeply rooted in the Bulgarian mentality. Many authors found the reasons for this in the constant deprivation of any chance for material progress. Whilst cultural and social progress here on the Balkans has occurred, it has differed from what some might see as a more guaranteed and protected social model in Europe. This tragic notion has strongly eroded the Bulgarian mentality and his cultural notions of a complex and less known world in which he tends to believe he is disadvantaged in a way. This, as we would like to illustrate below, has it's own grounds:

> »To get a full grasp of the tragic national fate of Bulgarians – as bitterly briefed by Iv. Shishmanov in his profound historical writings – all we have to remind here is that the epoch of the Western European renaissance is an epoch or great discoveries – the discovery of the new world and the Antic one, the discovery of America, from one side and Ancient Greece and Rome, from the other; this is the epoch of the invention of the printing art, which made easy in technical respect the distribution of the ideas through the book; this is the epoch of most genius masters of the words, painting and marble...
>
> From all those wonders of a rich material, intellectual, moral and esthetic culture Bulgaria has seen nothing. Right at that time... our semi-literate monks, the only representatives of the Bulgarian intelligentsia in those dark ages – copied in labors and scarcity the Holly texts and painted icons, which reflected the whole dogmatic conditionality and scheme of Byzantium arts.
>
> This was the point where a people, which in the relatively longer period of political tranquility, short before its fall under Ottoman oppression, at the epoch of Ivan Alexander and Patriarch Evtimij – did a most energetic attempt to revive his literature and even to add national color to it. One could say that Bulgaria in the epoch of Ivan Alexander was on the road of renewal in many ways. And indeed in some areas we can witness signs of a Renaissance, as feeble as they are.«[7]

Another significant reason for this most depressing but realistic conclusion is the difference between the way in which the traditional Bulgarian culture

7 Ibid.

developed – from the epoch of our Revival – as compared to that of most European people, who experienced new economic forms that opened the road for transition from the feudal economy to capitalism. Bulgaria never became part of the progressive trend of that time, which determined the structures of most civic societies in Europe. Consequently, Bulgaria never experienced this crucial structural and cultural change. Such a long historical period, with its related socio-economic consequences, has had a negative impact on its political culture.

> »The Western European Renaissance is one of the most significant social and economic phenomena,« Shishmanov goes on to say, »Its typical characteristics, its psychic, its theory and practice are to be explained today also with the deep changes in the social and economic order of the Middle centuries; the transition from old feudal type of economy to capitalism, but with the increased economic status of the Italian citizenship. Bulgaria not only in XI c., but also up to the end of its political existence (before the fall under the Turks) had no conscious citizenship, as was the Italian (later on the French, the English and the German). Bulgaria at that time was a feudal state, which just started to experience initial forms of community life«.[8]

Chained to his notorious primitivism and scarce lifestyle, the Bulgarian experienced a constant sense of *»material deprivation.«* Later on the prominent Bulgarian sociologist Ivan Hadjijski would find the origins of the eruptive revolutionary sacrifice of the leaders of the April insurrection against the Ottoman Empire (1876) in just this state. The Bulgarian lived for long in an extreme and introverted *parochialism* (Almond and Verba). The functions of the latter have been reduced to maintaining in latent form the potentially creative energies of a people, which were frequently dissipated in so many historical and political ventures, here at the heart of the Balkan.

However, as we can witness in a broader European context, the abstaining, the oppression and the *conscious postponing* of worthy spiritual and cultural self-realization in this Bulgarian existence, shape sustainable if not typical features of his parochialism in the era before the National revival (XVII c.). With the wisdom of hindsight we can say that this puts a dark spot on the Bulgarian soul and overrides most of the conditional chronic periods, used by historians in their attempt to rationalize and explain the series of down turns and pogroms, which occurred in our erratically shaped, yet *discrete* cultural-political »evolution«.

The lack of our own traditional patterns, as generators of significant national creativity, has many objective grounds and reasons. Among them all, however, we could clearly point out the failure of the Bulgarian people to re-produce own national aristocracy and spiritual leaders, especially after the

8 Ibid, p. 78.

fall under Turkish yoke. This abrupt collapse had the effect of marginalizing the Bulgarian nation as related to a common European pattern of transition to civic societies. Any attempt to grasp the internal dynamics and character of the Bulgarian political culture cannot ignore the crucial role played by the absence of *credible own-national elites*. Most foreign and Bulgarian scholars agree on this. Shishmanov's reflections seem clearer than many others and are worth quoting at length:

> »Left without aristocracy, without higher clergy, without leaders, the Bulgarian lived through the age of his slavery as a simple peasant,« he wrote. He went on to suggest that the most positive qualities of this psychological type are even though still to be appreciated, as they relate to: »a fanatic love to the land he works on, most close adherence to the native faith and traditions, parochial dedication to his family and it's virtues, iron industriousness, modest and thrifty way of life, feeling for democracy and a thrive to progress.«[9]

Thus the primitivism, the narrow mindedness, the stroked egocentrism of a type of most peculiar *Bulgarian individualism*, might be considered as a bitter fruit of his long-term cultural isolation indeed. This in no way diminishes a number of not less significant and still less studied virtues of his suffered soul. Many writers and scholars point out that Bulgarians succeeded to survive in a most unfriendly environment here on the Balkans better than others, despite rather, than »because of« their suffered history. One good reason might well be the capacity of a self-destroying traditionalism, which has been able to bid farewell to most precious values. It then proceeds to reshape them in new forms, which is another way to regain them again.

What seems more troublesome is a political orthodoxy, shaped in the *specific conservatism* of the Bulgarian social mind, that anchors him to the past and which enables him to believe in his own ability to survive better than others. This illusive notion has been a shelter for many years of a specific political philosophy that has accompanied him through different political orders and regimes. »All wonders happen in three days« – you will still here him say. His deep mistrust to the reality however, might well be a desperate hidden cry for some internal freedom, which has been constantly challenged and gambled by others, as to leave him powerless. It springs from his oppressed civic courage and reflects some deeper *philosophy of survival* that turns, as we believe, into a life style of selective ability to feed on fragments of his scattered social reality. No doubt the chains of this political orthodoxy prevent him from taking decisive steps ahead of others. Yet in a paradox way this strategy reduces risks in a world, which seems easier to understand, but hard to ignore…

---

9 Ibid.

This is the reason why so many »new ages« have turned to be only sunsets on the hills, that surrounded the Bulgarian in days of trouble and disgrace. What he has been looking at for most of the ages of survival is the sunrise from the East, which has promised and brought life, but also hope and dignity for him. The art of following this Orbit of old hopes and new temptations has always been (and is still) the most admirable advantage of the parochial Bulgarian.

Our Feeling of State and Statecraft

Bulgarians are bound to some multiple grounded notions of their ever-surviving state and nation. This feeling has shaped a rather dualistic, both destructive and creative pattern of state and states governance. It roots back in the foundation of three Bulgarian states (according some historians even four) and more than 1300 years of own history. This Bulgarian statecraft mission starts from the Asian territories under the peaks of Pamire and Hindou-kouch mountains, goes through the wide steps of Volga (Russia), passes through the foundations of the Second Bulgarian state (681) here on the Balkans, right next to Byzantium, and goes even beyond – as to the shining coasts of the Adriatic and South Italy. As short as the Bulgarian historical mind has always been considered to be, this long aged sates craft tradition, is a mighty spring of national pride and dignity. On this invisible, multiple constructs, we have less been able to upgrade some solid or lasting political architecture. Bulgarians most often preferred to start their ventures anew – especially after break downs and failures, leaving the ruins behind, to look for new scope of freedom and even inventive solutions This notorious lack of persistency and respect of sustainable efforts, typical for other nations, might well be the reason why most Bulgarian achievements have less to do with the learned experience of the past.

There is no way to draw out rationale features of the Bulgarian notion of state and governance except to rest on the historically confirmed, significant trends in the Bulgarian cultural development, as shaped through the ages. Let us try to restore this scattered mosaic of passed state glory, but most dramatic downfalls, as well, which have molded the »conglomerate identity« of the inheritors of Asparuch (Isperich) here at both sides of the Balkan:

> »Our state has its foundations on the Asparuch (Isperich) Bulgarians, as upper strata, and the Slavs, as subjects – a dualism, which is known to Russia, France, and England etc. – so the Bulgarian social anthropologist Najden Sheitanov. State power expressed itself on our lands in a rather resolute and firm pattern – something that caused resistance among the »democratic Slavs«, or denial of the state and the higher class. Added to this political and social negation, there comes a cultural one, when with the adoption of the Christianity, the alien Byzantine culture with the support of the state, aimed to destroy the indigenous culture of both

Slavs and Bulgarians. Something of that kind is to be observed in other European states as well, but what is specific for the Bulgarian case, is the rigorousness of the relations. The precipice that opened in this way between Bulgarians and Slavs, subjects and state, city and village, between the Byzantine-Bulgarian Church and people's paganism – was used by the heretic Bogomils, which is a continuous form of Manichean heretics, but shaped as purely local Bulgarian religious movement. Step by step it exposed in front of the people a whole program of negation: a denial of the state and all its institutions, negation of the official Church, while meanwhile and in another way, it pleaded in favor of the culture of the people, of its political and social ideas, in so far those concepts suit to the passed primitive and most of all religiously determined ages.«[10]

There are some reasons to relate those *arche types* of the traditional Bulgarian resistance against so many outside and alien cultural influences, as milestones of the Bulgarian collective identity, shaped through the ages. This notorious *»spirit of denial«* emerges on top of many historical turnovers, indeed. It is to be witness it times of deep crises and social perturbations, as it fills the gap of a discontinuous, evolutionary, »cut off« socio-political and cultural route of this nation. It is not to be related, however, to some idea of »war of all against all« (Hobbs). In a no lesser extend have Bulgarians proved their remarkable spirit of creativity. The deep, even though rather »idealized devotion« to their state and leadership, the cult of strong power, the sensitivity to justice, have in a no lesser extend determined the Bulgarian political culture. To grasp better what shaped the general, most permanent and significant traditional attitudes of Bulgarians to such objects as their political system, state and governance, we have to look back into the ages of the Second Bulgarian state. This means to touch a notorious *»barbarism«,* out of which the most contradictive metamorphoses of the proto-Bulgarian culture arise.

»Proto-Bulgarians and Slavs, of which the Bulgarian nation was founded, settled on the Peninsula as »barbarians«. The »Barbarism« was what initially united them – points out the same author. In this sense Byzantium has been initially felt by Bulgarians as representative of an enemy culture. The Bulgarian state founded its confirmation at this time in protecting and keeping its own pagan tradition. This is where it drew its internal strength. And this is the reason why the pagan period is the steadiest epoch in the Bulgarian history. The jumps and turns off begin after It.«[11]

10 Najden Sheitanov, Duhat na otrizanijeto u Balgarina, Sp. »Filosofski pregled», 1933, Nr.2, See: Zasto sme takiva. V tarsene na Balgarskata kulturna identichnost, Sofia, 1994, p. 270–79i.

11 Ibid.

Over this fundament of the Bulgarian collective identity, religious differences had additional and most decisive impact. The contradictions became even bigger, considering the deep demarcation line between culture and politics, which passed right through the Bulgarian territories here on the Balkans. The latter refer both to structural and contextual differences, reflected in the Bulgarian states and social life:

> »In pursuit of its vital interests and those of an independent development the Bulgarian state and society had to underline most often the moments that differed them from others and give priority to tendencies, which kept them at distance from Byzantium. This is where a most *insolvable contradiction* arises. Having positioned themselves through their Baptizing in the very gravity circle of the Byzantium culture, Bulgarians had to steer their state, their social and spiritual development in a rather fatal way along the roads, which Byzantium followed. This by itself would have been not a big trouble, had the problems which Bulgaria has confronted with in the middle ages been made even more complicated by a constant fact: for Bulgarians Byzantium was a carrier not only of a specific culture – it was a carrier of a hostile political culture, as well. This cultural antagonism was sentenced to death, after the Bulgarian Baptizing, but the political one remained and to a certain extend got even stronger.«[12]

These deep discrepancies with Byzantium, the most powerful political system in the East, form a consistent core in the Bulgarian traditional (parochial) culture. It never managed to develop a *subjective culture*, of the kind most Europeans people and nations did – say the Brits or Germans. A small people, consisting of most heterogeneous and culturally-contradictive elements, confirmed its right of existence under the sun, of own state and governance right »on the crossroad« of the Balkans, in permanent resistance against the most powerful, but still culturally most progressive Empire at that age. This shaped a steady pattern of constant opposition towards all »alien«, which continued long after the Baptizing. Even Christianity was forced in IX c. by King Boris I, whereby local paganism, a deeply rooted disobedience, the rejection of all »alien values«, norms, and even precious ideas, stayed to devour the Bulgarian soul and mind for ages on.

> »The self-protection and moreover the development of the Christian Bulgarian state has been possible – and now even to a greater extend, than earlier only in the fight with Byzantium. In order to fulfill its vital drive to unite the South Eastern part of the Balkan Slavs, it was bound to such a fight by its very geographical dislocation. But conquered often on the battlefield, Byzantium after all always stayed undefeatable: not only because of its affluent material resources, but the sophisticated organization of its strength, and its higher culture, after all. To disarm

12 Ibid.

> her from the weapons she used against them, and not only because of the organization of its new Christian society – the Bulgarian state and spiritual leaders had to consciously lean from her everything which they believed was of Byzantium advantage. There was no other way and here lies the tragic core of Bulgarian history: the epochs of upheaval in it have always started with an upheaval in the spirit and with some massive drive to complex national building, which inevitably turned into periods of rapid denationalization. The growing competition, and from here on the increased copy pattern from Byzantium, deviated the development from its natural roads, to push it in directions which gave no chance for anything solid and lasting to be created. And if those epochs glamour with unexpected achievements, this was because the implementation of ready made foreign patterns saved in their way the efforts of the steady continuous, real creativity.«[13]

This »*arched-back*« Bulgarian pattern of interaction with a hostile social, political and cultural environment, the notorious readiness of self-sacrifice at the alter of own pagan values, labeled by many foreign scholars as some »irrationalism«, has been repeated in many falls and in a most dramatic way after the fall of Bulgaria under Turkish yoke (XIV c.) It proves in its own way the right of some »barbarism«, which has guaranteed the strength and stability of the Old Bulgarian state. Here roots a peculiar instinct of many Bulgarian generations, as related to their devoted feeling of state and national dignity. Nothing has been more sustaining in times of falls and crisis, as this affiliation to ones own Bulgarian homeland, state and firm state leadership.

The Great-Bulgarian feeling of state and statecraft, the cult of power, or the deep appreciation of the »hard hand«, symbolized by the severe laws of Khan Krum the Terrible, the heroic wars of King Kalojan, less the »golden age« of King Simeon I, however, still fills the Bulgarian soul with pride. But as well as with some bitter nostalgia for the ages of pass states glory. In the search of a new life view, as to raise Bulgarians from the catastrophes of couple of sequential wars on the Balkans (1912,1913, 1918) – this appeal for a New national revival, dating from Paisij (XI c), shaped a most explicitly stressed people-centrism. It may be considered as a gravity of the Bulgarian political mind ever since. It is worth to illustrate it as summed so brilliantly as early as in 1920:

> »Here is the first milestone of Bulgarian politics: Bulgaria is an ever standing entity of land, people and state – so Najden Sheitanov master of Bulgarian nation building less known to the European scholar. Our people's or historical lands are Mizia, Thrace and Macedonia with their natural extensions. Our Fatherland is situated in the middle of the Balkan Peninsula. Bulgaria has been from ancient times the backbone, the brain

---

13 Petar Mutafchiev, Kam filosofijata na bakgarskata istorija. Vizantizmat v srednovekovna Balgaria, Filosofski pregled, 3, 1931, Nr.2, p. 27–36.

and the hearth of the Peninsula...The Bulgarian people are the first and legitimist inhibiter of our native land. All other people in this country of ours are our guests only. As our Fatherland is situated in the center of the Balkan Peninsula, so does the Bulgarian people has a central place in the historical life. People centrism is a creative historical premise...the state is an eternal crystallization of the people. We, Bulgarians, are the oldest state craftsmen on the Balkans. We have founded the mightiest state in South Eastern Europe. The internal politics of ours is life viewing. The external one protects our historical lands and the unified people...the people's army embodies our ideals. Economy, culture are only forms of politics. They are secularly understood and are managed according to plans...«[14]

Thus the Bulgarian feeling of state and statecraft, form the very springs seems most closely bound to the notion of a constant, everlasting challenge. The lack of own patterns of state governance after the Baptizing (IX c.) has been additionally hindered by the cultural barriers, which are ever since a source of uncertainty, as related to the further shaping of the Bulgarian nation. Commenting on this moment, P.Mutafchiev points out:

»It was even less possible, from another point of view, to implement on Bulgarian soil the real values of the most refined Byzantium culture. The latter had it roots in the ancient Classicism and exactly this heritage was unknown and out of reach for the Bulgarians, who only through the Christianity entered the stage of real civilization. This is the reason why Bulgarians stay alien to the Byzantium theological wisdom, which King Simeon wanted to implement in our lands. It could not inspire the spirit of this people to real creativity: it was not capable to answer the simplest questions, which moved the mind of the people, deprived from the faith of their ancestors.«[15]

There is little to be added here. One can only conclude that most threads of a proto-Bulgarian culture seem thorn off, as we try to trace them through the scopes of our privileged modernity. It is a real wonder that they still hold some cognitive patterns in the Bulgarian political mind, even so perplexed by sophisticated frameworks of the present. Let us draw the line in an objective term:

During the whole period of 546 years of Bulgarian state existence (The First Bulgarian Kingdom existed 339 years, The Second one for 207 years – its rule lasted as follows:

In Misia (North of the Balkan and Dobrudja (North Eastern Bulgaria) – 524 years,

In the region of Vidin (North Western Bulgaria and the river Timok region – Now part of Serbia) – 495 years,

---

14 Najden Sheitanov, Balgarskijat svetogled, Prosveta, 8, 1942, p. 193–204.

15 Ibid.

In the Region of Sofia – 404 years.
In the Eastern under Balkan region – 363 years,
In the region of Morava – 285 years,
In the region of Velbazd (now part of Serbia)– 238 years,
In Plovdiv, Thrace – 222 years,
In the Rhodopy mountain region – 113 years,
In Macedonia – 221 years,
The Black sea coast around Bourgas – 138 years,
In Albania 130 years,
In the region of Odrin (Turkey) – 284 years. [16]

This gives us reasons to consider Bulgarians as bound for ages to some role of »standing" for their vital interests on the Balkans, but in a wider European cultural context as well. This pattern has gone far beyond the mere egocentric idea of keeping ones own territorial and other interests. It is related to a self-confident awareness of Bulgarians as protectors of Europe's cultural entity as well. Whatever old historical sources have to tell us – this most committed, self-sacrificed contribution to Christianity is a steady milestone on which Europe can count and upgrade. Moreover – it offers its new vital forms that go beyond mere war battles and implement the idea of European integrity in its own way.

The Bulgarian Elite and its Foreign Influences

The Bulgarian political culture during the period of the National Revival and its immediate aftermath has been strongly molded by our political elite. After the Liberation this elite proved to be an important pool for the recruitment of a considerable part of the new political leaders. We will concentrate on those external influence sources, reflecting the more common interests of the dominant socio-political value systems in wider European context. Rather than being paraphrased, these value systems underwent, as we shall illustrate, a transformation process, strongly influenced by the Bulgarian national revival elite's activities. It finally induced a multi-facet cultural and spiritual change. In the context of the churches struggle for national liberation this aspect is well clarified by Bulgarian historians. What we are interested in here, are the secularized manifestations of the Bulgarian national consciousness, as can be traced in the cultural and spiritual activities of the Bulgarian elite of the age of our national revival.

During the national revival period and its aftermath, we can distinguish three primary and a few secondary influence spheres having the biggest impact onto the cultural and political orientation of the Bulgarian elite. Firstly to mention is the Greek, the Serbian and the Russian influence and secondly,

16 Petar Mutafchiev, Kniga za balgarite, Balgarska academia na naukite, Sofia, 1987, p. 124–125.

depending on their relation to the latter, the more periphery sources as the French, the Anglo-American, the German, the Polish and the Czech. Ivan Shishmanov has elucidated this subject in his remarkable studies, dedicated to this period.

For us Bulgarians, the Greek influence has been the most lasting and most powerful one. It took its beginnings whilst Byzantium was one of the most brilliant countries of its time. As Ivan Shishmanov pointed it out, we owe to the Greeks both our baptizing, as well as first literature attempts, art creations, the material and spiritual patterns of culture, especially the one of the high class. The Bulgarian kings and boyars copied the life of the nobles and Byzantine patriarchs. King Simeon was a half-Greek by education. By the time of the fall of Bulgaria under the Turks, the Greek influence ceased widely but in a way continued to persist in the circles of Greek patriarchs and subordinated clergy. The Bulgarian kings and the high class disappeared gradually, as they used to copy their modes from Constantinople. It was the simple *mass*, which was left only, placed under the imperative and direct devastating effect of the new master [17]. The influence of the Greek patriarchy seems not so powerful in cultural terms, however as:

> »Both the Bulgarian and the Greek clergy were equally ignorant – as the same historian witnesses. Gerald marks at the end of XVI century that even the Odrin Greek bishop was semi-literate, something not amazing, having in mind that the higher Church ranks used to be traded as tender, regardless of any educational qualifications...«[18]

All this reflects a most fatal *»oppressed parochialism«* typical for the Bulgarian mass from the past. That's why the manifestations of the national self-awareness seem not so much spiritually oppressed, but »erased« from the cultural map of Bulgaria at that time. Looking back at the initial phases of the Greek influence it is this ›Greco period‹, which had the most important and cultural effect on our secular elite, however. Being part of the ruling system, the high Greek clergy, determined the socio-cultural interaction in its own cultural patterns. The social climate of towns populated with Bulgarians was equally affected with this domination and behavior.

Seliminski assigns this to the Greco-Bulgarian bishops, which »... were mentors of the citizens and diplomats of the people. Such figures were almost in each Bulgarian town«. Aprilov during 1841 judging by own experience and convictions, points out that

> »... If here and there you see an educated Bulgarian, so he has received his honors among the Greeks and he is seeping with the spirit of the Helens. He turns his back to his origin and he wants to join the Greeks as

17 Iv. Shishmanov, Izbrani eseta. Balgarskoto vazrazdane, t.1, BAN, Sofia, 1965, p. 49.

18 Ibid.

> he hides his descent«. Macedonia was most strongly influenced by this Greek »megali-idea« nationalistic influence. In 1852 D. Miladinov gives evidence, that nearly sixth eights of the population of Macedonia was inhabited by one language speaking Bulgarians, but all they used to study from Greek books and call themselves Hellenes...«[19]

Bulgarian and foreign historians, who relate the dimensions and the depth of this Greek influence to the idea of *denationalization* of the Bulgarians and other nationalities in the XIV c., have own reasons to consider so. The Greek assimilation was rather due to the voluntary national betrayal, than to some forced influence of the Greek spiritual powers. More precisely:

> »... Pure economical interests made ... much more Bulgarians first to embrace the Hellenism, to ensure the privileges and the advantages, which the Greek traders had in the Turkish Empire and abroad. The Greek language was used not only in all bigger towns of the Balkan Peninsula, but in the Black sea and Mediterranean ports, where the Greek trade colonies used to be. The Bulgarians who identified with Greeks could benefit from some *political citizen rights* given to the Greeks by the High Porte«.[20]

The most positive manifestation of this Greek cultural influence was a vast network of Greek schools, where the first generation of activists of the Bulgarian national revival movement received their proper education. [21] Within the boundaries of the Turkish Empire famous schools, like those in Epirus emerged as on the islands – in Ago, Thessalonica, Redone and others. Greek schools flourished in Brasher, Zemlin, Pest, Viena, Leipzig and Venice from the XVI c. on. Discussing this influence, which had a crucial impact on the cultural integration process of Bulgarians into a wider European context, Ivan Shishmanov emphasizes:

---

19 Ibid. In his autobiography Gr. Parlichev points out that until 1861, the Greek influence had been so strong in Ohrid, that »Bulgarians used to call a Bulgarian »shop« (ethnic Bulgarian group inhabiting mainly South western Bugaria and the Sofia Reion) while the Bulgarian alphabet was known only to three people, and was called... shopska alphabeth«(!?).

20 Iv. Shishmanov, Izbrani eseta. Balarskoto vazrazdane, t.1, BAN, Sofia, 1965, p. 50–51.

21 In Kidonia-Seliminski, Fotinov and Georgi Zolotovich; on the islands Andros and Kairienia-Z.Makariopolski, G. Busilin, Mihailovski Bros., Atanasovich, Chomakov; on the islands of Sira and Aton, Ilarion Makrioplolski; at the high school in Kuruchishme founded in 1803 – Krastevich, Rakovski, Dobroplodni, Ivan Bogorov, Ilarion, A. P. Granitski, Stefan and Petar Pop-Izvorski, Bogoridi's sons, Nikolaki and Alexander; in Athens – the Michailoivski Bros., Atanasovich, Chomkov, Seliminski, Parlichev and others; in Bukarest – Atanas and Stefan Bogoridi, Peter Beron, Neophit Rilski and many others.

> »Most of those schools were praised for their teachers. They were humanists by the Italian pattern, philosophers, natural scientists, mathematicians or medical doctors as in Italy, France or Germany.«[22]

The deep respect for the Greek culture and science among the Bulgarian leaders of the revival age reflects in its own way the political metamorphoses of the time. In its early phase a complete identification with the Greek culture and language took place. During the age of the Bulgarian church conflicts all this turned into ›extreme hatred‹ and intolerance against all created by Greeks. The role of the Greek language is remarkable though, as it became a cultural bridge for Bulgarians to the outside world, as well as humanistic science and its significant achievements at this epoch. The Greek language was the window through which the curious Bulgarian mind first dared to look at the world of science and fruitful ideas, being deprived until that very moment of any secular horizons.[23] As Raino Popovich in his ›Reader…‹ points:

> »… Everyone should know that everything comes from the Greek language. Bulgarians should spread their curious mind as to grasp from the Greek classics, philosophy, history and literature, which has opened the eyes of enlighten nations as well…«[24]

Gradually, with the transformation of Greek schools into Slav-Bulgarian and finally into »pure« Bulgarian schools, the Bulgarian elite of the revival period seemed not so assimilated, but has practically profited immensely by the flourishing Greek culture, which exerted its influence over Europe, too. Ivan Shishmanov points:

> »We should say in favor of the Greeks that Bulgaria counts its best patriots between initial Greek followers. Everywhere, where the Greek influence acts more straight forward, the Bulgarian has a more vivid *and more accurate feeling of his own dignity.*«[25]

The S e r b i a n influence, though not as strong and diverse as the Greek, started equally by the end of the XVIII c. and had a no lesser positive effect on the intellectual shaping of the Bulgarian national elite. Nevertheless, as Boyan Penev brings forward, there is some difference, regarding the conditions between these two. This difference is determined first of all by the

22 In the preface to its »Greek-Bulgarian phrasebook« printed in Belgrad in 1835, Hristaki Pavlovich not only calls the Greek language »noble«, but also »most usefull«,… »Because speaking it you could go everywhere and don't have to worry since you could do everything successfully. Why: because you could find it spoken everywhere, in Thrace, Macedonia, Asia, at the Sea, in Italy, Germany, France and elsewhere« – See: Iv. Shishmanov, Bd. 1, p. 54.

23 Ibid., p. 54.

24 Ibid., ,p. 55.

25 Ibid., p. 58.

close similarity between the Bulgarian and the Serbian language and the fact that the Bulgarian Revival started initially in the Western Bulgarian districts. The Serbian influence is to be characterized by an intense commercial and spiritual interaction with the West, but most importantly by its lively trade relationships between the West and Northern Bulgaria. [26]

Among the personalities, which had strong influence on the ideology of older Bulgarian revival movements, as Sofronii Vrachanski, we cannot miss to mention Dositei Obradovich. His sympathies for the Bulgarian nation and deep knowledge of their suffering during the Turkish oppression made him plea for our liberation in front of Emperor Josef II. The commitment of people like Dositei or Raich (17591762), professor at the Shroud Virgin Mary school in Karlovtzi, serve as examples of this vivid influence, which transferred enlighten ideas of XVIII c, onwards and shaped the Bulgarian national awareness. Through Serbian and Greek learned community leaders it had a direct impact on the Bulgarian elite from the age of the national revival and »on their lives as well«:

> »... Apart from their rationalism, their cult of the healthy sense, their hatred against the religious fanatics and monastic parasitism, their belief in the omnipotence of education and science, their care for women's education e.g., the leaders of the Serbian revival undoubtedly had an influence on the basic ideas of the ideology of Neophyte Rilski, Bozveli, Photinov and others. To figures as Vuk Karadjich we owe the introduction of the grammatical rules of the Bulgarian language, considered in 1814 and even in 1882 for a Serb adverb«[27]

All this played an important role in the creation of the national awareness of educated and socially interested Bulgarian circles. It contributed to the development of political engagement of Russia and the Slav people for the emerging of the old/young Bulgarian nation

> »A founder of the whole Slav Church literature, shared by Bulgarians, Slavs and Russians altogether«[28]

The R u s s i a n influence has been the most significant of all outside influences, having an impact on the Bulgarian elite over a long historical period. It dates back to the XV c., when close religious ties between the Rila Monastery and the Russian »Saint Panteileimont« on Atone developed. Soon after 1774 and the conclusion of the Kjuchuk Kainardja peace treaty, the

---

26 This happened with the famous »Dodatak in Sanct Petersburg dictionary«, printed 1882 by the same author, who gives scientific grounds to prove the belonging of Bulgarian adverbs to the old-Bulgarian (Church) language. The first honorary patterns from the Bulgarian national poetry were also a work of Vuk Karadjich, See: Iv. Shishmanov, Izbrani sachinenija, Bd. I, p. 59.

27 Ibid.

28 Ibid., p. 61.

Turkish Empire allowed the re-establishment of direct trade relations of Bulgarians with Russia. This marked the beginning of a lasting commercial interaction, which equally permitted an exchange of social and political ideas. Russian culture and intellectual ideas had a great impact on a considerable part of Bulgaria's elite and finally replaced Greek influence. Yuri Venelin and his most zealous adherent Vasil Aprilov played a decisive role in this cultural turnover. The systematic »Russian orientation« of V.Aprilov synthesizes a typical pattern of cultural and spiritual fusion between Bulgaria and Russia's learned elites.

> »Today it is well known who created a convinced Bulgarian from the misled Greek follower, ready to sacrifice everything for his glorious, but slowly degrading tribe, who thought him to be proud of his name, who gave him the method how to work amidst the deeply asleep nation, to be able to recover, to remember his glorious past and rise to a new cultural life – points out Ivan Shishmanov«[29]

In his most remarkable opus »Denitsa«, V. Aprilov, with his typical vigor repeatedly turns to the young Bulgarian generations, encouraging them to grasp the achievements of the world culture first of all through educational contacts with Russia. This tendency, which found an expression in a most energetic appeal to all Bulgarians *»to pave the way not to the South but to the North«*, as expressed by R. Popovich, prevailed in the end. Plenty of studious young Bulgarians went in 1841 to Russian schools and later on became the first systematically educated ›messengers‹ of Russian culture and science in Bulgaria: Botyo Petkov, D. Chintulov, Iv. Bogorov, T. Mihailovski, Toshkovi brothers, N. Gerov, S. Philaretov and many others. By 1858–1868 all Bulgarian students at the Academies of Moscow and Kiev graduated successfully. Most of them studied on Russian government grants, or with the financial help of the Slavic communities.

The most significant result of this cultural exchange was the formation of own national system of Bulgarian schools. Almost all of the students, who graduated in Russia, became teachers in them, as in the Ottoman empire »... their careers have been closed in any other direction«, points Shishmanov. These teachers brought with them not only fluent knowledge of Russian language, which was introduced systematically in many Bulgarian schools as a new subject, but a new attitude of mind as well. These were people with modern understandings of national development, who had deeply grasped the European culture and were thirsty to convey it to a native ground – as Shishmanov writes. This was the case of the first prominent Bulgarian teachers as Joachim Gruev, Danov, Karavelov, Nesha Bonchov, Drinov,

29 Ibid. p.62

Botyov, Vazov and almost all our eminent social and intellectual workers from the 1870 on. These people were in *every respect European culture workers* .«[30]

The F r e n c h influence took its beginnings with the spreading of the ideas of the Great French Revolution and its echo in the Turkish Empire. This impact was however rather secondary. The French influence was carried out primarily by the Greek middle class and Greek newspapers in Viena, which provided information on Bonaparte and outstanding Republican personalities Amongst the books of N. Karastoyanovich, the first Bulgarian printer-publisher, who lived in Samokov, some bulletins of the French Convent have been found recently. This influence was strengthened by the intervention of French catholic missioners. Regarding the Bulgarian Church question and by their efforts to use the union of Tzankov for a political union with Napoleon III, this influence has slowly diminished.

France and the French culture played a most important role for the *political emancipation* of the younger generation, notably the Bulgarian elite of the national revival. There is enough evidence, that this influence can be considered as not some formal less even mechanical »transfer« of republican ideas to Bulgaria. It was more of an ideal challenge destined to waken up the Bulgarian political mind, to fuse progressive ideas of liberty and human rights with European values. Furthermore, it had a particular significance in regard to the Bulgarian national unification and it's linking with the progressive European political and cultural mainstream.

In the years 1820 protestant missionaries became active on the Balkans and in Greece, as English and American influence became noticeable too. After the opening of the first Greek university on the island of Corfu by Lord Gilford, the missionaries founded a large number of schools, offering primary education in Greek language. They also cared for the translation of books. Their biggest contribution was definitely the translation of the Holy Bible in popular Greek and in Bulgarian language.

Experiencing many obstacles the translation was entrusted to Ilarion of Crete, later Tarnovo metropolitan.[31] V. Barker and his role in the English

---

30 Ibid. p. 64.

31 Initially the translation was given to the abbot of the Bistritza monastry in Rumania Teodosii and an »anonymous Bulgarian«. The translation was printed and sent in 5000 copies to Petersburgh, but it was destroyed here since it was not up to the standards. Subsequently the society turned to the Odrin Greek metropolit, who confined this important task to two priests from the city of Sliven. Their work also turned out to be unsatisfactory, but 800 copies were bought by the translator Sapunov. »Here is a big merit of the protestant missioners – as Shishmanov points out – because of their persistent demands for the translation of the Holy Bible to be comprehensible for the ordinary people. This supported the development of Bulgarian literature«. It is known that Photinov translated the Bible into Bulgarian,

Biblical Society merits special recognition in this respect as the latter bought 800 copies of the Sapunov translation, considered as most adequate. Protestant missioners for Bulgarian schools translated various English works of literature, as well as moral teaching texts. The merit for the foundation of Robert's College, as well as several more educational institutions for girls and boys is widely acknowledged in Bulgaria and those institutions are still highly appreciated.

The G e r m a n influence was mainly noticeable in the context of the Lutheran Reformation of the XVI century, which did have a greater impact on Slovenians and especially Croatians, but less on Catholic Bulgaria. There was only one Bulgarian leader of this epoch, Dr. Petar Beron, oldest Heidelberg university Alumni (1825), who set this German-Bulgarian academic tradition and implemented it later on it to the wider public in his famous »Fish primer«. V.Aprilov, the founder of the first school in Bulgaria to provide a systematical education approach, went to Viena as well, »to become a medical student, but due to his innate nervousness – as the historian clarifies– could not bear blood and surgeries and soon had to leave the university« there. Similar to the French, the German influence had an indirect impact on the Bulgarian elite at that age of national revival.

The P o l i s h influence was directly related to the period, following the revolution of 1830 and in particular to the personality of Chaika Chaikovski (Sadak Pasha), organizer of the Turkish Kazakh regiment in 1854, where many Bulgarians served. Chaikovski supported Ilarion and N. Bozveli in front of the Turkish High Gate. He had an influence on Georgi S. Rakovski and backed his ideas in 1840 in front of Guizot. The latter argued for the opening of a high school in Bulgaria and the attendance of approximately 30 Poles in it. Even though this proposition was rejected, it witnesses the interest of the Polish learned elite for the Bulgarian cultural development. After the revolution in 1848, »Poles (together with some Hungarians) acted as the first representatives a proper bourgeois culture« in the Bulgarian regions of Shoumen, Rousse etc. They were deeply engaged in the cultural creating process in this country, as well as in the solution of the Bulgarian Church question.

This summary of foreign influence on the Bulgarian elite during the national revival is not exhaustive. We omit here the analyses of other most interesting details and secondary, but not less fruitful cultural and political influences, as the Czech, the Hungarian, the Italian, the Spanish, the Ukrainian or even the Finland ones. Historians have still a lot to discover in

---

but the Biblical society didn't approve it, because the language was neither Slav nor Bulgarian«. The merit of the society in supporting Photinov is not less important in shaping the first Bulgarian journalist and his magazine »Luboslavie«.

Ibid. , p. 67.

this respect indeed. What can be drown and specially stressed here is that the Bulgarian political culture is to be considered as a rather unsystematic, but still long-term syntheses of many cultural traits and political ideologies. It is even of greater importance that it was molded, as we tried to illustrate above, by mot significant and outstanding values of the European civilization. The Bulgarian national revival movement is thus to be grasped more as a process of re-creation and adopting (and less of adapting) of an old/new nation into its natural wider European cultural context.

In search of this strange »key code«, which shaped in its peculiar way the Bulgarian political culture, we may once more remind a most fruitful idea of Shishmanov:

»...Culture is a product of various factors, as a nation, or even a tribe does its best to avoid most foreign influences – it cannot preserve its *initial purity*, if it has to exist (or has existed at all). There is something, which is definite in any case, however and this is that higher cultures always involuntarily affect the lower ones... Still:

> »The originality of a culture often doesn't exist as anything else, except more or less as an *independent process* of imitating foreign elements. Nations – were they small or big – are great plagiarists. Lucky is the nation, which is able to plagiarize, as this did the great writers from the XVI and the XVII centuries, which profited without any shyness from the foreign literature. But put such an original stamp on it, which made other people regard it as heir own national achievement.«[32]

It seems so often that there is nothing new under the »sun« indeed. But exactly when it hides amid the clouds and the misty sky – a man of own vigor and courage decides to light the Fire. What if he had no idea of Prometheus? Or has even never heard of him?

The April Insurrection of 1876 as Pattern of Mass – Political Participation

One can look for different starting points for some evolutionary temporal dynamics of the Bulgarian political culture. As in the case of Bulgaria, we prefer to »start« from no other point as the first *public forum* of the awakening Bulgarian political mind – the Assembly at Oboriste as one of the most significant event in the Bulgarian national liberation movement – determining the date of Insurrection against the Turks in 1876. This event has been thoroughly analyzed by historians and there is less to be added in this respect. What we are interested in here is to »read« and interpret this historical act as related to an »eruptive« form of participant political culture, which lead to Bulgaria's liberation after 500 of Ottoman oppression.

---

32 Iv. Shishmanov, Bd.1, p. 373.

This political culture, as we believe, has a unique character. It not only managed to mobilize Bulgarians in the fight for their freedom and independency, but also, as we shall illustrate, accelerated a process of most admirable *civic creativity* and political involvement. All this occurred in relatively short period of time, »prepared« the Liberation in 1878 (as result of the Russian-Turkish war) and crystallized immediately after in the work of the National Assembly and the Tarnovo constitution.

As unique pattern of participant political culture, it shaped it's institutions and political leaders, added legitimacy to their immediate political roles and governing decisions, suspended from »above«, or generated at lower levels of power, to propel upwards. As we could find out on the base of a more profound analysis in the framework of Almond and Verba's theory, the April Insurrection of 1876 is a perfect case of emerging of a new political subject, with clear notion of his political rights and freedoms, as well as definite responsibilities in the shaping of own political system.

One can still learn from these »latent« (natural) and innovative patterns of civic participation less known to the scholar of the modern age. Their structures and forms shaped in most explicit way and are not to be interpreted in their trivial »militant« aspects or sheer historical context. This culture of mass involvement invented original structures and attributes of an own state and national creation. And in a most indisputable way has re-defined the European identity of the Bulgarian people, earlier than this country has fully shaped into a nation.

Bulgarians have many reasons to regard the April Insurrection of 1876 as a starting point in their new political history. As the prominent sociologist Ivan Hadjijski (1936) points in his most penetrating »*Psychology of the April Insurrection*«:

> »The April Insurrection was not the first one against the Turkish yoke. It was the one and only, however, that was prepared and carried out fully by massive, all-Bulgarian internal revolutionary organization – this firstly. And secondly – it was the one and only which was not inspired from abroad, being not as most other insurrection from the past a mere attempt for some military-rear maneuver. It was moreover a purely national act, an achievement of the revolutionary self-activity of our people«.«[33]

110 years after April 1876 Andrej Pantev commented the internalization of the so called »*Bulgarian question*« in wider context, stressing on this »delayed Bulgarian participation« in the process of national emancipation and modern political development:

---

33 Ivan Hadjiiski, Optimistichna teorija za balgarskija narod, (I, II), Sofia, 1974, p. 229.

»To cross the Atlantic as political problem, as moral dilemma and civic-religious challenge, turned to be not less important, than to stand bravely and challenge a still strong and vital Empire...This means that yet there is another explanation of the wonder of the Bulgarian insurrections, the wonder of the Bulgarian Liberation. This was not a capricious pity, but an *imperative of time*, in which Bulgarians made their entry with a rapid, impetuous and most durable participation. From here on started the road ...which had many turns, but has never been cut off...«[34]

The question of this Bulgarian »political wonder« and it's universal cultural significance is not to be discussed here. What we have claimed in another historically accentuated study of the Bulgarian political culture (Georgiev, 2000) it had a decisive impact on the awakened political mind of Bulgarians. Bulgarians have indeed joined later than other Balkan peoples (i.e. Greeks) the system of independent national state existence of XIX c. But did this in a most impressive and resolute way, making their cultural choice in favor of Christianity and civilization.

This »pattern of mass involvement« is closely linked with the personality of a legendary hero of the Bulgarian national liberation movement – Georgi Benkovski (Gavril Hlatev), leader of the Insurrection in IV revolutionary region, centered at Panagyuriste. Over 600 000 participants in the April 1876 Insurrection followed him »like one« in less than 3 months of preparation of the uprising. This *national sacrifice* has less to do with some phantasm, as post-modern historians try to »define« it in sophisticated way. It is a source not only of patriotic feelings, but a milestone of activist participation of Bulgarians in the shaping of their own destiny. Certainly with other means and instruments of democratic power, than some notorious *»vote of the daggers«* which ignorant, but most dedicated peasants raised in support of their leader, as they unanimously determines the date of the April 1876 uprising against the Ottoman empire.

And thus paid the high price of Freedom with own blood.

---

34 Andrej Pantev, Balgarskijat April 1876 v Anglia i SAST, Sofia, 1996, p.13.

Fig. 1: Georgi Benkovski leader of the 1876 Uprising against the Ottoman Empire

Fig. 2: Map of the April Uprising in 1876

Benkovski as Imperative of the Bulgarian Participant Political Culture

He just appeared – and it happened!
»Bloody song« – Pencho R. Slavejkov

How come that Georgi Benkovski (Gavril Hlatev)[35] and not Panajot Volov, the legitim elected commander in chief of IV Revolutionary region (see map), managed to raise in most miserable conditions 600 000 Bulgarians to follow him as *»one man and this in three months only*«? This is the question, which we find crucial to understand the »eruptive« political participation of the Bulgarians, as they raised against the Ottoman Empire in 1876 in fight for their national liberation. To grasp this unique Bulgarian pattern of political involvement, we have to »reincarnate« the figure of a most charismatic national leader as Georgi Benkovski [36] – a man who stayed for long years in the shadows of other »brightly« exposed national heroes, as

---

35 As Zahari Stojanov in his »Zapiski po balgarskite vastanija«(Notes on the Bulgarian Insurrections) mentions – the name of Georgi Benkovski belongs to a polish patriot, send into exile by the Russian government to the island of Sahalin. This polish man could flee and »stepped on Japan«, after which he was taken under the protection of the French ambassador in Edo. The latter provided him with a French passport on his own name – Anton Benkovski; so that he could return to Europe A. Benkovski chose as residence place Turkey and met Stojan Zaimov (Apostle for the Vratza revolutionary center) in Diarbekir, who was set as an exile there by the Turkish government. A.Benkovski sold his pass for 5 Turkish liras, so that Zaimov could flee. Zaimov was lucky to do so, fled to Romania in 1975 and when Gavril Hlatev headed to Istanbul in the same year, to take part in the action of »burning up the city« (according the plans of the Revolutionary committee), Zaimov gave him the passport on the name of Anton Benkovski. »Thus our Gavril Hlatev had to change his Bulgarian family name with a polish one« – explains Z.Stojanov. See Zapiski po balgarskite vastanija, Balgarski pisatel, Sofia, 1976, p. 359–397.

36 Short before his death, Benkovski shared as Z.Stojanov wrote in his »Notes on the Bulgarian Insurrections: My name is not Georgi Benkovski. They call me Gavril Gruev Hlatev, born in Koprivstiza. I kept secret my birthplace until now and my real name only because I believe in the saying that no one is a prophet in his own place...I have been first karaabadzija (producer of wool made coats – P.G.), then have tried as merchant of different stock. I have traveled to Istanbul, Asia, Egypt etc., but I could not save a dime. God has not gifted me with the advantages, which merchants should possess. The most important was that I had to lie both to left and right, and prosper only by this in my merchant ventures; I had to make deep bows to the Turks, to witness as they misuse the rights of others etc. something which my soul could accept in no way. I got rid of all this and crossed to Romania to look for free and better life. There I got to know some proper men of the people and this was the reason I had to come to the Fatherland under false name« Ibid. p. 596).

Vasil Levski, Christo Botev, Georgi Rakovski and others. There are many reasons why his name has been mentioned only on rare occasions of »revolutionary« celebrations from the near past. Less considered is his political role in its cultural context and meaning. What may be the reason is that Benkovski was the one »to be blamed« (Zachary Stojanov) both for the revolutionary achievements of the April 1876 insurrection and its bloody defeat (30 000 slaughtered Bulgarians). It was the »hard hand« of this most charismatic hero that pushed Bulgaria onto the road to Europe and independent national existence. Even though this happened in a most paradox »authoritarian« pattern, imposed by Benkovski on the April 1876 insurrection and the Bulgarian mass. This phenomenon has been for long years assessed into the framework of dogmatic materialist interpretations of the Bulgarian political history. Let us briefly tackle it here from another point of view, as it played a decisive role in the shaping of the modern Bulgarian political culture.

As a direct form of mass participation, that is an immediate interaction of the political subject with his ad hoc emerging political object (the long lost Bulgarian Kingdom), the April Insurrection of 1876 confronted the awakened Bulgarian political mind with two major and most contradictive forms of political orientation:

1. At one side was the spontaneous »*instinctive democratic drive*« (Iv. Hadjijski)[37] of the Bulgarian, who made its way and even found its realization in the dramatic days of the Insurrection. It rapidly shaped own

37 In his remarkable essay »Psychology of the April Insurrection«, Ivan Hadjiski points out 6 »source-lines« of which the participants of the April 1876 Insurrection arise: »the incapability of the decaying Turkish state to secure the property and life of its subjects«, »the religiously opposed state government«, »the robberies of some of the Bulgarian notables of the older generation«, »a proletarian line«, »the line of peasants deprived from any property«, »a parochial moral still vital«. Hadjiski does not exclude the role of other factors – as the immediate, major cause of the Insurrection, which he sees in the massive robberies of the Cherkezi (horse riding voluntary militants near to the oppresive Ottoman regime). Hadjiski briefly comments on another additional source of the Bulgarian political participation – the one of the »individualism of the inteligenzia« – as he comments: »Once emerged as social product, this individualism becomes relatively independent«. Thus his concludes: »For Rakovski and Benkovski the Insurrection was a way to receive from the freed Bulgarian people the crown of the old Bulgarian kings«. The Insurrection of 1878 has confronted a »militant« wing to the evolutionist one (the so called »cherkownitzi« – pleading of reforms through the Church). In one way or other a civic form of competitive political participance has developed, in which gifted sociologist as Iv. Hadjiski never doubted. See: Iv.Hadzijski »Psichologia na Aprislkoto vastanie« (Psychology of the April Insurrection), in: Optimistichna teorija za nashija narod (Optimistic Theory of he Bulgarian people), Balgarski pisatel, 1974, p. 307–319.

democratic forms of organization (representative Assembly, most efficient network of security, secret post, revolutionary committees, etc.), upgrading the secret organization for liberation, as founded earlier by Vasil Levski.

2. At the other side – there was the »authoritarian« pattern, which penetrated through the ideas of the French revolution and Bonaparte, as they echoed in the mind of the leaders of the April 1876 Insurrection. But, as we could find out, had deeper rotes in the Bulgarian traditional (parochial) mind:

A. The first form of political orientation, as represented by the learned, well off, (or what Benkovski called »philosophers«) participants in the April drama, failed to impose on the parochial mind of the Bulgarians. It is was not only the shortage of time, the lack of military experience, the scarcity of the material resources etc. that contributed to this, but, the specific *parochial-subjective culture,* as spread over the Ottoman Empire. Its »mix«, as shaped in the mainstream of the Ottoman system, determined a dual pattern of political involvement of most social strata of the Bulgarian community (except the notables, close adherents to the Turkish High Gate). This culture, which is considered to be the driving force of the Bulgarian Insurrection from 187, could not perform successfully, had it not been *converted* and pushed to revolutionary activity by what we call here the »imperative of Benkovski«.

B. The second form of political orientation – the one of a spontaneous but most resolute support of *»the strong hand«,* [38] as represented by Georgi

---

38 In the draft of the Statement of The Bulgarian Revolutionary Central Committee (BRZK) – the so called »Regulations for the workers on the Liberation of the Bulgarian people« prepared by Vasil Levski clear political objectives have been defined: »through an all people revolution to turn off and fully reconstruct the present state despotic-tyranny system and to substitute it by democratic republic (government of the people)...« and on the same grounds of our ancestors to »...raise a Chapel of Truth, perfect equality and proper Freedom« ,...« whereby ...consensus, brotherhood and perfect equality between all peoples – Bulgarians, Turks, Jews etc, no matter of faith, or any other belonging, or in any civic respect, or whatever...« as far as »all they comply to a general law, which is to be voted with the majority of representatives of all people« . This Statement had to be omitted though and a special Marshal law had to be imposed according the Regulations during the all people Revolution. »No one of the Bulgarian leaders or man of wealth had any right to represent the Bulgarian people in front of other nations and to negotiate with them without the knowledge of the Central Committee« – stood firmly stated in the original text of this document. The rapid development hindered the voting of such a Marshal law. The clash between the »notables« (democrats) and «peasants« (nationalist-republicans) – at the Oboriste Assembly (proto-National Assembly) which had to decide on the date of the Insurrection, showed that Benkovski and the Apostles adhered to this Marshal scenario claiming for exceptional rights according to its clauses. What actually happened after Benkovski succeeded to get those rights by a »vote of the daggers« (supported by his close followers mostly ignorant peasants from the village of

Benkovski, imposed as more vital and active pattern of identification, as it offered a clearer perspective to the Bulgarian parochial mind. This form achieved full compliance between »culture« and »system« (Almond and Verba), as incorporated in an *ad hoc* emerging Bulgarian political object. This proved the events in IV Revolutionary region, centred at the city of Panagyuriste. In no other region (except Tarnovo) the Insurrection had such a massive support and perfect organization capable to mobilize the Bulgarians. This traditional (parochial) culture, brought into compliance with its real political object, as symbolized by Benkovski, turned an »ignorant« mass into well organized revolutionary actions and inspired a devoted identification [39] with the cause for National liberty.

The thesis which we would like to raise here is that the April Insurrection of 1876 is an unique Bulgarian form of participant political culture, in which the *authoritarian premise*, as represented by Benkovski (and the Apostles of the Insurrection), has deeper roots and grounds in the Bulgarian traditional culture, to differ from all »modern influences« at that time. This political participation performed as ultimate cultural-political imperative, which forced the Bulgarian people into their real political existence and did this in a most resolute way. At the same time it re-confirmed the European identity of the Bulgarian people, as the only possible and rationale form of consistent interaction between culture and system, in the context of the 500 years of interrupted Bulgarian state existence.

Further on – this Bulgarian participant culture from April 1976 undergoes general (universal) and internal (specific) regularities, as it generated its own system, relevant patterns and forms of rationale political behaviour. Its imperative character has no analogue among the political cultures of other »young nations«, and is even less related to substitute, quasi-*forms* of modern political participation. This authoritative pattern in no way diminishes the

---

Mechka (near Pazardjik). This gave reasons to many analysts for the last 100 years to blame Benkovski for his »tyranny« and »despotism«. As far as his role of military leader demanded this, it cannot be denied in any way that he acted fully according the precise premises of the Statement of the BRCK and the ideas of Vasil Levski for National liberation in pace with the advanced democratic world. See: Vasil Levski, Dokumentalno nasledstvo (Documentary heritage), Red. Cyril Vazvazov & Prof.Nikolai Genchev, Nauka i izkustvo, Sofia, 1973, p. 110–116.

39 »Have a good look, you scoundrels! This one was to be your king« – so shouted the Turks, as they took the head of Benkovski, pierced on top of the sable of a Turk, as they passed through Orchanije (Botevgrad) to Sofia. Nearly 100 men were involved in this procession through the villages from the surrounding area. Ahead walked a man who forced the peasants to go at the outside of their village and meet the convoy. »In Osikovitza the convoy emptied 500 rifles. The head was carried by a Bulgarian, pierced on top of a long shaft«. See: Z. Stojanov, Zapiski po balgarskite vastania...p. 636.

consistent democratic character of the participant Bulgarian political culture, as shaped in the dramatic days of the April Insurrection of 1876. The deviations in the political life of this country, in which later most devastating effects of »one-man rule« occurred, are not to be considered as result of some »spirit of denial« of the Bulgarian »national character«. They are not to be ascribed to external factors only (even though they have also played their role). All this political and cultural complexity is being rationalized as the result of the defeat of a self-generated Bulgarian *parochial-subjectivism converted into subject-participant culture* in the glorious and tragic days of the April 1876 Insurrection.

Moreover, the defeat of Insurrection was a defeat of this self-generated Bulgarian participant culture, which could never (even after the Liberation in 1878) grass root into a *proper subject-participant culture,* as both the »subject« and the participant elements of this culture have been deviated and systematically alienated from their generic participant forms and patterns of cultural existence. This is the reason why the Bulgarian political development could never upgrade an evolutionary »mixed« culture to fuse into typical forms of some autonomous civic culture, as in the case of other European nations.

Let us only briefly illustrate this complexity, as related to the inevitability (but not irreversibility) of this peculiar »authoritarian pattern« of Bulgarian involvement in the process of National liberation and European integrity, as brilliantly explained by Anton Strashimirov:

> »In this epoch something crucial happened to our tribe. The regions of the periphery of Turkey, which were demographically more compact (Greece and Serbia), or geographically at greater distance (Romania), began to alienate administratively and economically from Turkey. Our tribe, as most near to the centre of the state, was pushed right into the opposite direction: it began to press to Istanbul. Thus psychologically the cause of the Turkish government turned to be a Bulgarian cause. This was equal to an Ottomanization of the Bulgarians. For it is a historical fact: Turkey got rid of the anarchy in the first half of the 19 c. – exclusively due to the support of several hundred Bulgarian industrial cites and mountain villages. This and no other historical fact created a positive attitude among the High Gate (Turkish government) towards Bulgarians. This continued for nearly half a century and culminated in the remarkable deeds of Sadak pasha's army, met by Bulgarians, supplied and cared by them with the enthusiasm of own army – and in fact it was Bulgarian. This speeded a conscious turkophylia among the wealthy class of Bulgarians – big owners of land, merchants, and part of craftsmen. Is it too hard within such consistent political and economic process to come to any theorizing on the decisive role of the internal wide markets in the Ottoman Empire for the prosperity and the future of

the Bulgarian tribe? Is it not most likely to accept that the *political turkophylia* among the Bulgarians of all social camps and ideological feathering during our Revival (until the Liberation, and even after this) was not only the result of diplomatic impacts, or some kind of Bulgarian opportunism, but an ideology with deeper political and economic backing «[40] (cursive P.G.)

Thus the Bulgarian Apostles, ahead with Georgi Benkovski faced a crucial choice – the one of fighting against the Ottoman Empire, and against a deeply rooted culture of obedient loyalty to the Empire, among the dominating part of the Bulgarian notables. This cultural and political choice could be met only by a most courageous, imperative pattern of all-Bulgarian upheaval and involvement into the process of national liberation, as achieved earlier by other European nations under different conditions. What Strashimirov called a »*most decisive historical turning point*« of the Bulgarian people towards Europe and the Christian civilized world, is no less worthy achievement of the »mass« revolutionary involvement and challenge against the Ottoman Empire. That this Insurrection »prepared« the war of Russia against Turkey (1878), which in fact »brought« on the bayonets of Russian soldiers the Bulgarian liberty, from which other Empires profited, is another story.

The »*all or nothing*« alternative of the Apostles of the April 1876 Insurrection might seem still a political gambling – but we prefer to let eccentric social scientist to ruminate on this, as they comment on some 500 years of »Ottoman presence« in Bulgaria (?). This »eruptive«, imperative pattern and most vivid form of political participation, as performed in the glorious days of the April 1876 Insurrection, is to be considered as un (typical) but ultimate solution of a most contradictive political and moral dilemma, which the Bulgarian national existence had to find out by itself only and this is what gave birth to its own values of freedom and liberty.

This act was only made possible trough a catharsis of a deeply thorn Bulgarian identity, which found its new centre of modern national gravity. That this culture never had the chance to grass root and flourish in its vital and deeply motivated civic forms in the long run of development of this country, is another dramatic story. The Balkans still hides stories of that kind. April 1876 will stay however as a milestone of both political and moral courage, as it gave legitimacy to a European identity of the Bulgarian people, even before the act of our National liberation.

---

40 A. Strashiirov, Nashijat narod, Sofia, 1925, p. 238–240 .

The »Fragmented« Subject in the Principality and after the Unification (1885)

It is hard to say if some »predetermined« pattern, or rather a most striking disrespect of an old Bulgarian statecraft tradition has played a more pernicious role in the process of cultural and political creativity of the Bulgarian people after the Liberation in 1878. First of all this blow damaged the fundaments of an originally created Bulgarian subjective culture, on whose ruins aster the Insurrection of 1876 no proper *participant-subject culture* could grass root.[41] The reasons for this are manifold. As we believe, the most significant of them spring from an imperial »new legitimacy«, as imposed on the state building of »young nations« on the Balkans in the end of XVIII c. In our Bulgarian case it seems in deep discrepancy, as related to the premise of congruency between »culture« and »system« (Almond and Verba). This determined the most uncertain pattern and forms of political interaction of the Bulgarian subject with his imposed political object.

> »Bulgarians did not start to build their state on a vacant lot. Even in the darkest ages of the oppression the people's mind kept memory of the great Bulgarian state from the past, which had played a significant role in the European South-East and contributed for the development of human civilization – so Ilcho Dimitrov in a penetrating essay, dedicated to the Bulgarian Unification in 1885. Sacral memory has been kept of Khan Eparch and King Boris, of King Simeon and King Samuil, of the brothers Cyril and Method, as well as their students ahead of Kliment Ochridski, Ivan Rilski and Patriarch Evtimij. This memory was one of the fundaments of the Bulgarian people's mind. It was a vital spring of the national revival and the Liberation movement.« [42]

---

41 What we have in mind here are not so much typical features of the civic cultures, as they emerged in the European catholic world, or even their more or less typical forms of establishing different systems of social and political order. All this differed from the regime which imperial Russia imposed in freed Bulgarian territories after the Liberation in 1878. What is of greatest interest here are the psychological impacts of a systematically oppressed and forced Bulgarian national spirit, wuch has been deviated from the mainstream of integration into the system of modern national states. This process in the Bulgarian case did not occur as in Italy, or Greece through sovreign autonomus activity (except in the months of the Insurrection of April 1876, when elements of a participant-subject political culture occurred in one of the 4 Revolutionalry districts under the leadership of Georgi Benkovki). See: Plamen Georgiev, Balgarskata politicheska kultura, K&M, Sofia, 2000 (Chapt. 2., Benkovski as an imerative of the Bulgarian participant political culture, p. 113–148).

42 Ilcho Dimitrov, Epoch 1885. A historical essay on the Unification of North and South Bulgaria, Sofia, 1995, p. 27–28.

The very fact that the Bulgarian political culture could not sediment into some homogeneous »mix« of more or less participant patterns of interaction with its political object and thus undertake *autonomous civic functions* in later stages of its development, is a sequence of the most abrupt »deviation« of the parochial subjectivism from the forms of participant subjectivism, as prevailing (typical) in most European nations from the middle of XVIII c. Let us briefly discuss this thesis here.

As it returned to life from 500 years of devastating Ottoman oppression, according the Treaty of St. Stephano (March 1878), the new established Bulgarian state spread almost all over the Bulgarian lands on the Balkans. In general its borders coincided with the two autonomous regions, marked by the Istanbul Conference (1876) with capitals Sofia and Tarnovo. Including all Bulgarians in the ex-province of the Ottoman Empire, the thus re-incarnated (as result of the Russian-Turkish war) Bulgarian, »state body«, in fact re-defined most of the Old Bulgarian ethnic territories. But in no way allowed an independent existence and own state creativity of this nation. This is the reason why the initial participant drive, as propelled by the April 1876 Insurrection, faced at the very start of the national independency, the »matrix« of a fragmented and most uncertain Bulgarian state's totality.[43]

Spread at both sides of the Balkan, in Mizia, Macedonia and Thrace, or even beyond the Danube, having just tasted freedom, the Bulgarian people felt deprived of full and fair state restitution and their national ideal. This had a most negative impact on the structural determining factors of the emerging »system«. The prostration seemed overwhelming. The old *parochialism* has been practically excluded from the process of shaping of a new subject, relevant to the established new Bulgarian state. The latter could not involve the individual on affective and normative, less even on cognitive level:

> »The re-establishing of the Bulgarian state busted into celebrations and patriotic upheaval all through the Bulgarian lands – so Ilcho Dimitrov, back to the spirit of joy and glory of »liberated« Bulgaria. The St. Stephano Treaty was seen as a deserved recognition of the right of the Bulgarian people to live free and united, compensated for their suffering through the ages. The most sacred expectations and hopes had come true. In the run of four month only, however, a thunder stroke from the sky, as the malicious news came from Berlin. The excitement turned into indignation. The situation of Macedonian Bulgarians was even worse.

43 The latter has been assigned only to part of the Bulgarian people – mainly the inhabitants of Mizia (North Bulgaria), which was included in the Principality. In the »excluded« rest of the Bulgarian lands, as many historical sourced witness, the Bulgarians have been reversed back to their old parocialism and it's adherent forms of »diffusive« comprehension of the state and political body.

> The fanatic rage of the defeated Turkish authorities fell on the helpless *raja*,«[44]

The psychological results of this partial compensation of the Bulgarian sufferings through the ages and the unfairly determined »*limits of freedom*« turned the national spirit into deep indignation and some internal resistance which we can trace to present. It had its impact on the character and forms of the shaping new Bulgarian subject in the Principality and beyond its formal borders. Millions of Bulgarians have been excluded from the Principality, as symbolizing the recovered Bulgarian state. They had to accept all old and new sufferings, which life under the »*dual-subjectivism*« and the adherence to the *Sultan vilaeti* offered. This was a most devastating »form« of political existence for Eastern Rumelia and especially for Macedonia, ever so close to most Bulgarian hearts, as it had to suffer under Turkish yoke for another 36 years![45]

Neither did the Kresna-Razlog insurrection (5–17 Oct. 1878), nor the attempts of Russia to support a movement against the decisions of the Berlin Congress succeed to »mild« the imperial will of the Great powers. They have immensely injured the Bulgarian people.[46]

---

44 Raja – deprived from all rights subjects of the Ottoman empire, usually from all lower strata of the multi ethnc social structure, adherents of other religion as the official Islam. See; Ilcho Dimitrov, Epocha 1886...p. 17.

45 All this was a result of the geo-strategic plans of the Great imperial powers (Great Britain and Austria). The formal model of a »frameworked« national state , ignored the emerging own subject aspirations not only of Bulgarians (as inheritors of the oldest states in Europe) but other Balkan peoples as well.

46 The meetings of the Congress in Berlin took place from June 1(13 to July 1(13) in 1878, where Russia, Great Britain, Germany, France, the Austrianuan –Hungarian empire, Italy and Turkey were presented. It's decisions are systematicly layed down in a document (Berlin Treaty). According it's clauses under Turkish administration have been left Macedonia, Eastern and Western Trace, whereby the Principality encompassed only North Bulgaria. South Bulgaria has been even deprived from the right to carry this name, and turned into an »authonomy region« within the borders of Turkey and under direct government of The Sultan.The authonomy was named Eastern Rumelia. This »innovative« idea originates from the diplomacy of the British empire. A special Commission had to work out the so called »Organic Chart«, which had to operate as Constitutional law. The decisions of the Berlin Congress are exemplary of an empire approach to the political architecture of the Balkans, which »spread the seeds of national and ethnic wars for years ahead« The sufferings of hundreds and thousands of people left again under tyranny of Turkey lies on the consciousness of the European statesmen but first of all on Dizraely and Andrishy...»Thus the Great powers predetermed a most uncertain and volatile development for the Balkans as historical events have proved nearly a century after« See Ilcho Dimitrov, Epoch 1886., p. 16–17.

With a most naïve belief that Bulgarian feelings could move the European empire diplomacy – 120 members of the just established Bulgarian National Assembly gathered on February 28 (March 12) 1979 in Tarnovo, to vote for the Constitution of the Principality, appealed in a special Memorandum addressed to the Great powers. The latter still reminds of the high and most bitter price of political illusions...

Thus the road to an independent Bulgarian national existence seems to be hindered at the very start of a generated parochial-subjective culture, as it spontaneously had moved to its participant forms of political involvement into the redefined political object. This turned Bulgarians to some *internal voluntarism*, which has rooted ever since into his subjective culture. This »fragmented« subject in the Principality and in South Bulgaria from the very early days of independent national life bounds Bulgarians, as we believe, to deeply alienated and most uncertain forms of political orientation ever since. Most of the *proper civic forms* of social and political life, as we could witness them to flourish in Europe, seemed crashed and suppressed forever again. There might be numerous reasons for this. One, however, as related to a spontaneously shaped, but widely spread republicanism at this side, may well be the cause for this »punishment«.

> »One of the most remarkable phenomena in the history of Bulgaria after its liberation is the *proclaimed equality guaranteed for all citizens* – so Ilcho Dimitrov further on. This happened after 500 years of barbarian oppression, after the slaughters in which the April Insurrection has been suppressed. Neither in the Principality nor in Eastern Rumelia existed any racial, religious or national restrictions. Equality springs from the very *character of the democratic regime, the politics applied, from the legal treatment of minorities and the methods applied.* Full freedom of political ideas and peoples belonging, of religion have been guaranteed...« [47]

Thus Bulgaria turned to be condemned to some *constant chasing* of advanced social and political development, as in the case of other European nations, with all devastating effects of this on the national spirit and its »against the tide« shaping political culture. [48] Possible sociological elements

---

47 Ibid, p. 46.

48 The young Bulgarian state, being both object and center of a new subject orentation (with all the attributes of a reincarnated Bulgarian state – King, Constitution, Members of Parliament (National Assembly) etc.) seemed provoked to re-determination. It had to pass through most sophisticated diplomatic labyrinths and balance between the interests of the Great powers. This »pattern« of state and political behavior had turend for ages not only typical. But had a most negative effect on the Bukgarian mind, who often is inclined to consider himself as »scape goat« or »victim« of conspirative theories of more powerful nations. In one way or

in the Bulgarian political culture after the Liberation 1878 could not be expressed through adequate forms of *compliance with the political system.* This has shaped a most inconsistent political orientation and uncertain political behavior for decades on. It also hindered the process of generating autonomous participant patterns and forms of political involvement, as in the case of other European civic cultures from the end of XVIII c. onwards.

Stoyan Michailovski, one of the most penetrating Bulgarian writers from the early XIX c. pointed this effect of an »overwhelming« and most irrelevant *political emancipation* of the Bulgarian nation. This process ignored first of all the character of the Bulgarian parochialism. It also neglected totally a most painful process of emerging of own Bulgarian *subject-participant culture*, as in the case of the April 1876 Insurrection. [49] This »suspended« pattern, succeeded to corrupt, but not to cultivate a rationally motivated state-subject orientation and interaction with the established political object. Paternalism seemed the only vital impulse for the institution of the newly shaped Bulgarian subjectivism. It determined the development of the political culture even long after the Liberation from 1878.

If we, Bulgarians, still live with the illusion of some »state without King or Sultan« (which we still prefer to call a republic), even when nearly »half of us« voted in favor of Simeon Saxe Coburg-Gotha 100 years after (!) – The only rational explanation seems hidden in a »dual matrix«, as implemented in Tarnovo Constitution. Thus an *old-new paternalism* still flourishes on its rubbles…

Having embraced the republicanism of Mazzini and Garibaldi, but as well as other progressive European ideas of civic liberty, the Bulgarian elite after the Liberation of 1878 has been excluded in an off-hand manner from the invented bureaucratic and most banal forms of political »participation«. The latter came to fill in the mentioned deep cultural gap in the established new Bulgarian state. The incompatibility between a »suspended« *political object*

another the »cut off« Bulgarian territories up to present still seem a »good proof« for this notion. (see. Il.Dimitrov, Epoch 1886…).

49 The emerging of a Bulgarian subjective-participant culture, as Toncho Zechev has brilliantly demonstrated in his penetrating study on the Bulgarian National liberation movement might be considered as early as from 1861 (the separation of the Bulgarian Orthodox Church form the Greek one). There are enough historical facts to consider that within the Ottoman empire own Bulgarian original forms of civic participance(as Church schools, Bulgarian community eterprices, or even own proto-juridical organs etc.) operated successfully. The offered analysis of the Aprill 1876 Insurrection, as form of mass political involevemet, is by no means to be opposed or in any way diminishes the role of the »Church Movement«. The latter is not less important for the National Liberation, as it searched for long years peaceful, evolutionary solution. See: Toncho Zechev, Balgarskijat Velikden I strastite balgarski, Sofia,1967.

(imperial by spirit and monarchist in form) and the *political subject* in the newly established state seem more than obvious. [50]

Let us discuss briefly on this.

At the time when the new Bulgarian state came to life in North Bulgaria, an autonomous region in South Bulgaria, according the clauses of the Berlin Treaty has been founded.

On April 14(26) 1879, as signed in Istanbul, the so-called »Organic Chart« was released. Its 15 chapters, 495 paragraphs and 13 amendments, enchained Bulgarians of Eastern Thrace into new vassal dependence to Turkey. This dependency was manifold and most humiliating[51].

While in North Bulgaria the constitutional »dress« of European fashion design has been pulled on the shabby Bulgarian »state body«, their brothers and sisters from the East and South were left in the old »hand made« woolen robes of the »Organic chart«.

Practically Bulgaria was deprived from the chance to progress, using the advantages of the national model of state building, relevant to other European states. In this way a »delayed return« of the Bulgarian people to its natural cultural and political European environment was left on the midway.

Thus most of the premises for effective state functionalism, through the system of participant-subjective orientations and interactions with the main objects and attributes of state and political power, have been excluded in the Bulgarian case. This relates to the 2 basic models, applied (as partially) and inconsistently as it appears:

The first model was the one of a »*democratic national state*«, as established in the Principality. As a paradox of history – it found its most energetic political support mainly by Russia. (!) Emperors have also »democratic sentiments« – is all we have to add here.

The second one – was the model of an »*autonomous vassal state*«, applied in Eastern Rumelia. This most exotic political hybrid, as some scholars claim,

---

50 On April 16(28) 1879 The Foundation Assembly adopted the Constitution of the Principality. On the very next day, in Tarnvo again, a Great National Assembly has gatheed and appointed (by vote) for the first head of the new Bulgarian state – the German prnce Alexander Battenberg. As disputavle as his figure has been according to differents historians in this country and abroad, his »only merit« (Il.Dimitrov) was that this 22 years old yound man was nephee of the Russian Empress and was nominated by Alexander II – the King Liberator (!). By the end of June the Prince took an oath in the Constitution in the Great Assembly of Bulgaria. Two years later he suspended it and preferd a »one man« rule.

51 Anually East Rumelia was obliged to pay 3/10 of all it's incomes for the budjet of the Turkish government. The Sultan had the authority to impose military forces into the region. He appoints as well the governeur and the high rank officers, the secrtary in chief and the »law enforcement« sdministrative posts (gendarmery and militia).

is rather »a contribution of British snobbism« than a realistic political solution. None of the two »form«, turned to be adequate and sustainable. As in 1908 at the ruins of the last Bulgarian Kingdom (Tarnovo) the National independence of Bulgaria was proclaimed, this incongruence between an authentically emerged participant-subject culture and it's irrelevant »system« stayed, to deepen through the ages even. Why, so? Let us tackle this here from our point of view:

Firstly – within the constellation of the Principality, for part of the Bulgarian people, who survived 500 year of Turkish oppression, the formal right of democratic involvement as citizen has been proclaimed indeed. But this occurred on no fundament for a proper *participant-subject culture.* Using the »rubbles« of what was left of the Turkish Empire, the subject in the Principality was not able to make sense, less evens use of his political advantages, given by the Tarnovo Constitution. As progressive as it was (based on the Belgium one), it pushed aside the parochial-subjective mind, excluding it from it's generated and already explicitly expressed participant orientations to an own political object. Thus the formal movement to the new (national) political system did not allow the individual to live through and experience an intermediary »chain« of consciously adopted »subject-parochialism«, which might have later sediment into a consistent participant-subject culture, bound to the system. This led to the devaluation and loss of relevance of the latter.

Secondly – within the other »constellation« – the one of Eastern Rumelia, the Bulgarian practically faced the role of a »non-*participant subject*« – an absurd quasi-civic status, as related to the dual subordination of the autonomy (once to its governor Bogoridi, in charge of the »Organic Chart« and secondly to the Turkish Sultan). Thus the enforced Unification (which occurred as »massive« protests and annexing of Eastern Rumelia to the Principality) has been accepted as act of restored justice by most Bulgarians. Practically it overwhelmed a cognitive gap in the parochial-subject culture, dominating in the Bulgarian mind. This has been felt as s »second try« of the historical objective to quit once and for all with the »rests of ottoman-phylia« among Bulgarians at both sides of the Balkan.

The Bulgarian Unification (or at least the pattern in which it occurs) had not only positive impacts and sequences for the further development of this nation. It has in a no less »voluntary« manner cut off the Bulgarian roads to a civilized planned national and cultural development, as it brought to extreme the links between Russia and the Principality. It sharpened the contradictions between the Great powers, which took part in the Berlin Congress. Battenberg's politics of *fait accompli* gave grounds to a kind of political mistrust as related to Bulgaria, which is in a way latent to present. In one way or another, the act of the Unification of Bulgaria in 1885 was a result of the failed attempts to reach some congruency between »culture« and »system«, a

»matrix« which this nation had to follow for decades onward. The »gambled« institution of the Principality has been analyzed as passionate critics of the personal role(s) of Battenberg, or even Alexander II. What we prefer to stress on, as related to the »systematic output« of this process, is the failure of consolidation of a most *»fragmented subject«* at both sides of the Balkan.

This might well explain the perplexity of the Bulgarian political mind, as reflected in crises of identity, or the attempts to re-position itself in a »hyper-centric« political system and/or a most uncertain «regionalism«. Neither the »witty« procedures by which the III Great Assembly tried to »bring over« the Dutch prince (relative to the St. Petersburg court) to carry the Bulgarian crown (Russia rejected this option), less even the nomination of the Georgian prince (offered by Russia as counter step), could fill this cultural gap in the political orientation of the Bulgarian people. As »imaginary« as it could appear to formal political scientists, an originally re-discovered and re-defined political »object«, as in the case of Bulgaria on the road of national independence appears to us deprived in a »secondary« way. As Dr.Stojan Chomakov, the first professional politician in this country had brilliantly put it: *»an enslaved people can be freed, but a fragmented people are not to be united...«*

This missing »chain« of some own Bulgarian »participant-subjectivism« in the evolution of the political cultures, the fatal deprivation of our authentic political object, with all it's institutions, attributes of power etc. differs the Bulgarian case from most European cultures. This might explain the ambivalence of Bulgarian attitudes not so much to »a less known« world of politics, but a still existing cognitive dissonance, as related to the »mix« of systematically alienated patterns and forms of »interaction«, less relevant to the emancipated civic cultures of most European nation. Still Bulgarians seem less inspired by some cosmopolitanism. A core in our mentality still keeps the memory of Great ancestors as »men of war«, but less of crafty governors or even politicians. The only fear of the »participant subject« of the present seems still driven by the nightmare of some possible »death« of his national. No nostalgia can add meaning to a political culture, however, as deprived as it is from it's originally rediscovered and predetermined shapes and forms. Therefore their substitutes still seem to suit others better, but less to us, Bulgarians.

The »Catastrophic Matrix«

A most sinister continuity of couple of national down falls determines the *»output«* of the Bulgarian political culture in the period between WWI and WWII. This *»catastrophic matrix«* puts its dark legacy on most of the cultural and political efforts of this nation and has in a way »predetermined« the Bulgarian state and national development. The defeats in two wars on the

Balkans (1912–1913), and shortly after this in WWI (1915–1919), as Bulgaria made its choice at the »wrong side« of the »losers« (Germany, Austria-Hungary and Italy) might still appear as some process of »raise« and »fall« of a young Balkan state and nation. But this is only formally to be considered. They had a most devastating impact on the Bulgarian mind. The culmination of this was the Treaty of Neuilly (1919), which buried the Bulgarian dreams to live under the roof of »a united Fatherland«.

The two national catastrophes (some historians considered the collapse of communism in 1989 as another one) have cut off first of all the chance of an *evolutionary pattern* of economic and political development of the Bulgarian state. It enjoyed such a chance only for a short period of time (1900–1910). In a no lesser extend they have »nailed« the suffered national body to a most humiliating and unworthy status on the Balkans and in a wider European context. The cultural and historical mission of Bulgaria in the Orient was undermined. Even though the Bulgarian army won all battles on the front – and did this with brave courage and self-sacrifice, which are highly appreciated, ever since – it became clear that this country has been deprived of worthy politicians. The consequences of the wars doomed this state and nation to isolation from the progressive civilization processes of the modern age. The fatalism that springs from those days of down fall fills most Bulgarian hearts with resentment – canalized into sequential authoritarian rules that followed.

> »As Nikolai Genchev – one of the most penetrating political historians in this country – compressed it in a remarkable essay: »Three fatal ›fives‹ mark and cut off the tragic path in the newest history of Bulgaria from 1878 up to the end of WWII – *five failed Insurrections*, unsuccessful participation in *five wars* and *five coup détaté* interrupt the natural and normal state development of this nation «[52]

Most elements of an *»aspiring«* subjective culture, in search of participative forms of interaction with »it's« political object (cognitive, affective and evaluative orientations) carry an explicit positive load, as related to this period. At the »input« of this process one could find out so much self-sacrifice and uncorrupted patriotism in favor of ones own sate and nation. It is beyond our capacity to draw the line of those »investments«, which end in an overwhelming resentment. What is of greater significance is that at the »output« of this process we can witness a still bleeding wound. The »forced« and most exhaustive attempts to capitalize on ones nation only left human resource and sacrifices it for mere nationalistic ambitions, result less from some rationally steered political activity, or even ideology. They are result of extreme political ambitions of *quasi-national elite,* bound to the

---

52 Nikolai Genchev, Balgaria I balgarite v kraja na XX v., in Dumadaily, Nr.80/81, April 3–4, 1996.

interests of great powers and their monarch egocentrism here on the Balkans and in a wider European context.

What counts more in the Bulgarian case even is that the crashes of the National catastrophes from 1913 to 1919 (Treaty of Neuilly)[53] deviated irreversibly the relations between political system and political culture in this country, as they have driven the latter into an overwhelming apathy and resignation. This might help the modern scholar to better grasp a constantly reconfirmed »pattern of mistrust« of ordinary Bulgarians to most »great national ventures«. Or see beyond some »theory« of conspiracy on which his suffered national dignity still feeds. This systematically pressed and deeply alienated interactions with ones political object, as frame worked by the monarch institution (a trend we can chase back to the Unification form 1886) has shaped a most popular pattern of »blaming the King« for all that happened. The »input-output« relations between »system« and »culture« seem less effective, but more extreme, as compared with other European nations. This notion drives the Bulgarian national spirit to the specter of total *nihilism* towards any political object. The widely spread *»hatred towards any power«* (Marko Semov) is a most bitter result of consistent system failures and deeper structural discrepancies.

Let us brief on this here[54]:

As historians assess the results of two dramatic clashes on the Balkans (1912–1913), which took place in 9 months only, they stress mostly on their impact on the Bulgarian state. Most of the analysis in the last decades offered their »balanced« comments, according the established tradition of obligatory socialist »neighborhood«. Less has been commented on the impact of those wars on the national dignity and their most devastating effect on the shaping political culture of this nation.

What we can witness in this respect is a drastic rupture of the process of system involvement of the Bulgarian »subjectivism«. The wars damaged the process of national identification both »in« and »out« of the formally defined territories of the Fatherland.

The synchrony between both poles of the political process, as performed in 1913–1918, could never be achieved in the Bulgarian history. This relates not so much to some »militant« motivated aspects, but to a mass national upheaval considered for impossible ever since.

The *»catastrophic matrix«* of this nation in a drastic way crashed both subject and *civic* orientations of Bulgarians at »both sides of their bordering Fatherland« – in so far no other state on the Balkans borders with it's own ethnicity.

53 See: Treaty of Neuille-sur-Seine, 27 Nov 1919.

54 Marko Semov, Narodopsichologia. Balgarinat i vlastta, II, Slavena, Varna, p. 65–7.

Thus an irreversible transformation in the »instinctive« readiness of Bulgarians to sacrifice their life not so much for some wider *Lebensraum,* but for a dignified cultural position in wider European context has occurred.

All this has paralyzed for long the Bulgarian national spirit and made it apt to other (Eastern) influences. An Occident future of this nation has been denied indeed. .

The massive drive to the fulfillment of a massively followed, but *failed national ideal,* is the fundament of a most devastating resentment, as related to the idea of some emancipated involvement of this nation into the cultural building processes of the XX c. A bitter political realism springs from this period of Bulgarian existence ever since. They still regard themselves condemned to watch as others spend what belongs to them. Blood has always been too costly for us, Bulgarians though. Some prefer to explain this with an irrational instinct of ours to survive »by all means«. Others blame ancestors for some »genetically embedded« fear, or even »inherited obedience« from the years of Turkish (or even totalitarian oppression) what tasteless jokes, indeed!! System political experience might still turn most precious »cultural software« in a risky and too schematically »coping« world. Thus abstaining from conflict involvement seems a marker of proper politics to us.

Output:

After the two Balkan wars of 1912 and 1913 Bulgaria increased it's territory from 96 000 to 120 000 square kilometers, the country received 1/9 part of Macedonia and access to the Mediterranean, but had to give up South Dobruja to Romania. The price of this was the death of 70 000 Bulgarian soldiers. The total losses amounted to 2 billion Bulgarian golden leva.

Even worse effect had the losses at the »diplomatic table«. The political life between WWI and WWII confirmed the impossibility of an explicitly propelled national upheaval and the crash of the ideal of complete unification of the Bulgarian people.

To the losses of those two wars we have to add another 11 000 square kilometers as result from the Treaty of Neuilly, signed a year after WWI (1915–1918). The western parts of Bulgaria have been given to Serbia. A government of the Antantè has been established in Western Thrace. This territory inhabited by compact Bulgarian residents was later added to Greece.

For 37 years Bulgaria had to pay reparations amounting to 2, 5 billions French franks. The unbearable »natural contributions« – animal stock, foods and coal brought the land to starvation.

The army, together with the police has been reduced to 30 000 people. The victims of the failed attempt of Bulgarian unification amounted to 100 000 people!! Weaves (and abandoned graves) still remind of the victories at Ljule Bourgas, Bulair and Odrin (Edrine)...

> »Ivan Evstatiev Geshev – a most prominent Bulgarian politician in the early XIX c. called 16 July 1913 »the beginning of the end«. Fair

> enough! For 1918 was another sinister continuation of 1913. The sequence of »historical mistakes« is to be related to the personality of Ferdinand Saxe Coburg-Gotha.«[55]

He ruled the country for 31 years! According the Constitution of Tarnovo he had immense power. After his abdication the territory of Bulgaria increased with less than 7 000 square kilometers. The price of this »gain« was the death of 200 000 Bulgarians (!!). This has crashed totally the national ideal for generations ahead. The questions of the national identity in broader Balkan terms were (and are still) open.[56]

The hazard policy of most Bulgarian regimes in the past have deprived us from some *civic privilege* of most European nations, as shaped through hard years of post-war recoveries. Still the Bulgarian political mind has suffered more from a notorious *»voluntarism«* of it's own politicians. They have explicitly performed their authoritarian character and extreme power ambitions, ignoring basic values and self-generated civic structures. That this could also shape into disgraceful »modern« political oppression is still to be rationalized.

We seem to be in a way sharing some of the bitterness of the Germans – as related to the notion of some *»dagger in the back«* (Momsen). National betrayal(s) have haunted the Bulgarians ever since, even though we have rarely dared to challenge them by democratic means. We still feel more vulnerable than others, and have own reasons to call us a »wounded nation« (Noelle-Neumann). The sense of being severely punished for our courage and aspirations for a better position under the sun of the Balkans and in a wider European context is still with »us«. It hides in our »twisted« attitude to »big politics«, in which we prefer not to interfere. But seem still tempted to pace along with the conqueror...

55 Dimitar Michalchev, Za roljata na sluchajnostta I na velikite ljue v istoriata, Philosofski pregled, XIII, Mai_Juni 1941, p. 229–251.

56 National identity in the aspect of the comparative analysis of politicsl cultures is related to a complex of beliefs on the integrity of the individual into his national state. While E. Erickson stresses on the necessity to solve »crisis of identities«, so that a stable personality could be encouraged, L. Pye discussed the way such crises of identity influence the mentality of the national elites. Untll the individuals, which are physially and legally members of some political system »do not become psychologically members of this system as well (i.e. feel themselves as such- P.G.) no orderly patterns of change can occur.« See more on this in: Lucian Pye, Politics, Personality, and Nation Building, New Haven, Yale UnivPress, 1962; L. Pye, Comparative Political Culture in: Political Culture and Political Development, L. W. Pye, Sidney Verba(Eds.), Prinston Univ.Press, 1965, p. 529–30.

Liberalism and Conservatism (1919–1939)

The establishment of a modern political system in Bulgaria can not be considered as some exception from a nearly 100 years of traditional challenge between liberal and conservative ideas. It is a *»dualistic quintessence«* (Dahrendorf) of the political development of capitalism in Europe from the end of XIX c. The couple of »older« and »newer« waves in this process reflect an own Balkan way of transition from agrarian and craftsmen to industrial forms of economic life. This process flows in delayed, reluctant and rather primitive forms, even though it undergoes general principles of capital development and accumulation. It reflects the emerging of a new class division of the Bulgarian society. Parallel to this determinist triviality, both liberalism and conservatism on »Balkan soil« seem loaded with a pluralism of an own breed. This quality of the two major value systems and their relevant patterns of behavior are of special interest here. [57]

What comes first to differentiate from a common European trend is that most of the ideological and political forms of interaction between labour and capital, as performed by the mass of petty and independent entrepreneurs at this side and the industrious cohorts, appear as most inconsistent and contradictive in the context of a longer temporal shortcut, dating from 1919 to the very eve of WWII (1939). This might well explain the »hybrid«, »diffuse«, and as critics define it, »a priory« deprived of significant meaning both liberal and conservative ideas in Bulgaria. This period is related with the rule of a »republican monarch«, as in moments of sentiment King Boris III preferred to call himself. A »thorny crow«, which decorates the Bulgarian political culture of that age, is another national catastrophe, as result of the

---

57 The socio-economic development of Bulgaria after the Liberation (1878) up to the WWI shaped two major periods, – initial capital accumulation, which lasted till the end of XIX c. and a period of advanced capitalism, dating from the early XX c. to WWII. These have been rather schematically evaluated by dogmatic Marxist social science, especially considering the cultural impact of both major ideological streamlines. Prevailing was the interest to liberalism, as far as it reflected the interest of broader masses in Bulgaria. Both patterns are in fact a product of most primitive productive forces, feeded on extractive forms of capital accumulation and were based on unfair distribution, as well as a specific »cultural conservatism« (Iv.Krastev) that hindered modern developments. The gap between a missing conservative »chains« in the misbalanced political culture of this country before WWII became obvious only after 1989, as quasi-liberal and/or conservative parties emerged out of nowhere. None of them could offer a rationale set of reformist ideas – and it was not just some interrupted tradition to be blamed for this. But more likely, as we could witness. a rapidly liberalizeation of the political market who neglected rational criteria of defining both liberal and conservative ideas in their modern terms and context.

fatal alliance of Bulgaria and it's joining to the tripartite pact on the side of Nazi Germany.

What strikes most is the epigone character of both liberalism and conservatism in their Balkan context. Both patterns of interaction with the political object draw their ideas from abroad indeed. What is even more destructive is that they are less a product of internal objectives and social realities. This *ideological plagiary* has a long tradition and has found most sophisticated forms of political mimicry through the ages. It is not to be blamed alone for a delayed, unsystematic and most uncertain social development of this country. But, moreover, for a notorious »idealism«, which has nourished political unrealism of most peculiar kind. This mere resonance of liberal or conservative ideas has most often ended with sequential fiascos, which seem typical for most Balkan cases. Both patterns of political behavior are loaded with constant contradictions and rivalries. They sooner or later failed (each in their way) to contribute for significant social change, less even for the emerging of consistent civic cultures. The latter peddled between both liberal and conservative »poles«, but have rarely gravitated around proper notions of individual rights and freedoms, independent creativity or social progress. As »vague«, as liberalism has always considered to be at this side, it offered more freedom, at least in its popular sense, and enjoyed support from the broader mass. It never managed to mobilize significant cohorts, less even to cultivate a long lasting tradition. Conservatism, on the other side, is a product of most extreme efforts to feed on primitive means and sources of wealth accumulation, irrelevant to the progressive technological and social innovations. This deficit of potential is in a way reflected in the social and political structures, as shaped by eclectic notion of nation building. Let us discuss those cultural patterns, which in a most paradox way reflect the incapability of both ideologies to organize the indigenous political mind into consistent and socially efficient forms.

***

From the early naïve liberalism, free lanced among the ignorant peasantry immediately after the foundation of the New Bulgarian state (1908), to the grim faced conservatives of the 20 ease and 30 ease, not to miss the hyperactive Bulgarian »Jacobins«, »broad« and »narrow« socialists, anarchists, radicals and liberal democrats – the Bulgarian political life seems to have been created according the rules of some Oriental Babylon indeed. It has offered a most inspiring social environment to anyone who decides to »lead« even »his father's friend's gang«. This popular saying reflects the tradition of mobilizing old clans, nepotisms, or neighborhoods as »critical mass« of party generation. The result of those efforts has been most often the emerging of quasi-political structures, which mushroomed but vanish as unexpectedly as they have appeared out of nowhere.

The pathetic liberalism of warm-hearted peasants and semi ruined independent craftsmen confronted in most passionate and bloody street battles the »stubborn« conservatives. This pattern could hardly be changed, since ideas of social progress went rarely beyond one's own yard, surrounded by high stone hedges and barking dogs. Neither liberal, nor conservative parties in 1919–1939 could reflect, less even implements significant trends in the social and political development of Europe. This »home made«, provincial, character of both major ideologies and their most intense »pulse«, have often ended in ambushes, murders of political leaders, imprisonment and most oppressive terror of both »libs« and «cans« contributions to a specific *culture of political revenge* [58].

Rational and pragmatic ideas have been brutally crushed or systematically ignored, as the notorious »*passions of ours*«(Zhechev) »reigned« and determined the political philosophies even of learned and experienced leaders. Most of the conventional criteria used by modern political science seem in a way helpless to reflect these internal controversies, which are less compatible with civilized patterns of social and political interaction. Observers have often pointed out the unpredictability of Balkan political behavior. Leading sociologist as Iv.Hadjiiski explained those features of the local political culture with the »law of the hesitating nature« of the small owner. The latter rapidly changes his feathering according the unexpectedly turning political environment and is loyal only to his own egocentric and primitive pragmatism. No wonder that the latter could give birth to a sheer »instinctive democratism«, but rarely allow proper individual freedoms to flourish on Balkan soil.

The amorphous social class structure of the Bulgarian society from the early XIX c. has often been pointed as a mighty spring of this vague *liberalism*«. Another point is the cultural conservatism of the Bulgarian social existence long after the Liberation from the Turkish oppression. A third one is, as some consider, an Asian-Oriental mentality »mix«, which has cultivated sustainable patterns of despotic behavior, ill polished by the mimicries of some »European outlook«. Authoritarian and openly oppressive patterns of behavior have been regarded as status symbols here in the Balkans.. Humiliating attitude to women, intolerance to the weak, or even

58 To explain in a most popular way the ideas of liberalism to the semi-ignorant peasantry P. Karavelov (founder of the Liberal party) used a words connotation of »libe« (love, being fond of) and »ralo«(wooden plough) – hence »liberal«. In other words »all who are fond of their wooden plough« as he claimed, should join the ranks of the new Liberal party. Similarly the word »can« (konserva – Bulgarian) is still used to label the conservative political wing in this country.

disabled people, the show off style and most repulsive egocentrism of the »well off«, the cruelty of the »money usurer«, are symptomatic in this respect. Arrogance is often considered as a proof for some self-determination. Those that profit by »tricks«, or even »open cheating", are still admired and appreciated. Even losers seem inspired by such »creative capacity«, as they publicly condemn the rich, or the man who has been lucky to secure his prosperity by corruptive practices. This moral discrepancy especially refers to attitudes towards the state and its institutions. It has shaped a twisty, self-devouring and most erosive quasi-social behavior, which has rarely reached a commonly accepted consensual, less even positive social effect.

The traditional *paternalism* has been another structure shaping factor of both liberals and conservatives at this side. The notorious contradiction between *»Russophiles«* and *»Russophobes«* (pro- and counter Russia supporters) has for decades been the source of constant impulses of rivalry and furious »political« battles. Having Russia behind one's back was a must for most of our liberals, while conservatives did all they could to stick to Europe. Most often those attempts ended, however, with failures (especially after the 2 national catastrophes) and their only significant outcome was to enrich few clans. This *quasi-ideological pattern* of rivalry (less proper democratic competition) adds an irremovable scar on the Bulgarian political culture up to 1939. It has been less motivated by significant ideas of social progress, and relied on some pervert notion of a political »value« added to ones own lack of political substance imported from abroad. This »zigzag« political behavior of couple of generations has for decades eroded the emerging of modern nationalism on which other European nations upgraded their social and political development. The Bulgarian political culture seems deprived from the chance to initiate own significant social change, and is to be considered not just alienated, but in a way insensitive to its own national demands and interests.

Some political scientism considers this as a spring of some culturally implemented radicalism, which has often tempted both Bulgarian liberals and conservatives. The demarcation line of the two major »wings« is still to be witnessed even though in more sophisticated forms of some mainstream of the new »market pragmatism«. The latter embraces gladly the idea of »second hand bargaining« policy in which national interests are often is interpreted in most speculative and perverted way. Neither liberalism, less even conservatism in Bulgaria have rested on rationale, system bound notions of civic rights and freedoms of the individual. They have most often ignored the integrative role of democratic institutions in the system of the national state, as well as its attributes of real power, i.e. all significant elements that give meaning to political life. In their Bulgarian paraphrase both ideological platforms seem loaded with a most repulsive *internal voluntarism*. The latter has demonstrated its evils both in »libs« and »cans« forms of government, as to prove the temporal inconsistence of each policy and deepen the mistrust and cynicism of many Bulgarian generations. This is synthesized in the lack of proper political philosophy generated at this side, capable to make use of the political energy of a small, but sober people. The latter has never been too late to grasp his interest and even look for retribution. This occurred, however, only after drastic and massive social falls and political turnovers. A systematic, patient upgrading of social structures has rarely been the case. The lack of a non-compromising public control over the deeds of »the strong of the day«, has been only an unrealistic dream, and object of passionate discussions in pubs and in the open. Never, except in days of upheavals, has this capacity been able to find its adequate and system relevant forms. Instead the genuine »liberal« (irresponsible in its own way) pattern, has dominated to avoid political involvement and thus deepen the crises. The »step by step«, eclectic pattern of conservative political engagement, from the other side, has most often betrayed its own national credo, even though so explicitly proclaimed by best heads of the Bulgarian intelligentsia.

»Land is which gives birth to aristocracy« – wrote Alexis de Toqueville as he touched the new world. This rule is less relevant, considering the genesis of the Bulgarian representative political structures immediately after the Liberation.[59] To differentiate from most European nations, the Bulgarian political subject has always been doomed to find his own way, with no proper ideological support from its aristocracy. This self-made political existence has been much exploited by the Bulgarian high political class, offering cheaper (populist) political stories to the naïve Bulgarian mind. Right at the threshold of the new Bulgarian national state, 30 years after »Democracy in America« (Toqueville), the leader of the movement of Bulgarian Church independence P. R. Slavejkov pointed out the need of a *principally different* Bulgarian road. This road, as he claimed »must learn the Bulgarians to rely

---

59 The agrarian turnover after the Liberation as reliable sources point out did not change the status of big land property owners. Only the lands of Turkish owners, who left the country have been redistributed The Bulgarian rich agrarian class even enlarged their land property, occupied illegally, or bought at cheap prices from the Turks. Thus, along with the process of parceling out of Turkish lands and enrichment of poorer Bulgarian peasants, a process of accumulation in favor of the rich Bulgarian land owners has practicallya occurred. A counter process of secondary accumulation of capital (land), taken from ruined Bulgarian farmers also took place. This process contributed to the modernization of older and bigger private land estates. All this occurred not in the forms of »reclamation of new lands«, as in the New world. In this way the the old land aristocracy in the case of Bulgaria has been deprived of re-establishing into the political structures of the newly found national state. See: Jacque Nathan, Economic history of Bulgaria, Sofia, 1957, pp. 250; Angel Bankov, Razvtie na filosophskata missal v Balgaria, Sofia,1966, p. 194–195.

first of all on himself, on his own strengths and to wake up in them a sense of their own social and political interests«. Those appeals have rarely been heard, less even followed. The Bulgarian political development has been most often a painfully delayed offspring of the *collective suffering*, less some lucky achievement of political midwifes, as symbolized by our self-made and self-proclaimed aristocracy. It might well be the reason why most of our cultural and moreover political thriving performs most often as extreme mobilizations of the scarce internal energy of the Bulgarian people in each attempt to raise from the rubbles and stand up equal to other nations. This has rarely been the result of some altruistic wisdom or inventiveness of noble men indeed.

This most eroding »lack of existential minimum«, out of which our civic culture had to raise from so many ashes, ghosts until present in the Bulgarian mind. It determines the humble, servitude and most *humiliating obedience* of the Bulgarian, confronted systematically with an unfriendly and less social environment that others enjoy. »A well feted man never trusts a hungry one« is a common Bulgarian saying, reflecting this bitter helplessness of the small man. But, we can read it in proverb collections of most Balkan people as the Albanians, the Romanians, or even the Turks. The »hungry cohort« of a Balkan in emergency established political class after the Liberation and immediately after the WWI, has devoured in relatively short period the scarce national recourses. Both liberals and conservatives have equally profited from this nourishing a specific tradition of corruption. A special Bulgarian contribution to the corruptive clienteles is considered the turning of »politics into most profitable profession«. This »upside Weber pattern« in its Bulgarian case (and in broader Balkan terms) is still successfully feeding on the naïve democratic or even »rightist« sentiments of the Bulgarian and their dream of proper social order, justice etc. Political partisanship is a theme that is worth to be studied separately. Corruptive patronages often appear only as icebergs under which a prehistoric monster still breathes and threatens to strike back. This is the reason why many political scandals, rarely end in court. And if they do, it is a part of the »political laundry« which repairs the reputation of the strong of the day to leave the weaker and poorer in their traditional uncertainty and desperation.

A notorious »material scarcity« marks the life-path of the Bulgarian self-mad man, moreover the representative of our intelligentsia; usually victims of political pogroms and systematic spiritual oppression practiced successfully both under Liberal and Conservative regimes. This Balkan severe environment demanded more than mere civic courage and commitment – as we can judge from few empirical studies of that age.[60]

---

60 Graduates of leading European universities, in Berlin, Munich, Zurich Prague and even Paris as Geo Milev (poet, founder of the German Secession art movement),

> »This is the start of the career of Todor Kozarev from the city of Sliven, prominent tradesman, and founder of the famous Kozarevi family. His father was a goat's shepherd. He left the world when the boy was 12 years old. From this early age the orphan had to work hard and earn money for bread and living. Initially he started as ash cleaner at the local »Horse bath« for 20 pari (small coins) a day. He saved 40 grosh (a bit more valued coins) and bought a donkey. He started working with his animal for other people's vineyards. The donkey died from overloading, and having no extra money, he had to take off the donkey's shoes and sold them for 1 grosh. With this capital he started a more profitable trade. His bough pressed goat's meat and carried it each Saturday on his own back (some 30 miles away) on Sundays at the open market in the city of Jambol. This trade he practiced for quite a while, until he earned 3000 grosh. His nephew Belchev appreciated his qualities and involved him in his shop. This is how the rapid career of this most capable and entrepreneurial Bulgarian started to flourish. To reach this peak later in the years, the iron shoes of his donkey and his personal qualities have backed him only. He had a sharp mind, was quick and witty. His math's was perfect. He could remember thousands of names and recognized with no hesitation many faces. He was eloquent, a man of humor and excellent, brave kind of speech. He had a remarkable memory, which he kept until his old ages .«[61]

To add a bit more:

> »...The same process – sums up Hadjijski – took place among the representatives of the Bulgarian trade and industrial capital. All hose were new people. The ancestors of the prominent families from Koprivstitza, the Chalakovi, and Doganovi, were simple shepherds. The first Bulgarian industry businessmen – Dobri Panajotov, the »Factory man«, as they called him – started his career as simple factory worker in Russia and on his own, with no education whosoever, managed to prepare wooden models of the weaving and textile machines he worked on. He smuggled them secretly and organized his own factory in constant resistance against all craftsmen, citizens and the state authority even«.[62]

Joseph Herbst, (leading columnist and passionate democrat), Dimcho Debeljanov, (one of the most inspiring Bulgarian lyrics), or Boris Vaptsarov (king Boris III gave hopes to mercy him till the day of his execution being close friend of the Vaptsarov family in Bansko) have been »liquidated« according the clauses of the so called »Law on the defense of the State« and the junta regimes from 1925 to 1934.

61 See: Ivan Hadjijski, Rodoslovie na semeistvata Kozarovtzi OT grad Sliven, (The kinship origin of the Kozarovtzi Family from the city of Sliven), Sofia, 1925 in: Ivan Hadjijski, Pojavata na individualizma u nas (The emerging of individualism among us«, Philosofski pregled, XIII, Nr.3, p. 13–209.

62 Ibid, p. 198.

Can we really »explain« a long lost tradition and most industrious self-sacrifice of personalities as mentioned above? Or is it the Spirit of capitalism again to be praised? One way to rationalize these phenomena is the inventive »obsession«, which has served as a guiding star for many Bulgarians, who had to rely on themselves only. And even carry life long battles with a notorious and most primitive conservatism of their own social environment. This anti-gravity social field hindered (and hinders still) most progressive and even useful ideas. The metamorphoses of initially admirable values have turned in few years the cohorts of the »new riches« or self-proclaimed notables into disgraceful figures. The Bulgarian »self-made man« of the years of modernity strikes with one major capacity only: he consciously forgets where he comes from. And if in a moment of sentiment, or for some other reasons he dares to remind on the genesis of his Ego – this is to put a most dramatic stress on his own immense sufferings, his »iron will«, but less good luck, or recognition by others, who have contributed in one way or another for his well being. This notorious Bulgarian *ungratefulness* goes well even with one's own religious believes, which rarely have anything to do with a most disputable business ethics. This self-appraisal is no less a reflection of a deeply hidden *self-unawareness*, which we can witness only if he turns his back to ordinary people…

A *homo politicus* (Dahrendorf) of local Balkan breed rarely claims that his achievement is the result of some life view, even less any ideology. If this still happens, however, one finds with astonishment a naïve »ideological« and most contradictive »value« system on which his social behavior rests. Its simple premises in a paradox way »operate« in a semi-ignorant social environment, deprived from proper economic rights and freedoms. Most irrational ideas are in this way successfully freelanced and even »politically« backed. All this creates a constant vacuum in the Bulgarian political culture, which has not been able to sort out rational forms of public control and get rid of a »swarm of political horse flies« (Marko Semov) biting on the suffered national body for ages. The Bulgarian political participation has been less a product of ideological evaluative efforts of the mind. It could never flow into a generally accepted mainstream and instead has most often left the Bulgarian political life into its unconsolidated, raw shapes and forms. Politics is done »by the way«, rarely with commitment. This dualistic discrepancy is apparent in the political behavior of prominent politicians even and »strong men of the day«. Being well aware of their transitorily status and privileges, which they might soon loose – most of them rush to misuse power and positions »as long as this is possible«.

A most introvert life style made all this possible and characteristic (if not typical for the Bulgarian), even though modern ages add more sophisticated forms to this traditional *social escapism* of ours:

> »The Bulgarian has looked with mistrust and prejudice to all common actions, to which he has been summoned or his involvement has been needed. Most often of he has ever decided to take part in such activities, he has done this only if he has been convinced that his private, egoistic interest would not be offended. – So Bojan Penev, commenting on P. Slavejkov's critics on the Bulgarian national character. For the Bulgarian »I« is the sun, around which all planets rotate. »He lives with his family for himself, he is deprived of the feeling of his homeland as entity; this is why when he considers his work done, he comes back home and does not care much what happens outside his home... He is fond of his privacy and hates if bothered and feels thus most happy. As lonesome in his ambition, he thinks of nothing more but his tomorrow. This tomorrow offered often-terrible ghosts, his forehead wrinkles, his eye darkens, his heart shrinks, and his hand even more so. Could we than expect that his plans drawn succeed?«[63]

This selfishness has less in common with the conscious withdrawal of the German, or the French citizen, who is capable to run even quicker from the vanity and vicissitudes of public life. Not to mention the pragmatism of the American self made man. While those cultural types, seem in a way inclined to temporary withdrawal in the sharing circles of their family and kinship (as long as they can change their »social skin«) before they jump into new social ventures – the indigenous at this side still prefers to hide behind his »shell«, as it gets cornier with time passed. This most primitive conservatism is notorious and consistent element of the Bulgarian political ego. This might well explain that in times of slight hesitations even, not to mention deeper shifts in the political life, both the indigenous »liberal« and »conservative« equally rapidly get rid of feathering and ideological platforms, persuasions and/or civic positions. Both they hurry to re-write their political biography (Draganov) using cheap pencil, or even most expensive brand ink-pens. This rapid transformation of the Bulgarian political ego has impressed the alien observer. It is only the external, facade appearance of a much deeper political Ego. The Bulgarian political history offers numerous examples of such a *»swap« of political identities.* The period of »transition«, as we could witness, offered new chance of this chameleon culture to flourish and even merit from the vast political changes in a wider context.

This quasi-pluralism of ours, determined by the level of development of the social existence, as well as by the reflective, epigone character of the quasi-ideological orientations of most political parties and movements, dates far back to the early days of our political life. The temporary, transitorily character of most parties and structures, has added only to a quickly fading political tradition in this country. Most parties that emerged immediately

---

63 Bojan Penev, Istoria na novata balgarska literature, (History of the New Bulgarian literature), Bd. III, p. 331.

after the Liberation up to the early XX c. vanished in a remarkable way, while few of them managed to play any role in the political life of this country. Let us brief on this »quick rate political mortality« at this side:

The *Conservative party*[64] – which endured a crash in 1884, came off the political stage relatively quickly. Its leaders joined later through new combinations other parties and movements. The split during the plenipotentiary rule among the Liberal party continued and lead to further political rivalries. Out of the wing of the »irreconcilable« liberals (shaped 1883) couple of new parties emerged.

The supporters of St. Stambolov, who took part in the counter coup d etat, turned their back to the pro-Russian oriented old Liberal party and founded in 1886 the organization *»Bulgaria for itself«*.

On its base in 1887 the *Peoples-Liberal party* was found know as the Stambolov's party. This formation has couple of times been involved in the government of Bulgaria. Inspired by the idea of an independent economic welfare in this country, it worked to shift the old political gravity from Russia to the West. Its most oppressive style of government became notorious. Later

64 The party of the so-called »old« before the Liberation acted as conservative in the new political conditions after 1878, while the party of »young« – as liberals. As D. Blagoev points out »...the ideology of the conservative party appears as representing the transitions, the ideal of the diminishing class of usurers and big owners of land, i.e. the rich (chorbadjii) class before the Liberation«. Its ideal is the monarchy, concentration of power in the hands of the Principal and the senate and restrictions of the rights of the people and the National Assembly. At the Foundation Assembly (1979) the liberal party represented most actively by P.R.Slavejkov, fought most passionately for the voting in favor of a democracy constitution (Tarnovo Constitution) against the conservatives. Todor Ikonomov is considered as one of the most prominent Bulgarian conservatives from that age. The Bulgarian conservatism, as A.Bankov claims, has deeper ideological roots. It builded it premises on a most disputable »sociological« theory of the Bulgarian society. According to it Bulgarians are not to be regarded as »rich« or »poor«, but more likely as »industrious« (rich) and »lazy« (poor). The conservatives »proved« that the Bulgarian people, who lived for 500 years under Turkish oppression and have not the needed education and culture, should not be given freedoms and rights »right away« , since they might most probably misuse them. The victory of the young Liberals, which lead to the division of power, and democratic rules is notorious for political life in this country, who has most often followed this mainstream of mass political preferences, even as vague as they are. Under the pressure of the conservatives, however most of the ideals for a republican political system proclaimed by leaders of the national liberation movement as Vasil Levski, Christo Botev, Ljuben Karavelov and others, have been abandoned. See. A. Bankov, Gravities Na filosofskata missal v Balgaria, (Development of the philosophic thought in Bulgaria), Sofia, 1966, p. 195.

it suffered the same political »revenge pattern«, as being banned in 1894. St.Stambolov and D.Petkov became victims of the political terrorism.

In the summer of 1887 as result of the contradictions between the Regent Stambolov and the Prime minister V.Radoslavov, a new political formation emerged – *The Liberal party (Radoslavists).* Most respectful scholars find no significant differences between both. The Radoslavists ruled, but acted in opposition only in collaboration with other political forces. They were not capable to form a stronger political movement.

In 1904 out of their rank and files the *Young Liberal party* of Dimitar Tonchev appeared on the scene. It became famous« as the smallest Bulgarian political formation. The two liberal newspapers »Peoples rights« and »Free speech« of the two parties mentioned offer almost identical ideological platforms – something common for other parties representing »different« wings.

The Democratic Party is an inheritor of the old liberal wing, ahead of Petko Karavelov and Petko Slavejkov. It adopted this name in 1896 during the rule of Stambolijski, when it was in opposition. Its leaders are A. Malinov, R. Madjarov, A. Ljapchev, M.Takev, N. Mushanov and other. The party is related to historic events as the pronouncing of the Bulgarian independence. Its printed organs »Flag« and »Banner« reflected brooder interests of the middle and upper-middle class in Bulgaria.

In 1905–1906 around T.Vlaikov and N.Tsanov the *Radical Democratic Party* was founded – as political formation with most limited membership. It claims for democratization, but has no significant influence.

The extreme Russophiles of Dragan Tsankov formed the core of the *Progressive Liberal party* named so in 1899. It ruled only in the beginning of XX c. and for a short period after during the II national catastrophe. After the withdrawal of D.Tsankov its leadership undertook Dr. S.Danev. Its printed was »Bulgaria daily«.

The people's party – founded 1984 by the prominent Bulgarian politician Constantine Stoilov united part of the ex-conservative with activists of the South Bulgarian Peoples (Union) party. It strived to economic development and modernization of the ruined country. As ruling force it works for a more or less balanced foreign policy. Its printed organ is one of the most prestigious newspapers in this country »World«. Prominent representatives of the Bulgarian business as Iv. Geshev, M. Madjarov, T. Todorov, A. Burmov, are to be mentioned here.

In the last decade or XIX c. (1981) the *Bulgarian social democratic party (BSDP)* ahead of D. Blagoev, J. Sakazov and N. Gabrovski appeared. It split in 1903 into so-called »narrow« and »broad« socialist. The party reflected from its early days the socialist ideas that began to spread in this country. Its social bases stayed limited and it was not before 1944 till it gained on influence as result of the communist period.

At the very end of the XIX c. (1899) *The Bulgarian agrarian peoples union* has been founded. This political formation reflected in a most adequate way the agrarian character of the social structure of this society. It turned under the leadership of Ts. Tserkovski and J. Zabunov, later A. Stambolijski into the mightiest political party and played a significant role in the Bulgarian political life especially after the wars.

The rapidly shaping political infrastructure in Bulgaria has been less commented as related to an initial both cultural and political deficit. In most European countries up to 1913, as recent findings show, the voting right does not refer to more that 25 % of the population. In some countries as UK this share is 17 %. From all who disposed with voting right, an even smaller share practically made use of it. This, as respectful European sociologists have pointed out, brings us to the empirical conclusion that not more than 10–15 % of the European population before WWI had real chance to participate in the political life of their countries through the forms of representative democracy. The *use of the voting right* is in advantage of the modern age indeed. If we turn back the newsreel some 30 years ago in Italy for example, the voting right involved not more than 2 % of the population. Only 1 % made use of it there. Even in UK, considered as exemplary of representative democracy, only 4 % of the population took part in the national elections until the reform in 1885. Slightly bigger is the share of those who used their voting right in Germany. This fact does not differ from a common European trend, which seems obvious here. [65]

There are all grounds to claim that Bulgaria has formally related to the political structures and procedures of the Western European representative democracy. At least considering the period up to WWI. Thus the above-mentioned *pseudo-political pluralism* is relevant not only to lower and broader social strata of the Bulgarian pre-war society (WWII). It has in a way infiltrated and has shaped a most uncertain and inconsistent political culture of the prewar *capitalist elite* in this society until the very eve of the dramatic »turn to communism« (Sept. 1944). It is a painful but realistic conclusion to reach here that as primitive and unsophisticated as it seems to us, those capitalist forms of social existence could not contribute for the emerging of a proper civic culture of European type. The Bulgarian political culture seems deprived in a »secondary way« indeed. This relates the Bulgarian political sub-culture(s) with some oriental arche-types, inherited, which feeded on the scarcity of this society even in days of »advancing capitalism«, which practically delayed the political emancipation of this nation in a common wider European context.

---

65 R, Dahrendorf, Recent Changes in the Class Structure of European Societies, Dedalus, Winter, 1964, pp. 225–270.

The motto »*One man one vote*«, that became symbol of the fight for social and political rights of mankind all over the world, turns inapplicable in its proper sense in the case of Bulgaria. Thus the civic culture founded on the premise that all people are born equal, even long after the massive social movements after WWI and up to the 30 ease of the XX c. is a chimera for the broader Bulgarian mass. Along with the voting right which an insignificant part of the Bulgarian population practically made use of until 1919 the equality to the law as part of the civic emancipation turned a no lesser deprived chance. The same could be concluded as related to a system of social and health care, the right of education, security of labour and unemployment, or health care for aged people. Therefore, »social wonders«, as unavoidable compromise between capital and labour, and its basic tributes – representative government, power of the law, moreover »welfare state«, etc. have never fully occurred in the Bulgarian case. Thus the Bulgarian prewar society seems deprived in general terms from basic democratic achievements for quite a while, and it was not as early as 1930, when this trend began to have some positive impact of the Bulgarian political life. The exposition of the European people in the light of social a *political participation* by the end XIX c. seems a process from this country has been systematically alienated. This process occurs not only in delayed but as we have tried to illustrate in quasi-forms, which hindered a creative reproduction of this nation and kept it away from a common civilization effect relevant to other, especially Central European states and nations. A significant shift in this respect was possible and has partially occurred after 1944, but in principally different social and political context. The very fact that the so called »socialist forms« of political life rapidly turned into authoritarian, centralized forms of state-party control over most spheres of the Bulgarian society, has its external but not less internal logic and grounds. If this »phase« of the social development could contribute to a relative material and cultural advance of the Bulgarian society, this could be realized not through a total denial of some civic potential of this society, but trough the canalled mainstream of mass-mobilization. This accelerates a fatal initial deficit of the Bulgarian political culture pushing it into the realm of deprivation from universal civic values as fundament of proper complex social and political progress. Bulgaria could never cultivate and less even implement those precious civic values into its political system and its adherent institutions, as most European countries managed to do this. One solid argument in favor of more rationale patterns of transition of number of central European »new democracies« is, as we believe, this specific deficit of the Bulgarian political culture which had less civic culture traditions to upgrade on. The latter seems to us a missing »chain« in the Bulgarian case and is well to be regarded as fundamental disadvantage.

»The misfortune of the Bulgarian people springs from the very fact that we have started our free life (which demands creativity from us) without an organized vital energy – so Geo Milev in his magazine »Scales«, in one of its issues from 1925. Therefore the elected sons of this people, who undertook the ruling in their hand and in their consciousness, had one supreme duty only: to organize the vital energy of the people, to organize it in creativity. But: here stars the tragedy. The leaders of the people became »managers« of the people. And not the fate of the people was their priority but their personal ambition, their personal egoism. For those were elected sons of the people – people's managers – and not chosen sons. They were always the most unworthy sons of this people – fully opposite to those self scarified idealist as Rakovski, Botev, Levski, grandfather Slavejkov and other. – who was the father of the Bulgarian nation. Today even, until present, we witness the eased bridle of demagogy. All come with shining slogans of this party and that, but behind those slogans cunningly hide the dishonest rapaciousness and greedy egoism. »Power« is the occupation – the most profitable occupation of the Bulgarian so called »political actors«. Their »political activity« by the way has always been only »fight for power«. And this fight has devoured the vital energy of the people... The people feel, the people knows that.«[66]

The end of what we prefer to define here as »quasi« – conservatism and/or liberalism in the Bulgarian political system between WWI and WWII has certainly more complex dimensions and specific reasons. But even those mentioned here suffice to draw the general conclusion – both ideological streams and their relevant structural incarnations, as shaped earlier and repeated in the »era of transition« in this country, are most irrelevant to the objectively emerging new political culture of this nation. They are less relevant to the grass rooting autonomous structures that have overwhelmed their political leaders. Liberal and conservative ideas could not be re-born in their old shapes. They can even less be leased for a day use as a »brad« store network. It is people who live with ideas and they still are to be born, learned and brought up to those ideas in their modern shapes and forms. It was a rather unrealistic euphoria of the newly defined scopes of freedom to declare ideologies for dead. They still have to contribute for a world to get better. Thus a process of political resurrection seems as inevitable as it has always been in Bulgaria.

A laconic in its empirical findings survey, dedicated to the dominating values in this society from the end of 1994, shows that liberal ideas are more popular among medical doctors, lawyers, private businessmen and civil servants. Among them dominate those engaged in the state sector though (68, 5 percent), independent businesses (11, 6 percent), owners of companies with

66 Geo Mlev, Balgarskiat narod dnes (The Bulgarian people today). »Vezni«, 3., 1921, Nr.3.

more then 5 employed (6, 5 percent) and other 10, 5 percent as employed in private companies. A general characteristic of potential liberalism in this country is the »pattern« of a »self-sufficient reproduction«. Professional occupation turned to be a stronger correlation factors than markers as »property«, »material status«, or »political popularity«. [67] The economic stand of the Bulgarian »liberal cohort« seems so far a painful replica of the failed neo-conservative experiment of a most disputable breed. In a way it reflects the »vagueness« of Bulgarian liberalism between WWI and WWII. But it added a lot of hazardless and most extravagant social engineering schemes. The roles of those political actors gravitate around »middle« standards, which are not yet up to the demands and standards of advanced European nations. This does not mean that their political culture will tolerate this disadvantage for long. Therefore the »assassination of the third class« proclaimed pathetically in the early years of transition by street democrat's leaders, gives no reason to prescribe such a sin to the shaping new Bulgarian democracy. Less relevant is this populist outcry to the controversial performance of our neo-conservatives as saviors of post-communist devistation. That both fundamental political patterns deepened the precipice between politics and citizens is another disgraceful result from over 17 years of transition in which quasi ideologies used the chance for a »second breath«. Alas. It turned out that Bulgarians still prefer to breathe on heir own, as far as this determines their pragmatic social demands and a sober political mind.

---

67 See: Choveshkite tsennosti (Human values), Patriotic union, Sofia, 1994.

Chapter 2: Shaping the New Bulgarian Political Culture

As far as history is not written with capital letter and stays more or less an *enigma*, the political culture of a nation is not to be tackled in the old self-determined or even objective plan, to which we are still bound at this side. It is a misunderstanding in this sense to grasp the turn over from »capitalist« to »socialist« forms of social order – marked in Bulgaria by Sept. 9, 1944 – as a transition from one »class form« of constrain to another. Even though many people at this side have their own arguments to link the establishment of communist power in Bulgaria with the dramatic »signs« of a new age, the »passions of violence«, or the »reflections of Stalinism« on Bulgarian soil – those descriptors are hardly to be accepted as fruitful scientific indicators in the framework of a system theory of political culture. More over they are incapable to unveil the driving forces of most complex cultural change that is taking place after the fall of the Berlin wall. The »concepts« of perverted Marxist determinism, or even most sophisticated modernist reflections of this reality; are equally helpless to rationalize trends of significant but also desired cultural and political change.

Each fundamental form of such change (as the Reformation for example), along with the denial of the old culture, through religious, cultural, social, economic, ideological and political counteracts, seems loaded with not less significant qualities of an emerging new system. Number of values and structural elements of the old social and political life have the capacity not just to »vanish«, or even destroy each other, but to *converge*, or *proliferate* and thus »give birth« to new forms of social existence. This process results not necessarily into »hybrid«, less even in »perverted« shapes – but into qualitatively different forms, which exist parallel. They can last for relative longer periods of time. And it is this *capacity* of the system which gives to them homogeneity, and under certain conditions guarantees their stability and chances to flourish. This is, one of the most significant postulates of Almond and Verba's theory, which we prefer to stick to.

We have no reasons to claim that social systems are »born«, »grow up«, »decline«, or even »die« in the sense given to these concepts by biological science – as Parsons warned us. Biological science is still in high demand of some general theory on the »life cycle«, which could explain social processes by some general law. This gives reasons to some sociologists (Rex and others.), to argue on continuous »metaphysical attempts« to explain the nature of social change. In this context we have more grounds to relate the so-called *»real socialism«* in Bulgaria with the shaping of a political culture of specific, own breed. Even though it looked as «opposite«, »different« or »counter standing«, to most liberal democratic cultures in the West – this specific culture, »mixed« in its own peculiar shapes seems still adherent to universal common features, which relate it, as we will illustrate on empirical grounds most closely with the European, continental political culture. These general (gender) and specific (class) characteristics, relate the Bulgarian political culture most closely with political cultures of Eastern Europe. But they are loaded with structural and qualitative characteristics, which link it with West-European cultures, even though in »interrupted«, discontinuous patterns and forms. This »kinship« goes beyond spatially prostrated cultural constellations even, and in one way or another makes it compatible with them, as we could find. Thus some Eastern European political cultures appear to be not so much »frozen«, stagnating, or deeply alienated. They are more successfully to be rationalized as deviated from a common civilization root, to which they gravitate by new cultural and political forms and patterns.

As specific »products" of certain historical, political and other conditions and factors, those cultures are of *common genus,* but belong to specific *internal origin of species,* as it appears to us. As far as their traditional, subjective, and participant patterns of orientations do not »vanish«, whatever rule or power comes (change of property, indoctrination, recruitment of a new political elites etc.), those cultures have cultivated specific forms and patterns of political behaviour, that gives *own meaning* to their system. They are a »backbone« of societies, to which they refer, and on which political structures and systems usually feed. In this respect of a dominating interest for us is to answer the questions:

To what extend do we find in the »deeper strata« of present Bulgarian society (or even on its surface), elements of a civic culture of a participant type.

And if they exist – how far could this sociological premise back the idea of some activist (if not »mass«) involvement of Bulgarians into real political life, of which we seem even deeper alienated than other nations.

In a nutshell we will try in this chapter to:

First: Revise in cultural systematic plan the notion of the »totalitarian rule« in Bulgaria, by throwing more light not so much on its remnants, but concentrate on the generated elements of civic consciousness even under its dark shadow.

Second: Explicitly draw the sociological premises of an emerging type of a »mixed« civic culture in Bulgaria, which already undertakes autonomous functions at the complex social development of this country.

Third: Answer the question: »is an *activist type* of political culture still possible in the present Bulgarian society?« And if yes, what are its driving forces in a broader national and common European context?

We do not intend to turn the »newsreel« of Bulgarian political life as far backwards, as to the post-war years of WWII. Too shabby are the portraits of ancestors that look at us with so much hope and the joy of freedom offered in illuminative events and most passionate rhetoric. Instead, we shall approach another constellation of an Orwell breed – the one of Zhivkovism.. What was this – totalitarism, despotism, or a kind of a »Balkan Leviathan«, that not only ruled and dominated, but also shaped the life and mentality of couple of generations? And thus determined the destiny of Bulgarians as far as some »inertia of the passed« finds its new vital forms? We shall read in other words some pages of the latest political history of this country, left in shadow, which most East European nations not only dared to open and read but rationalized in a new universal democratic context. This might help us grasp better a notorious *Bulgarian civic deficit*, which has deeply rooted in the 34 years of reign of the »last despot« on the Balkans.

Totalitarianism and Civic Culture in Bulgaria (1956–1989)

Many people prefer to define the political regime in Bulgaria after 1956 as some *»soft«* form of *»post-totalitarianism«* on Bulgarian soil, which reflects the transition from Stalinism after the 20th Congress of KPSU and the subsequent eras of Khrushchev and Brezhnev. [68] No matter how arguable these terms appear to be, some hidden forms of the Bulgarian authoritarianism and despotism, which in this country took the form of *»Zhivkovism«* give reasons to consider it as peculiar deviation from an »authentic totalitarianism« (H. Arendt). What is worth pointing out here is above all that terms like *»authoritarian state socialism«, »command-administrative system«, »barrack socialism«* and other »descriptors« of the phenomenon, which gained popularity after the fall of communism at the end of the 1980's, in the Western, as well as in the »ex« and »post-Soviet« literature, appear to be unrealistic or less relevant for the Bulgarian »totalitarian reality«. As a deeper analysis shows, they have no serious scholarly contribution to the objective sociological and above all immanent characteristics of this form of Balkan despotism, which not only manifested itself in the last 4 decades in

68 The idea of certain »deviation« of Zhivkovism from some »authentic totalitarism« in the terms of H.Arendt has been articulated immediately after 1989 in local Bulgarian media by Prof. Peter-Emille Mitev. It stressed on some untypical features of the political character and structural forms of totalitarism in Bulgaria, but was in a way neglected by a most vague public political discourse in this country.

Bulgaria, but also in a way »survived« long after in new shapes and forms. [69] Such descriptors, as applied to a the authoritarian-despotic rule in Bulgaria since 1956 (the April plenum of BKP) obscure the subject of our *»structured despotism«*. But in some way still veil the moral limits of this phenomenon, which is often presented to as historical »inevitability« in the search of its own justification and legitimacy.

Moreover, plenty of reasons and arguments exist in support of the thesis that the huge cultural-political deficit, which could be sensed in a painful way by the Bulgarian society only after the fall of »Zhivkovism« as regime, stems from the ill-guided *»traditional« »subject« and »civic«* forms of interaction between the political object and the subjects of Bulgarian political life ever since 1956. That is why we find as more adequate to define »Zhivkovism« as a system for reproduction of typically alienated *»quasi« forms* and patterns of participation of individuals and groups of people in the immediate political life of this country from the mid and late 20th century. In the same time, being a pivotal element of the real Bulgarian political culture, »Zhivkovism" should be interpreted as a prolonged, most burdensome, but still inevitable process of reproducing (even in such extreme conditions) *participant forms and patterns* of autonomous civic culture. The latter has objective perspective now that Bulgaria has »entered« Europe.

As we could find out, certain typical participant forms and patterns of political behaviour, which constitute the contemporary Bulgarian political culture, provide an *internal system resource*, which is capable of carrying out a substantial social change through the painfully emerging Bulgarian civic society. All this relates Bulgarians to an *»activist« type* of participant political cultures. And in a lesser (or even insignificant) degree with some »subject-participant« type, as some observers claim, providing evidence to rank this country lower ladders of some »evolutionary« hierarchy of new democracies and political cultures in transition.

We shall provide enough arguments in favour of this thesis, whereby we shall deliberately try to avoid too hasty, moreover unrealistic assessments. The relative stability of this society nearly two decades after the democratic change of 1989, supports in a way such an analysis. Although this period reminds with its devastating of the years after the WW II, indeed, when other scholars made similar attempts to analyze the nature totalitarian control and severe brutality against the spirit and freedom of entire nations. This they did (as the author in his own way) with the »sufferings and the pains of the experienced«, rather than from the standpoint of some *sine ire et studio…*«[70]

---

69 See: W. F. Haug. Der befehladministrative Sozialismus ist historish am Ende., in: Wahrnehmungsversuche. Beiträge zur verstandigung in der Krise des Sozialismus, Berlin, 1990, p. 23–30.

70 Hanna Arendt, Totalitarism. (bulg. Totalitarizmat), Sofia, 1993, p. 5.6.

Totalitarianism »par excellence« and its Zhivkovist deviation

The Bulgarian totalitarianism is by its nature closely related to the despotic Balkan regimes in Yugoslavia, Romania and even Albania. In this sense it carries something of their radical, if not by all means, extreme ruling potential. »Zhivkovism« has always appeared to be to some greater extent guaranteed and even, »confirmed« by some »own tradition«, as well as its ingeniously exploited political closeness to Russia. That is why it remains aside of the ruling extremes of the neighboring authoritarian-despotic regimes on the Balkans. While most of then faced the need of constantly redefining the one-man authority, upon which they are based by definition, »Zhivkovism« sort of stood out as an exemplary political symbol of the stability of socialism, here on the Balkans. It even glittered in the 1970's before the civilized democratic world with some of the luster of the famous golden towers of Alexander Nevski Cathedral. And it has acquired »the aura« of some »moderate«, »enlightened«. Or even »bearable« form of Balkan authoritarianism, guaranteeing the *status quo* and the stability on the Balkans and Europe as a whole.

Meanwhile the power pyramid of »Zhivkovism" constantly »rounded-up«, »went down« and »landed«, as it adjusted, with an amazing ability to bow and adapt, to the political changes of several »general lines« of Moscow. In this sense »Zhivkovism« is to be rationalized as a much more consistent, condensed or »balanced« variation of Balkan authoritarianisms. This is valid for the nature of the state-party institutions, which derived its vitality through the loyalty of a follow-up, if not necessarily a successive state-party bureaucracy. In no lesser degree this was valid for the widespread and systematically cultivated governing style and »class defiance« of any liberal-democratic forms of political life.

Having found its justification in the »entire people's support«, »Zhivkovism« operated even under the illusion of some unique contribution to the world civilization, being obsessed with this self confidence till its very end. A quasi-centrism, stemming from the traditional paternalism and feeding upon the notorious social-class amorphousness of the Bulgarian society, the well-displayed political loyalty to the ideology of »real socialism« and a kind of »European decency«, appear to be *the three sources* of this more mature, if not absolutely undisputable political status of »Zhivkovism« on the Balkans. And even in a broader geopolitical context. Selectively open to the values of the outside democratic world, it was in no lesser degree than the regimes of Tito (Yugoslavia), Chaushesku (Romania), or even Enver Hodja (Albania) defending its own despotism. »Zhivkovism« still remains, however, closer to some *political supremacy* than to other variation of modern authoritarianism.

Symptomatic for that is the deep attachment of »Zhivkovism« to the idea of its historical eternalizing. But not so much through some merely physical grinding of »human material«, which Bulgaria never experienced. It was rather at the cost of the astounding and repelling with its Asian flamboyancy overspending of this »scarce material«, the limited cultural-spiritual potential and above all the suppressing of the self emerging *civic values* of the Bulgarian society from the second half of the 20th century, with which this regime operated. Through »detaining« the process of natural evolution, mutual diffusion, and inevitable reproduction of universally established cultural-political, rational patterns of real political life, »Zhivkovism« carried out in this way practically a deep and massive *despotic transformation* of the civic spirit and mentality of most Bulgarians. Here roots the historical self-awareness of this political patronage, which relates it to a *tyrant of all times*.

The real power resource of »Zhivkovism« stems from nothing else but the intuitively realized, though completely erroneous idea, that the natural genesis of the typical forms of traditional, subject and civic orientation and interaction of any people, or nation with its authentic political object, could be »delayed« (if not violently interrupted). This *lethal effect* came through a systematic crash above all of participant patterns for immediate interaction of the individual and social communities in the system of their political life. It is this, which gave to our »political object« the appearance of the many-faced Janus. He was seen, however, not as first among peers, i.e. a *citizen*, to whom a rational ruling system has given certain functions for some period of time. Time had »stopped« for most of us Bulgarians, while the clock of history seemed to go for him and his entourage only.

Why inspire of all claimed, »Zhivkovism« cannot be viewed as totalitarianism? The answer to this question seems to us pivotal for the shaping of a new *civic philosophy* in Bulgaria. But above all for the rationalizing of a most diverse and rather perplexed spiritual environment in which »budding« forms and patterns of a new participant Bulgarian political culture emerged after 1989. We are less concerned with the highlighting of some »special« nature, »inner« logic, less even with some haunting idea of a possible »*second breathe*« of »Zhivkovism« that could »return« and determine the Bulgarian social development in the future. Let us discuss and bring forward some more arguments in this respect.

In her profound study »The Origins of Totalitarianism« (1949), which was only published in Bulgaria in 1993 – that is 7 years after Zhelev's »Fascism« (1985) gained popularity, the prominent German scholar Hannah Arendt relates the totalitarianism above all to the following basic characteristics: totalitarian personality, respectively the cult of it, dictatorship and one-party government, mass society. Last but not least, she mentioned also »*an idealism, no matter how stupid or heroic*« but always stemming from a »*personal decision and a conviction, leaning on something experienced, on some arguments*«. Let us remember these benchmarks, which are of great importance for the comprehension of our thesis for a most peculiar deviation of the so-called »totalitarianism«[71] in the Bulgarian case, as related to its authentic forms. But no less a hardly possible »secondary« reproduction, or »cloning« of a totalitarian rule, in the Bulgarian political reality even after the emblematic 1989.

Most of the influential studies of the totalitarianism after Hannah Arendt, many of which remained out of sight for the Bulgarian dissident and »post-socialist« literature distinguish between the so-called *»totalitarian movement«* and the *»state-party structures«*, which follow its absolutely dominating power. It is the latter phenomena and their impact on society that are defined as totalitarianism. Clashing all convictions, and even those of its followers, which could outlive the collapse of the movement, totalitarianism is above all grasped as an emanation of the *extreme fanaticism* and the *»total conformity«* of the masses. It determines the character of the institutions and the social hierarchies, which emerge upon the debris of the old class bourgeois society. This is carried out through the elimination from the political life of not only the multi-party system, but also the whole system of previous vertical and horizontal class links and relationships as well.[72]

The end of World War I overwhelmed the whole old continent by an extremely antidemocratic pro-dictatorial surge of the so-called »semi-totalitarian« movements. From Italy to almost all countries in Central and Eastern Europe fascist organizations came into existence (among these the Czech Republic is a fortunate exception, which could be partly attributed to a not completely shattered from the war, civic culture in this society). However even Mussolini, one of the political leaders that are most associated with the idea of a totalitarian state, did not dare, as it is well known, to establish a full-fledged totalitarian regime. It seemed enough for him to have a dictatorial and a one-party government. Such dictatorships emerged in Romania, Poland, the Baltic States, Hungary and Portugal, as well as in Spain, during the Franco rule.

> »Unlike the ›totalitarian movement‹, so Arendt, the so-called *totalitarian supremacy* is above all related to the condition that it could emerge ›only if limitless masses are at hand‹. Or there, where and when ›they could be sacrificed without this leading to a fatal decline of the population. In this sense a first substantial characteristic for an objective genesis of the totalitarianism turns out to be nothing else but the availability of the so-called ›sufficient human material (no matter how sinister this term used till present could sound), which could be sacrificed‹.« [73]

71 We use here the concept of totalitarism with quatation marks to make difference between a specific form of Balkan authoritarism in Bulgaria, and differenciate it from some »authentic totalitarism« in terms of H. Arendt.

72 Hanna Arendt, Totalitarism,... Ibid. p. 25.

73 Ibid.

The second significant element necessary for the appearance of totalitarian movements, as most respected scholars after H. Arendt have pointed out, are the qualitative characteristics of the »building material«. It is unambiguously stressed in the serious academic literature that totalitarianism emerges only when there are masses, which for one reason or another, have developed *aspiration to the political organization*«. Awareness of some common interest itself is far from being an integrative factor for the emergence of such masses (Arendt). They do not possess the elements of the specific class solidarity, which could set visible and realistic goals. That is why the totalitarian movements in Europe from the 1930s consist mostly of such masses of people, who, because of the strength stemming from their huge numbers, or because of their indifference to political life (and sometimes for both reasons) cannot be classified into any organization, based on common interests at all – political parties, municipal governments, professional association, or unions. In this sense they are being recruited from the available sufficient number of people (potentially existing in every country), who in fact are attracted among the myriads of »neutral« and »indifferent« citizens, that never join a party or even do not participate in elections.[74]

A third substantial and most important characteristic of the existence of totalitarian movements and relevant forms of government, is the emergence of a »*strong personality*«,[75] who one nice day undertakes the responsibility to

74 According the totalitarian movements the discords inevitably are rooted in »deep, natural social and psychological grounds, that are out of control of the individual« and are thus unyielding to his rationality. (see H.Arendt,Totalitarism... p. 29 and further on)

75 The qualitative benchmark of *power* into *Herrschaft* (Weber) is the transition from personal to institutional forms of leadership. This is a characteristical feature of most European societies. The Balkan case seems bound to not only an evolutionaly delayed – but more likely »converted« into it's »archetype forms« type of domination. This might explain the difference between modern political leadership and the kind of *vozdism* (one person encorporation of all kinds of power), as elevant to the Balkans. It's markers are extreme voluntarism, oppressive style of a most unpredictable character, as well as totall submission of his followers. The cult of Stalin in Soviet Russia – is a more systematically studded form of this variety of coersive power, as related to Eastern political cultures. As most dramatic cases of voluntary sacrifice of soldiers and officers of the Red Army during the 30 ese and even after WWII show – »*Za Stalinu – za Rodinu*« (For Stalin – For Fatherland« has been decades after his death (1953) a last out-cry of hope and most dedicated faith in the »true idea«, mis-interpreted by »internal enemies«, or conspiratively discredited. In one way or another – the cult of personality in Russia (and more over China), has less in common with its »*sultanisive pattern*« of power that has shaped among Balkan despots. As Sir Ralf Dahrendorf points out in this respect – eventhough history has given us enough examples of charismatic political fugures, the general trend in politics as well as in modern social

look after all communal affairs. The indifference to the communal affairs and the weakened civic will of the majority, are not the only reason however for the emergence of totalitarian movements. Thus, the long time-period of a more or less »court moderation« during which the bourgeoisie in Europe was content with its position of a civic-dominating class (as it left voluntarily the political rule to the aristocracy), has been followed by more open, negative attitudes towards the existing national institutions, and demands for self-organization and exertion of political power. The so-called »indifference« and apathy of the masses towards the political life, as well as the subsequent tendencies towards monopolistic dictatorship, stem therefore from nothing else but a certain *way of life* and a *specific life philosophy,* concentrated first and foremost on the success or the failure of the individual, surrounded by societies that lie upon the principles of merciless competition.[76]

It is these views, as H. Arendt and other influential researchers of totalitarianism argue, that appear particularly useful for the authoritarian dictatorships. An individualism of a special breed that is in principle different from the widely-spread beliefs, extremely sensitive to the infringements of the individuality (regardless the reluctance of the »apathetic groups« to assume civic responsibilities) forms the »substance core« of this mass attitude, upon which totalitarian movements are based, respectively the structural forms of totalitarian control. This fact makes it extremely difficult, if not impossible, to distinguish qualitative differences between the so-called *»organizations of the mob«* of the 19th century and the *»mass movements«* in 20th century.[77] Few scholars managed to do this and this happened only after the collapse of the traditional class society. It is this suddenly emerged vacuum between *mass* and *class* that is filled up by the totalitarian

organizations is the *reduction of the unlimited power,* which is characteristic for its personallity centered types. It seems exactly this redused to positions and mandate bound type of leadership.that the Bulgarian political culture has been traditionally deprived of, but moreover systematically in the last 45 years of communist rule. See: Ralf Dahrendorf, Recent Changes in the Class Structure of European Societies,in: Dedalus, Winter, 1964, p. 225–270.

76 Hanna Arendt, Totalitarism, p. 28–29.

77 Modern totalitarian leaders differ not much as related to their psyche and mentality from »old time despots«, whose moral norms and political manners very much remid of the initial norms and methods of the bourgeous class from the beginning of the 19 c. None of those leaders (as the »10 of October Society« for example which has backed Lui Napoleon to power), has had such a total control over his members – as H.Arend points out. This referrs to the »liquidation brigades« from the time of the *pogroms* in Russia before 1917, or the so called *»pan movements«* . This experience seems utilized and chanalized by similar »law enforcement supportive« groups or nationalist movements in favor of the »stong hand«.

movement. That is why even today they appears to be a sinister product of the process of some natural reproduction of the totalitarian social order.

This complex »amorphousness« of the social-class structure in many European civic societies, organized upon the principle of the nation-state and their total disinterest in politics, appear to be the most common characteristic markers of totalitarianism(s) in the epoch of a transition from class to a mass society. They become possible in spite of (or because of) the value diffusion and the formal fading of the class systems in epochs of bigger historical and political upheavals. [78] That is why most respectful researchers of totalitarianism [79] relate the first symptoms of the party system collapse not so much to the leave, or the outflow of a long-lasting member mass from the traditional parties, but rather to their failure to attract new members among the younger generations. First and foremost this was a loss of the »mute« approval and support from the unorganized masses. The latter, as we learn from experience, suddenly get rid of their previous indifference in order to find new political spaces and forms for manifesting their realized discontent. It is these *»sleeping majorities«* that are moved and forced in the »river-tide« of totalitarian movements and their structures. Their »solidarity of negation« is not related to one or ideology or another. It is rather an expression to the need to concentrate a »diffusive« and mutually inducing energy, which is mobilized to »defeat the enemy« that threatens the state, the national community, or the »race«. This enemy was considered to come not only from »outside« but also from »inside«.[80]

---

78 Masses are generated – as H.Arendt definitely proved – out of the »ingredients of an extremely atomized society«, whose competitive statement is the inevitable and constantly accompanying *lonesomeness* of the single individuum. The latter has been cultivated in the realms of a more or less »closed« adherence to certain class that shape the mentality and indoctrinate both mind and feelings. D. Riesmann has penetrated deep in this painful process in his »Lonesome Crowd«. Modern sociologists have turned their back in a waz to this problem of contemporary cultures and if mentioned it is relates to »communication deficits« (Habermas), or sectarian withdrowals into the niches of a pluralistic, multi-cultural world. This is another source of an extremely dangerous nationalism(s), emerging in Eastern Europe, where populism and demagogy flourish and nourish ideas of »deprivation of the masses«.

79 Kornhauser, Wiliam, The Politics of Mass Society, Glencoe, 1958, pp. 227–238.

80 One of the characteristic features of totalitarian regimes – as H. Arendt claimed – is the *neglecting of material problems* and orientation to »ideological« questions, that might solve problems for decades ahead. The belief in some »common fate« that reigns over the national identity, accelerates this long term strategy of behavior and suppresses individual differences, or »cases« of unfair treatment by the authorities etc. At the same time the prevailing »all leveled« notion of social justice, keeps the integrity of society in a most paradox , but still efficient way. (see: Heinrich Himler on »Organisation and duties of SS and the Police«,

The discussion above seems enough to clearly point out not only the formal resemblances but also the substantial ideological and above all *contextual differences* between the so-called »totalitarian movements« and the »structural forms« of the totalitarian domination. Without that it would be impossible to grasp the common, but in a no lesser degree the peculiar features of the so-called »totalitarian« performance of Zhivkovism in Bulgaria.

***

What do our main arguments in favor of the thesis that »Zhivkovism« should be considered as some deviation of «totalitarianism« and more likely a »Balkan form of despotism« in the sense suggested by H. Arendt and many other penetrating scholars examining this phenomenon, boil down to?

First: Bulgaria is no exception to the general flow of mainland totalitarian movements, which emerged in Europe among the 1920's and 1930's. However, it only appears to be so. In fact, Bulgaria stays aside from their joint »mainstream«, i.e. from they're powerful and extreme forms of acceleration of the vehemence of the apathetical masses. The reasons for that could be manifold. The most important ones are to linked, however, to the qualitative specifics of the traditional Bulgarian political culture from the end of the 19th century and the beginning of the 20th century. As we have pointed out already, a special place in this traditional culture is held by a »*remnant parochialism*«, respectively the elements of what we defined as »rest« forms of *dismembered subjectivity*, respectively emerged *quasi-civic culture*. The latter, as special cultural institutions, has not been able to undertake typical political functions, relevant to most European countries and their cultures. That is the reason why authentic totalitarian movements could not rise upon these forms and patterns of partially, but not totally, alienated type of political culture.

Second: With its population of nearly 7 million (as of 1939), Bulgaria counted among the small, at best medium-size Balkan countries with limited, if not insignificant human resources. Furthermore, the mere structure of the Bulgarian society from 1926 till 1956 is of such nature that it does not allow the reckless waste of fit for work population[81], which was typical for the

National-politische Lehrgang der Weltmacht., 15–23 Januar, 1937). The idea of »melting the individuality« has found its explicit and most repulsive sznthesis here. Cit. from H.Arendt, Totalitarism, p. 34.

81 In 1926 the population of Bulgaria (activly working) amounted to 2 912 000. In 1956 it increased up to 4 487 000, as the number of persons in unactive age – i.e. not workingg (on the base of 1000 in active age) , has declined from 873 in 1926 and 697 in 1956 to 718 in 1965. The aging of the Bulgarian population has been

Stalinist rule in the 1930's in the USSR. In this sense, Bulgaria does not offer the objective resources for a massive totalitarian movement, not to mention *nation-specific forms for total control.*

Even in the years of the so-called »massovisation« or in the era of »building of socialism« in towns and the founding of cooperatives in villages, as later on, the Bulgarian society, did not obtain the qualitative characteristics of a *mass society*.[82] It is due to its relative inner homogeneity, stemming from the lack of deeper economic differentiation between the main classes of medium-size producers and entrepreneurs in the pre- and post-war Bulgarian society. This objective sociological fact did not provide inner resource for attracting the *»mobs«* that could have been accelerated in mass totalitarian movements in Bulgaria.

Third: Last but not least, at the end of World War II, Bulgaria had to face the reality of being on the losing side of Germany. The Patriotic Front that came on power on September 9th, 1944 included at first representatives of the opposition that was crashed down in 1947 and later on fully eliminated from the political life. Those sentenced by the People's Court in the first years of communist rule in Bulgaria (between 1944 and 1947) amount to approximately 2600. From these, 600 have been »prosecuted« out of court. Those perused in different periods of the 45-year communist regime for their political beliefs amount to 26 000. Most of them were not political prisoners in »correction camps«, such as the one in Belene, that were closed after 1956.[83]

---

one of its most characteristic features for decades. This determines the failure of couple of forced« »mobillyzing« reconstruction plans before and after WWII. Demographs at this side are unanimous that this demographic decline in Bulgaria starts from 1920–1925. It determines to a great extend an »exhausted« pattern of most extractive 4 and 5 year plans during the age of »real socialism«. Most of them failed to pace with the trend of modernization and complex social development in Europe. See: Acad. Iv. Stefanov, Pof. Z.Sugarev, Prof. N.Naumov, E. Christov, Ph.D, A.Atanasov, Ph.D., Demography of Bulgaria, Sofia, 1974, p. 516–517.

82 A mass society is »a mass society in so far as both elites and non-elites have an access to each other, based of the weakness of the groups that play the role of intermediaries between them« – so W. Kornhauser in an older debate. This gives a different notion of mass(es), less known to the traditional political cultures on the Balkans. See: W.Kornhauser, The Politics of Mass Society, Glencoe, 1959, p. 227–238.

83 Up to the end of 1960 couple of »placements for correction« of Bulgarian citizens who had «deviated« from the norms of socialist laws functioned indeed, even less known to the broader western public. They were closed at era of Khruschev immediately after the XX Congress of The CP in Soviet Russia, which dismantled he cult of Stalin and lead to some liberalization of the regime in Bulgaria.

These facts, though controversial and argued still, do not underestimate in any way, neither are supposed to justify, the oppressions of the communist regime in Bulgaria. They rather draw attention to the objectively limited opportunities for some Bulgarian massive forms of »total repression« of the so-called »human material«, that are typical for Germany at the end of the war and in Russia in the 1930's.

The Bulgarian »*meek authoritarianism*«, which shaped as *Zhivkovism* however, deserves our attention because of a no less devastating erosion of the Bulgarian society, that has been going on since the 1950's up to present. Above all it leaves its most sinister mark on the civic consciousness of our people by reconfirming typically alienated, quasi-forms and patterns for interacting of the Bulgarian subjects with their real political object ever since 1956. This is what makes the Bulgarian political culture particularly bitter until 1989, but long after this symbolic date as we could find out. Why and how, we will try to explain below.

On the reversibility of a despotic transformation of the Bulgarian civic spirit

What are the arguments that back the above-mentioned, not particularly optimistic thesis? And if it is true, what makes such a pernicious transformation of the Bulgarian *civic spirit*, after all, reversible? It is not possible to give a right answer to these questions without examining the damages. That is why we will concentrate on them here mainly. As to the grounds for such an approach, it could be summarized in one main claim: Here we build on the proved and validated in the contemporary social theory idea of latent, more or less *implicit ability* of each social system (the Bulgarian being no exception) to change by itself. This relates to its capacity to determine not only the direction but as well as its typical and specific forms and patterns of significant general and individual change.

We have more reasons to believe that the idea of human rights and liberties of the individual, the elements of a clearly structured consciousness of the role of the individual, respectively the social groups, in a civic society could not be considered annihilated or »cognitively cleared off« in the collective (less even in the individual) mind of this nation. The things rather boil down to the same this conscious mind and its capacity to revive not so much a long »forgotten«, but rather systematically alienated, still existing forms and patterns for participant interaction with its real political object(s). Only in this way (and in no other) the system, as we believe, might find its inner rejuvenating as well as new rational impulse. This impulse could not spring from anywhere else but from the »sub-layers« of an *accumulated political culture* and its authentic forms of participant interaction with the political object, that belong both historically and culturally to us Bulgarians. To put it in other words, they stem from a generalized own national complex cultural and political experience and not from some »shady«, less even secondarily alienated, »quasi« forms of such cultural experience. That this is the case remains to be checked first, before we comprehend it fully indeed.

***

Above all it is the perfidious, and in effect, Asian-brutality of political oppression, worked out during the 34-year long rule of the Zhivkov's regime, that deforms the Bulgarian political culture. They demean most reasonable forms and patterns for rational interaction between the political object and the political subject. In this way the pivotal elements of a real political system are being deeply corrupted. This brings a pervert content and direction of the political process with all subsequent negative effects. We have all the necessary grounds to speak of an *»a priori excluded«*, quasi-participant political culture in our cultural-political case, upon which most democratic and civic societies in Europe in the last 100 years, and even earlier, have upgraded.

All formal characteristics of the famous *»fusion«* between party and state, the use of the oppressive apparatus for establishing the Zhivkov's tyranny, the total persecution of the members of the Bulgarian intelligentsia, those that thought differently, among them even members of the former communist party, are nothing, in its deepness and intensity, compared to the gigantic damages which Zhivkovism caused to the *civic status and self-awareness of the Bulgarian people*. It is not that every civic idea in this country could be considered »obliterated«, »wiped out«, »incriminated«, less even »crashed by the tanks«, as one of the leaders of the democratic opposition emotionally claimed in an interview for »Spiegel« (1990) short after he had delivered his consecutive bouquet, (once as a student at Stalin's monument in Sofia) this time at the grave of ex-German Chancellor W. Brandt...

What seems more relevant is that Bulgarians have systematically been strangled in the sinister grip of a ubiquitous party-bureaucratic control and a most humiliating »ideological«, if not necessarily »total custody«. All this paralyzes the natural gusts of the free and creative Bulgarian civic spirit. Generations of Bulgarians shaped their view of life, as well as their »political self« under a constantly grim, Orwell-like blood-freezing look of a legendary police control. This deformed the social and public life in this country till 1989, but long after this as well. Numerous arbitrary »interventions«, interferences and methodical »processing« practiced by thick-fingered guards of the ideological hygiene of the »system«, impress even those acquainted with power ruling absurdities. This leaves deep trauma, not only in the conscious mind, but also on the mentality of couple of Bulgarian generations.

This sociological phenomenon alienates systematically the individual from most rational patterns of political behavior and real participation in the social life. It still multiplies a *specific fear*, which crashes the human dignity. It is bred by the socialization of the individual. This somber and most humiliating *»legacy of Zhivkovism«* continues to exist in its explicit or latent forms and patterns. In its own way it corrupts the future generations, which do not even suspect what severe damages, have been inflicted upon the independent nature of their national civic spirit.

The violation of basic human rights and civic liberties leaves not so much a »fierce wound« for generations to go, it rather promotes an especially impudent *social cynicism*, ready to crash down any right of the »other«. A *»high tech«* despotism disguised as »state managed socialism« in a no lesser degree relates this country to the Orwell world. Many Bulgarians had to suffer and live through it, long before they had the opportunity to read some pages of the famous »black utopia«. The legendary spiritual isolation of the individual was based on the omnipresent system for control on convictions, the constraints over residence and work permissions, the brutal interference in private correspondence and even the intimate life of the individual in the form of »ideological« or »moral control«. The »voluntary« system for spying of co-patriots took paradoxical size. After 1968 it encompasses almost every third Bulgarian citizen, as a »countermeasure« meant to enhance the regime of Zhivkov after the events in Czechoslovakia. Since 1989 quite a lot has been written on all this. It seems that something else was left aside, however.

A special inner resource for the Zhivkov regime here, on the Balkans, appears to be the scale of a most obsessive and *amoral »social-class engineering«*. From it the »father of the nation« and his closer circle seemed to be taken over from the mid-70's, until the very eve of the »collapse«. Some 60–70% of the rural population on Bulgaria was forced through all kinds of rude measures of compulsion to carry out gigantic and most often senseless from their very start »projects« for industrial development. This political megalomania with a technocratic flavor generated infeasible material, moral and human deficits in the Bulgarian society. They continued until the eve of the »beginning of the end«, as crystallizing in the in 1990 moratorium on the paying off a most burdensome and irrationally piled external debt, which generations still have to serve for decades to come.

All this »materialized« in the unseen devastation, incomparable chaos and spiritual crisis, that took over the Bulgarian society after 1989. Series of reforms of the agriculture and the economy, reflected by a couple of migration waves in the 60's and the 70's, mark the Bulgarian »socialist development«. They resulted in the abandonment of the Bulgarian villages and instead huge masses of people were concentrated in the industrial centers and the big cities. This led to a fatal *marginalization* of couple of generations in this country. Torn between the organized groups of the »working class« and the »agricultural workers«, (always for the cause of a constantly delayed welfare), and elementary *civic progress*, the Bulgarian »masses« acquired the characteristics of systematically humiliated, degraded and rights-deprived »mobs« of which Europe managed to get rid of only after the end of World War II.

Feudalism found its materializations and specific regenerated forms in the forcedly publicized patch of »prosperous« Bulgaria. In this same *»Garden of Eden"*, that was presented to the introverted free democratic world through a particularly shameless propaganda, generations of Bulgarian peasants and semi-city-inhabitants, i.e. the base of real builders of this society after WW II, have been virtually enchained to an Asian-primitive and above all a *civic-rights-deprived existence.* Many people cannot, or prefer not to think of all this. And this is understandable, as the self-respect of Bulgarians has always been of special worth. Even as they had to face the axe of Ottoman tyrants...

In the same time one amazing with its oriental character and financial scale system for privileges motivates the *»nomenclature«* of the Zhivkov regime to support his dictatorship. This system of patronage allocation in a way helped a cohort of some 200 clans of the nearer Zhivkov's surrounding – to survive and inherit new forms of economic power in this society long after 1989. Such systems for »political encouragement« have been invented by a number of other Central European communist regimes, as Eastern Germany, Poland, or Hungary until 1989. Nowhere did they dare to exploit the so scarce national resources, as that happened under the Balkan dictatorships. It seems that a notorious traditional greediness, cultivated by new-feudal habits and oriental customs, concealed under the »red-orange« veil of the socialist reality. In order to rank this country in the years of the loudly-announced »transition to democracy« and »market economy« on the top of a completely diverted and distorted scale of some »ethic« of capitalism with most repulsive and unacceptable features.

Spread in »concentric circles«, depending on how close one is to the party top, but above all on the *personal loyalty* to Zhivkov, these privileges corroded the normal values cultivated traditionally by the Bulgarian nation. And through their distorted transformation a *parasite meritocracy* was systematically credited. In fact the methods of »totalitarian« supremacy of the Zhivkovism were not based on some open, less even brutal manifestations of despotism. It rested rather on some »quasi-liberal« and systematically cashed power innovation capacity of this same meritocracy. A special inner dynamics of this conscious and deliberate split-up of the Bulgarian society was a »reserve cadre« human resources army of the Party, that was left to »breathe« into the neck the »chosen« by the regime. Through their most zealous aspiration to top positions of governance, this invisible cohort generated a constant critical mass of division and separation within this society.

This »wolf cohort« of careerists and »loyal« supporters of the regime would cultivate repulsive patterns of ill-corrupted competition and political rivalry. It would keep up the fire of little known to the modern social science endless inner struggles between »guerrilla« groups, all kinds of »wings« and »fractions«, temporary »coalitions«, »alliances«, crony circles etc. And all of them unified upon the frantic, ever worse hidden aspiration to benefit at the cost of a deeply tormented society. After the depletion of the limited social resources since 1985, they have entirely directed their energy to the *»pure forms of authority«!!*

In this shape – definitely not by chance – has the emancipated Bulgarian *»new liberalism«* materialized little after 1989. In fact, the policy of privileges in the so-called »transition« to a market society in this country accelerated a process of a most robust but impotent aspiration of the new established political elite to the attractive, but culturally out-of-reach, values of the bourgeois-European lifestyle. This has its deeper system grounds, but we shall discuss them here, rather from a moral than some other point of view. With all the risks that this »discourse« might still bring.

First. The persecution of the opponents of the Zhivkov regime, especially after the reinforcement of his dictatorial authority after the events in Czechoslovakia in 1968 and the insinuated, as some insiders claim, »plot« of gen. Gorunja and some political enemies of the regime, had been replaced with a strategy for an in-phase, conscious *»enlargement of the nucleus" of* loyal, selectively chosen supporters of the regime, »late« recognized antifascists, add-ons of »fresh blood« in the party ranks, the state hierarchy and »nomenclature«, recruited even among the heir generations of the former bourgeois-class »enemy«.

Second. This systematic involvement of new »ideological followers« through the means of ideologically controlled growth and advance in their career, the accommodation-communal policy, moderate permission rights to travel to the West, and selective control over contact with the democratic world, etc. took the shape of some »liberalized«, if not necessarily »enlightened authoritarianism«. Its public face was the platform of »real socialism« in this country, developed from the positions of estimated ideological and class compromise. Many people, however, maintain that it was a consciously planned process of *»embourgeoising«*. Thus a more or less systematic social-psychological transformation among certain part of the top and middle party elite and nomenclature occurred.

Third. The established »style and method« of »dialectically« upgraded »real socialism«, and in fact ever worse-concealed ideological and class compromise combined with most uncompromising authoritarianism. This generated a special breed of *conformism* to the »system«. Its pillars were an ever more open and arrogant mercantilism, which took the scale of deep, if not all-encompassing corruption, the double-fakeness of the moral and ethical standards, the cynical compromise with recent »ideological« convictions, political »principles«, etc.

That is how the Zhivkovism generated a »new«, unknown to the modern sociology *»quasi-awareness«* for social, political and even creative activity and initiative. Through it typical behavioral patterns of »ours«, that are to be characterized by a particular corrupted elasticity of universal social and even all-human values, manifest themselves. Their philosophical motto is *»everything is possible«*. In a country that still survives among complex devastation, this might well be true. All this turned into the conviction of an overcoming even the lethal laws »justification« of a non-transition, eternal legacy of the regime, the illusion that was upheld till the very breakdown of the system. This obsessive idea would keep its initial cultural inertia. It would leave its marks on the mentality of a *»quasi-civic«* minority in this country even after the change. And as many people believe at this side it motivates at least one or two generations in their efforts to delegate their civic duties and responsibilities to some irrational form of « stateliness«, whose successors they believe to be.

This *self-inseminating legitimacy*, redefined within the chaos that followed the transition to democracy after 1989 in this country, has nothing to do with the idea of an actually recreated in its authentic and living forms Bulgarian political culture. And, as most readers might well agree, with the initially corresponding, participant civic forms and patterns relevant to the generalized cultural experience of this nation. But, what seems most fatal is that within this »secondary« alienated *»new Bulgarian etatism«* a considerable part of Bulgarians still grasp their seized democratic scopes as guarantee of »prosperity« and »survival«. This same source would be taken over by the »captains« of the enforced capitalist transition in Bulgaria, as if to confirm some inherited legacy of rule by other means. That perverted »values« cannot determine significant and desired social change, less even modern social reality is a lesson they might never learn. There hardly exists a bigger political and cultural paradox indeed.

That this same »driving force« of the quasi-democratic change after 1989, in a most enthusiastic and cynical manner would embrace the values of some »Thatcherism of an Albanian breed"«, that it would identify with the pervert status of both »owner and holder« of a commonly accumulated wealth, that it would find in the few nights of an embargo its illegally gambled new role of a »mega-mediator« of between a »Dealer State« in a suddenly globalized for us world; having the insolence to call itself »social«, while exchanging under the table summarized »strategies« of most brutal and exhaustive Far Eastern capitalism, that this attitude would take over »corporative« structures, which hastily proclaimed themselves as »nationally responsible« – all this would not stay hidden much longer for the public.

What stands out at the input and the output of this »system«, that devastated in its destructive way the civic spirit of the Bulgarian?

First and foremost, the centralized state bureaucratic control on the distribution of social means sustained the necessary »critical mass« of an all-encompassing *civic conformism.* Its functions are to hold back, with an enviable for any tyrant devotion any significant democratic advance of the Bulgarian society, pressing it down to the »old« marsh-land. A considerable part of the intelligentsia, merited workers and agricultural activists (not to mention the »reserve« cadres among the Komsomol members and even those from the »pioneer« youngsters organization), indoctrinated with the ideas of most perverted notion of »real socialism« and the loyal paternalism to the Zhivkov regime, would go later through series of chameleon metamorphoses. Having stepped on the ladder of a directed from above social-class progress and career planning, their »left« and/or right »foot« would prove all of a sudden to be hanging in the space. That would unleash unsuspected power-thriving potential and voluntarism inventiveness of the native post-communist *Homo politicus.*

The so fragile structures of the »civic society« in Bulgaria after World War II (whose existence scholars still question in the years of »Zhivkovism«) have been deprived of the opportunity to develop normally under the circumstances of a real competing and fair social milieu. Moreover, the personal and individual qualities had no chance to flourish freely and with a significant social effect. Such attempts proved often to be not only meaningless, but also depraved in a special way. The initiative of most former »subjects« of the regime was not allowed to exceed the limits of material benefits set – as »the house, the car and the country-house«. Or to materialize into more than a mediocre career in certain »sphere« of social life, regulated through the individual-degrading balance system. In this way, the *scarcity* to which the »common people« that were left out from the circle of privileges were doomed, resulted in a widely spread misuse of the collective and communal assets. The legendary embezzlements of small, middle, and with the appearance of the appetite for privatizing, larger state assets, the overstatement in time-sheets, the corruptive affairs of the »corporate« deals, privileging some bigger or even selected smaller actors of the economic »order«, would remain a badly concealed from the society »enigma«. Instead, the public would be entertained with the sentimental memories of the »good old time of *Tato*«....

All this eroded the civic moral of many Bulgarian generations, their notion of good and bad, of fair and unfair. The truth requires pointing out that it was not so much some »collapse of communism« and a most chaotic transition to quasi (facade) forms of democracy and market economy that caused those devistation. They rather stem from system damages and moral *corruption* inflicted by the Zhivkov regime both on the »horizontal« and the »vertical« of the Bulgarian society from the mid- and late 20th century. This regime smashed the most values of a traditional *Bulgarian asceticism* from which century's long industrious and ethical virtue used to spring.

This many-head »hydra« determines most of the manifest and imitation patterns of some Wild-South-Balkan capitalism in a »virtual paraphrase« which so insolently has showed its teeth to the robbed-in-few-nights Bulgarian people since 1990 and onwards. Its »political philosophy« rests on the idea a forcedly deviated subject consciousness, slavishly »condensed« in the years of »Zhivkovism« but accelerated anew in the years of transition. Hence, all the »plays« with a possible monarchic form of a state rule, capable of consolidating the nation from inside, as well in a pan-European context. Not to mention the media-manipulative models of a new »daddy-president«, of statesmen promoted by fancy hairstyles, inspiring experts rhetoric etc.

It is not that difficult to see how the self-proclaimed »builders of new Bulgaria« would develop and what forms of interaction in the system of the real political life they would take. The Bulgarian »corporative« structures mainly recruited from the same circles, destined to »move« both business and politics in its »integral« oligarch structures, turned to be however far more inclined towards wealthy life, over expenditures and the »macho« lifestyle, rather than something else. Most of the »independent« companies, trade, financial and other structures, generated own networks for direct and indirect social privileges and all kinds of patronage benefits. An unleashed »order of capital" that is unimaginable even for Westerners established its reign on post-socialist ground at this side. This totally alienated from most European and democratic values »remnant Zhivkovism« came back to life among the calls for class revenge and violence, which obsessed our street democrats. It will be remembered with a *»new-old« group-corporate despotism,* capable of brute violence over anyone who dares to oppose this ego- drive in the name of a self proclaimed but nationally irresponsible ruling elite

Thus, behind the facade of strengthening the state Zhivkovism carried out a systematic, pernicious transformation of the hard-budding (in spite of everything) real civic culture in this country – especially since 1968. An active role in this process of methodical destruction of the few sensible forms and patterns of rational political behavior, played the »socialist« law-making and juridical system. The latter readily followed the party dictatorship orders symbolized by the invisible interventions of the »strong of the day«.

The memory of the eternal »parliamentary« conformity and unproblematic practice of a shared »state responsibility«, with which most laws strengthening the »socialist relationship« in different spheres of Bulgarian social life, were passed, has not faded away. The National Assembly was entirely dominated by older and well-»tested« cadres. A silent »clergy« of the eternalized Zhivkov's rule, playing with the principles of the socialist democracy, »even at the cost of its personal self-esteem«, constantly strengthened its social and political status quo. The State Council which consisted of a few generations of senior officials and counselors (among whom even famous writers who gave up the role of idea-generators in a civic society that appeared absurd) played the role more of a representative, protocol organ of state authority, than anything else. The cabinet of the Chairman of the State Council (Zhivkov again) remained empty for most of the year. The only visited hall was the one in which state awards were conferred. Practically, all state bills were sanctioned and most often prepared by the apparatus of the Central Committee of the Bulgarian Communist Party. That is why they resemble decrees. The same style characterized the procedures in the »decision-making« of the Council of inisters.

With all that the so called »*Bermuda triangle*«, i.e. the impressive bastion of the unshakable dictatorial Zhivkov's rule, symbolized by the stone composure of the Stalin-type architecture and the City-largo in Sofia, usually crossed by »escorts« of black Mercedes-Benz and Russian Volga cars – seemed closed forever. That this bastion would prove to be not so rotten from inside as thrown out of the political stage (i.e. a victim of the same methods with which it ruled for 34 years – through its system isolation and deprivation of huge segments of the Bulgarian nation would become obvious only after the fall of the Berlin wall. But not before the dust from its ruins mixed with traditional Balkan »dust« on so many Bulgarian city squares and village centers. This symbolic – blue-red- smog – as ordinary Bulgarians preferred to describe the visible effects of a "behind the door" quasi-Democratic New deal never turned into a rainbow, that it has been designed to blur the sight of million Bulgarians, who gathered on November 10th 1989 at the Alexander Nevski Cathedral in support of proper democratic progress, became clear much later. But this is a new story, which is still lived through and might never be retailed again.

The Perestroika in Russia and its Political »Periphrasis« in Bulgaria

The idea of launching a new project to revive socialism in the ex-Soviet Union has been publicly proclaimed first at the April plenum of the Central Committee of the Communist party of Russia (1985). It was the first one – after the election of Gorbatchov for general secretary. Practically it raised an anti-thesis of the stagnating system of »*real socialism*«, and the attempt to overcome its deep crisis from the early 80- ease. As Ernst Bloch commented in one of the first reviews on this event – the Russian *perestroika*[84] was a

---

84 Perestrojka – russ. »reconstruction«, »upgrading«, »re-arranging«, »adapting« etc. had the political conottaton of radical change and abolishing morally discredited principles of leadership under »real socialism«, the corruptive style of the nomenclatura (ideological and technocratic) etc. Another »core« of interpretation (as related to the broader public) was the threat of an apocalyptic nuclear war in a most dangerously polarized bipolar world, the demand to go beyond the paranoia

radical political turn aimed to overwhelm the counter fight in a bipolar world that had reached the limits of its self-destruction. Gorbatchov's speech dedicated to the democratization and »work with the cadres« – has been given the significance of Krushchev's speech at the XX Congress of the Communist party of Russia (1956), which dismantled the cult of Stalin and his most devastating regime.

> »The perestroika idea has a short history of 5 years before Gorbatchov came to power. Initial signs of such a discourse are to be found as early as 1983 and in 13 texts of Gorbatchov's speeches held between 1985 and 1986. The most controversial debates in the Russian media – short before the spread of the Soviet Union – give no arguments in favor of the existing of some strategy, related to this vast political venture. The paraphrased ideas of Lenin, Gramshi, Bucharin, or Kamenev (The New economical politics from 1920's), mixed with neo-conservative »innovative practices« of M.Thatcher (her notorious »Green file«), added less to what leftist intellectuals believed to be a push to some »integrative socialism«.«[85]

Three years after »perestroika« was launched and a year before the fall of the Berlin wall, observers as Ernst Mandel (1988) shared their impression that it would be an illusion of some »historical idealism« to consider Gorbatchov's ideas as Marxist. [86] Others warned that Gorbatchov's ideas are hardly to be related to any theory whatsoever. [87] This »sediment skepticism«

---

of the Cold war, the dangerous milutarization, the dramatic lagging behind of »real socialism« from modern technogical and economic development. Russian debates even argued on some »degradation of the human factor« (Zipko & oth.) as result of this erosion of the soviet structures. This was an attempt to involve in the perestrojka the older generation, mostly victims of the Stalinist regime. In one way or another the perestrojka had a wider political resonance in Eastern Europe...

85 M.Thatcher's »Green map« has been mentioned as a source of innovative ideas related to a new conservative push of the stagnating UK economy during the 80 eese. The strategy of a privatization of unprofitable sectors of the UKh economy: railroads, the public sector (including jails or even graveyards), strict monetarism, raizing of taxation etc. has been propelled short after the arrest of Gorbatchov and the coming to power of Eltzin.

86 Authors as the German social democrats Peter Glotz claimed that Gorbatchov's reformed commnism in the next decades »will not succeed to challenge the western market economies«. Number of leftist writers shared their bitter dissapointment, as related to expected »new forms of some integrative socialism« as result from the perestrojka that could network leftist movement both in the East and in the West. See: W.F.Haug., Gorbatcshow. Versuch über den Zusammenhang seiner Gedanken., Argument, Hamburg, 1989, p. 38–39.

87 Some commentators argued on this »theoretical deficit« of Gorbatschov, claiming that the »ideological priority in Gorbatschov is not only clearly expressed«, but that he seems inspired by »the ambitions in this respect to follow Lenin« . See: W.

increased, but was overwhelmed by the rapid political developments in Soviet Russia after reformist circles took control of power by a most dramatic »revolution« of the street, backed by the tanks. The »revolution from above«, performed in similar scenarios in most Eastern European countries. It had its resonance in Bulgaria too. It still leaves questions opened, but less related to some missed »*chances of the crises*« (Dahrendorf). Less is this phenomena to be rationalized as some brutally crashed »real socialism«, or a »counter-revolution«. The appeal that the left has to »kiss capitalism« (A.Giddens); to adapt to a changed global world, is even less inspiring as years pass by. It is not of our concern, to discuss the Russian perestroika however, less even its failed attempt to abandon some type of »barracks socialism«, or whatever critics label the collapsed system in the ex-Soviet Union.[88] What is of greater interest is its *catalyzing role* in the democratic transition in Bulgaria.

Couple of questions, relate to the shaping new political culture in Bulgaria which we have to answer briefly. The Bulgarian political mind may never have the capacity (or courage) to find the right answers of most of them. One is certain – Gorbatchov's perestroika, even as a failed attempt to mobilize huge masses into a propelled process of involvement into the system of socialist »self-government», had a decisive role and impact on the most uncertain (and practically impossible in other civilized forms), democratic transition in Bulgaria. It was Russia that »allowed things to happen«, as it gave not only signs, but through active diplomacy, encouraged the replacement of Zhivkov and his regime. To get a better notion of this »backing« of the idea of abolishing one of the oldest totalitarian regimes left on the Balkans (as related to Albania, or Romania) we have to remind on the specific role of Russia in the traditional political culture of this nation. It dates back in the dark ages of 500 years of Ottoman oppression, passes through decades of struggles for national freedom, and culminates in the National Liberation (1878) bayoneted by the Russian »*bratushki*«, as result of the Russian-Turkish war. This pattern of *Russia as savior* – has been re-defined in 1944, when the Russian Red Army entered the borders of Bulgaria – at that time satellite of Nazi Germany. This led to the establishing of communist power (Fatherlands Front) in Bulgaria.

As paradox of history the process of rapid industrialization and modernization of Bulgaria coincided with the era of communism, labeled later as »real socialism», as the utopia had to be extended beyond the near future. In this way most subject-participant elements of the real Bulgarian political culture after WWII are deeply rooted and culturally linked to Russia. Russia (long unrecognized by Moscow) adopted the Cyrillic alphabet from

F. Haug., Gorbatchow. Versuch über den Zusammenhang seiner Gedanken., Argument, Hamburg, 1989, p. 15.

88 Ibid.

Cyril and Method, who were Bulgarians. Still Russia preferred to nourished its »soviet-imperial« self-confidence in Slavs on the Balkans in other ways though. A widely popular Russian saying reflects this pattern of specific empathy: »Kuritsa *ne ptsza – Bolgaria ne za granitsa*« (A hen is not a bird – as is Bulgaria not beyond a border«. It still reminds on a traditional respect and recognition expected, which Bulgarians have paid in their own way.

***

The perestroika in Russia was the first politically significant impulse of democratic changes within the »packed« (Fotev) Bulgarian society until 1989. As paradox of history its initial driving force was no other but the ex-Communist party in this country. And to be more precise a »reformist« wing within its leadership, pressed by history to adapt to the new realities after 1989. This was done in a »step by step«, less »fluent« but what counts more »bloodless« pattern of transition. This output has also its premises. Even in the years of Cold war, communism in Bulgaria stayed rather more open to the West. This is to be related to the intermediary status of the Zhivkow's regime, as »bridging« both East and West (by transfer of high-technologies in the years of embargos, re-export of crude oil and energy from Russia, exploiting trade links with advanced European countries (in the era of Brezhnev) and even with the rich resources of the Near East. This *»multi-vector«* hub-policy has been a spring of »managerial« self-confidence of couple of generations of the ex-communist (technocratic) nomenclature in Bulgaria.[89]

> »The very fact that Zhivkov survived for 34 years, as a closest satellite of Kremlin – that he successfully adapted to several sequential »general political lines« in the Soviet union is a special case to tackle. What most Bulgarians *believed* at the time of the »boom« of the Russian perestroika – was that it could only re-define the communist rule *status quo* in Bulgaria. But in no way undermine the solid irremovable fundaments of communist power in this country. Zhivkow seemed to had kept a »reserved« place in history of communism indeed.«[90]

---

89 Nearly 80 percent of the BNP, according to less known to the wider public data. Have been »generated« by trade and re-export. The standard of living in this county reached higer levels as compared to most Balkan »neighbours« in the 80ees. Or even »upper-midle« in Western Europe. The only limits of those operational scopes seemed to be the »ideological one« – as carfully watched by Moskow.

90 This might well be true – he left this world at the age of 83 , surrounded by grand children and family at his comfortable residence (though some believe this was a kind of house arrest) . This gave a sence of relief not so much to old »party soldiers« but scattered remnants of Zhivkow's nomenclatura. As for the broader

The general difference between the impact of the Russian perestroika in Bulgaria and in most other ex-communist countries in Central Europe could be briefed as follows:

The perestroika in Russia failed rather »too quickly« for the clumsy, but most cautious steps to reforms, as performed by the Zhivkov's regime in Bulgaria.

Once the political scene had been »cleared off« by Eltzin's democratic reformists, (supported by close military circles) and the Communist party of Russia was »banned« – the spread of the Soviet Union had a propelling impact on the internal political developments in this country.

The ruling political class in Bulgaria initially stacked to Gorbatchov's rhetoric of a possible »second breath« to socialism in this country. Once the dramatic events culminated in the shooting of the Russian parliament, dismissed by Eltzin – all seemed »clear enough«.

A rapid *transformation of power* and its allocation to hasty designed »home made« dissident opposition and »incubated« quasi-political structures, started to fill the political vacuum.

The output of this was a deeply controversies »transition« to what has shaped in a decade or so ion a most peculiar (and unacceptable) *Balkan breed of »capitalism«,* as licensed and steered by the Old Party itself (!). The scheme seems simple enough at least to the public eye. Most of the available state capital has been initially »exported« through different channels, and not long after distributed (under certain conditions) among loyal »cadres« and »shadow credited« millionaires. Most of them have been selected from the ranks of ex-economic nomenclature (and/or its »straw men«), representatives of the sport movements, ex-law-enforcement servants and others. This cohort of »one night made capitalists« formed the »critical mass« of a quasi- *market transition* in Bulgaria. The default in 1997, as dozen of »private banks« bankrupted, has blurred the traces of this »scenario« of rather desperate transformation of totalitarian power into an economic one. That it will reach its limits of competence in a most sophisticated, but still rationally controlled global market economy, has been of lesser concern.

Thus Gorbatchov's perestroika, which in a way promised new socialist forms of production and democratic self government, ended in totally discredited left and pseudo social democratic alternatives of social recovery of Bulgaria. Couple of shifts from »left« to »right« government(s) have only worsened the economic situation of huge segments of this society. The alienation (and isolation) of millions of Bulgarians from proper democratic involvement seems to have reached its peak right at the »threshold« of EC entry. The emerging of couple of nationalistic movements from 2005 on – as

»people's masses«, they seemed to be less moved by the idea of »strengthening« the old system, as the perestrojka opened new horizons indeed.

»Attack«, or even a new cohort of populist right centered »new riches« – GERB (Civic movement for European development of Bulgaria),[91] seems the bitter fruit of a fragmented and perplexed culture of transition, brought to its exhaustion.

The roads to civic society, freedoms and rights, as relevant to European values and democratic life-style, seem still under a recycled new-old »Sward of Damocles«, as a strong hand has stretched to get hold of power and »put order« in this country.

The »Knights« of the Round Table
Or How to Design One's Own Opposition

The perestroika in Russia initiated an intensive aggregation of new political structures in Bulgaria from 1990 on. The energy of the masses catalysed from beneath in some late *»Prague spring«*. It rapidly lived its romantic phase though. The candidates for new political leadership in this country immediately after the fall of the Berlin wall, seemed only formally inspired by the »Polish model« and its revolutionary experience carried out by »Solidarnost«. The latter could not be implemented in Bulgaria and there are many reasons for this, which we will avoid here. What counts most is that the Polish experience was only partially copied. This has been done in the forms of »spontaneous« street protests and quasi-civic activity under the steering of the still ruling communist elite, which experienced a political *Zeitnot* in a wider European context. [92]

This gave grounds to first rank leaders of the democratic opposition to comment on »missed chances« and brief bitterly:« We did what we could do«.

The Roundtable in Poland, which culminated 10 years of passionate resistance against the regime and couple of strikes at Gdansk, Warsaw and Krakow, »happened« in Bulgaria in the form of a *public forum* (called also Round table) that involved selected circle of a »nominated dissidence«. The

---

91 This Movement has founded a Party under the same logo (GERB) on Dec.3, 2006. Informal leader of it is a police general of the reserve, ex-bodygard of both Zhivkow and Simeon Saxe Coburg-Gotha – at preset major of Sofia – Boyko Borisov.

92 According to some European observers the fall of the ex-communist regimes from 1989 to present has followed a common outlook if not centrally directed scenario. W. Haug points out some similarities to the revolution of 1919 in the case of the fall of the regime in the GDR. »It happened as if not to occur« ,which is a sharp dialectical reflecton of this quasi –revolutionalry pattern, which in the media era might be of interest for future comparative studies. See: W.F.Haug. Versuch beim täglichen Verlieren des Bodens unter den Füssen neuen Grund zu gewinnen. Das perestrojka-Journal Argument, Hamburg, 1990, p. 132

»knights« at this table, (chaired by ex-members of Politburo of the Bulgarian communist party), had to accept what was to be allocated to them. Both representatives of the »older« and the »fresh-recruited« democratic opposition were thus sacked in their power temptations, offered by the still ruling communists.[93]

Most of the chairs at the Round table, have been »reserved« for close adherents to the old »masters of power« – representatives of the Zhivkow's regime nomenclature and their relatives. This democratic *»nepotistic mix«* according to most penetrating observers as Valentin Vatzev, ex-member of the renamed Socialist party's steering gremmie – was a step-by step »transfer of power from the old comments regime into the hands of their children from the ranks of the UDF. This, as he claimed »has the output of *›a restitution of power into one's own hands‹*«. The Round table had only to add legitimacy

93 Three days after the foundation of the Union of Democratic Forces(UDF) in Dec. 1989 at the first gathering infront of the »Alexander Nevski« Cathedral in Sofia, the leaders of the new Bulgarian opposition proclaimed the political demand for a Round table. The Trade union movement »Podkrepa« (Dr.Trenchev) threatened even »a round table or a massive strike...« On Jan. 3 and 4, 1990 initial negotiations between representatives of different political and social organizations took place in the National Assembly, as releted to the procedures of the Round table. The UDF actively negotiates with the BCP on the terms and issues to be discussed. It has been decided that the Round table discussions should take place between Jan. 16 and 24, 1990, but its sessions have been actually scheduled for May 15, 1990. Similar round tables have been organized in the rest of ex-socialist countries, but they ended their negotiations a year earlier. The general issues discussed at the Round table in this country were 4: the political system, the division of power, the national question and a new votiog electoral law. Under the pressure of time – the Bulgarian communist party was facing it's 14 th Congress which had to separate the state from the party power and rename the ex-Communist party into Bulgarian socialist party – the representatives of the ruling communist party had to agree and accept most of the demands of the democratic movement. A deficit of significant political ideas became obvious however. As UDF raises 12 demands which reflect in a way the perplexion of unexperienced democrats: »control over an application of a popular humour newspaper »Starshel«, as to use it for its political pamphlets«, »abolishment of the customs control on import of political, scientific, and religious literature«. Different organization insist to be involved in the Round table too. Two »co-chairmen« steered its working sessions – the ex-member of Politburo Alexander Lilov and Zhelju Zhelev – one of the few diccidents in this country (his book »Fashism« has been banned for the publishing short before the fall of the communist regime). Additionally 24 leaders of different delegations sign the negotiated results of the Round table. The delegation of BCP includes Andrej Lukanov, member of Politburo. After his election for Premier minister his Chair as Chairman of the Round table occupies »the young Knight« Georgi Pirinski – at present Chairman of the Bulgarian parliament (2006).

to this scheme. As the control on the economic structure by the »working collectives« has been put under question – »the privatisation appeared a more modern and adequate means« of re-establishing the status quo in a new political context guaranteed even by the West.[94]

Democracy gambled:

> »This processes – so Vatzev – developed under the sign of myths. The one was the myth »Lukanov« – »if there is no Round table we are to facie a civil war«. The image of some »threatening revolution« was projected on the wall. Under the motto »Let us perform a bloodless transition« – a transformation of power occurred. The second myth was the one of »Lilov«: »Let us not allow them to split our party«. And this has been discussed in a period when the Bulgarian communist party had *already spited* into Bulgarian socialist party and the Union of democratic forces. (?) The Bulgarian communist party could not split at that time – as Vatzev witnesses. Much more dangerous things might have happened to it – as to be banned for example. This alternative has been probably discussed, but those who could have done this, had no guts....[95] This was the alternative in Russia – the right wing in the Communist party of Russia got hold of the state resources and banned it's own party.«[96]

Outputs:

The transformation of power in Bulgaria has thus to a greater extend than in other Central European countries been steered through a pattern of political »baptizing« of a selected »new political elite« and nepotistic »cadre sources«.

Five years after the Round table activists of this still disputable political venture tended to define the Bulgarian socialist party as having identified itself more likely with some *conservative* (and in this way right) role in the process of movement to a pluralist society.

The UDF to which initially the role of a democratic »movement-party« had been prescribed, performed more likely as *leftist.* According its first leader Dr. Zhelju Zhetlev the UDF had to dismiss its ranks (or dissolve into smaller parties), as the process of democratisation advanced.

---

94 See: Interview of Iva Petroni with Valentin Vatsev »The New elite and the New order«, 24 h daily, March, 30, 1996.

95 Ahmed Dogan, leader of the Movement for Rights and Freedoms (Ethnic Turks party) represented in the Bulgarian parliament as »unorthodox« political respond to the ethnic and minority problems in neighbouring Yugoslavia that lead to the disasters of of couple of wars, Bulgaria believed to have invented own original »ethnic model«, as quarantee for etnnic pease in this country and on the Balkans. Recent debates on this rather disputable constellation blamed leader of MRF Ahmed Dogan for prescribing to himself mostly a collective achievement of relative ethnic stability in this country..

96 V. Vatsev, Ibid.

This not only did not occur but also practically reproduced a most dangerous bipolar model of extreme rivalry. The diffusion of »left« and »right«, within the notions of the mass electorate – propelled a spiral of confrontation, which reached unpredictable and most unacceptable limits.

All this only briefs a most disputable contribution of the »reformists« in Bulgaria for the so-called »peaceful transition« to democracy and market economy. The output was a widely spread public notion that the Round table had less to do with proper legitimacy of an emerging democratic political order. The achievements of the negotiations seem less relevant to the shaping new civic culture in shape. This refers not only to a quasi-democratic opposition generated *in vitro* (by the same old-communist guards), but the »weaver-dealer« pattern which has unveiled the character of some »gambled democracy«. As prominent representatives of the so-called »democratic idea«, joined a coalition with the Socialist party, this »buttoning« of a most discredited new political elite became obvious. Thus, they practically supported the return of the Socialists back to power in 1994. In this way a notorious »returns to the Party only creator« of part of the democratic opposition occurred. This pattern shaped a most heterogeneous »opposition against totalitarism, but not against BSP«.[97]

The fragmentation lead to a deeper split within the ranks of the Bulgarian socialist party itself. As V. Vatzev brilliantly puts it: »this process turned then to the right, since a right upper leadership within the BSP was much stronger. The old party demonstrated that it can rule in its own interest, by standing on one leg in BSP, the UDF, the Movement of rights and freedoms, the presidency...«. Moreover, to the question: »How come that this right upper leadership in the Socialist party came to life?«, the same sharp minded analyst gave a most definite answer:

> »At this time something of great importance happened. The managerial elite of BSP and its political representatives, having got rid of the control of Zhivkov, got the legal right and juridical ground to lead Bulgaria on a road, which they preferred. The party had to be persuaded that this is the only road left...« (! -P.G.)[98]

---

97 »In this broad opposition« – as ex-member of Politburo A.Lukanov points out in one of his interviews – »figures of most different featering joined as one flock: centrist, future liberals as Z.Zhelev and P.Simeonov, extreme rights, including legioneers (supporters of nazist ideas before WWII), monarchists. The very process of events at this time put up the dilemma – ›what am I‹. A democrat – yes, but of what type?. By the end of January 1990 those people could not cope together anymore – And they have defined themselves. ›Eco Glasnost‹ did that later. In my oppinion this happened under the shock which all real democrats lived through at the time of the non-democratic rule of Philip Dimitrov...« (Ibid.)

98 Ibid.

Now that the heralds of »perestroika« in Bulgaria are gone, it is obvious that it was more of a political failure, than some *»betrayal of socialist ideas«*, or whatever some still prefer to label it by. What is of greatest interest for Bulgarians and the democratic world is not so much a process of some tiresome »grass rooting« of civic culture »revisited« I this country. But an activist pattern of its involvement in shaping its own, even though »gambled« democratic destiny in a new European context. The idea of some new big social »experiment« in this country seems deeply buried at both sides of the Balkan. It might »ferment«, or be »recycled« historically some day, to find its new forms and shapes, as wise men believe. But this concerns less the pragmatic Bulgarian mind. *»Alle, aber nicht jeder«* (All, but not each one) is now the inspiring mantra even here on the Balkans...

Demoskopy as Maidservant of Democracy

»Opinions as many, as people« – thus the skeptic Bulgarian mind most often has referred to public opinion. There is no such »animal« for most of us yet. It seems that long before Bordeaux threw his glove, claiming that »public opinion does not exist«, the indigenous mind at this side has outstripped this modern reality. From Hume and Locke to Machiavelli and Habermas the discourse on rulers and ruled goes on. Bulgarians say: »the caravan strolls by, while dogs bark at it...« In a world of Internet we also »chat«, but we barely hear each other. Some »repressive tolerance« of which the Frankfurt philosopher Iring Fetcher wrote, rooted on our lands too. Thus the »multi faced Janus« – symbolizing public opinion, turns into an everlasting stake of a hasty implemented modernism of ours, in which vice and virtue – to remind of Derrida – make the present shorter than yesterday. In this unprecedented acceleration of time and space majorities become more transitorily than ever. How do they manage to express public opinion then?

Public opines is neither the common will, the nation, or the ideology. Less it is the sum of private opinions strictly registered by sociologist. It never speaks in first person. It is its mediators that articulate it. It is neither an object nor a subject, even though expressed in most boring way through media and at round tables. They make it speak »through the stomach«. It mumbles on TV debates. This is why it prefers to keep silent instead of talking loud. For it is obvious that there is no one to listen to it. Despite of this, public opinion in this country hides it's vital force between an ocean of apathy, and all the »fictions of the mind«. Not to mention the mountains of prejudices still haunting. It stubbornly opposes, despite the disrespect, or even drastic violations. This is why it will always be related to »the art of change« – as Rousseau stressed – something that »neither reason, nor virtues, or laws« posses.

The Bulgarian public got used to the old idea of Lippmann who defined public opinion as »counting the armies« and prescribing the victory to the stronger one without coming into a combat. Still the political passions in this country are less channeled in the framework of parliamentary democracy, which takes public opinion for granted. The rapid merchandizing of the political market offered new chances for »mushroomed« public opinion research agencies and even quasi-marketing actors. In one way or another most of them managed to go beyond the initial political servitude and even offered reliable prognoses of a most »twisted« (and media blurred) political development. Still experienced sociologists in this country warn that the empirical data registered (as in the case of media ratings, corporative PR images et.) are to be considered in a very precautious way indeed. During the »street performance« of the young democracy in this country the results of voting intentions of Bulgarians have been obviously manipulated. Results have »over-exaggerated« with 7–8 percent, as dependent which party the agency was »backing«. (Venedikov, 1994)

Thus the phrase »Demoscopy as maidservant of democracy« became popular. To reduce this still operating »political market temptation« we use here only empirical results from established research agencies, and even more objective results from electoral voting in the last years. Before we present a »bird view« of the shaping new political culture in this country, we have to once again remind on what our study generally refers to, as related to the theoretical framework of Almond and Verba, to which we still prefer to adhere:

»Political culture... is not to be reduced to the patterns of interactions between the political actors – who says what to whom, who influences whom, who votes for whom. It is related to the *system of beliefs* about the patterns of political interaction and the political institutions. It is not to be reduced to what happens in the world of politics, but to *what people believe that happens.* And these beliefs could be of several kinds: they could be empirical beliefs about the *real stand of the political life*; beliefs about the *objectives and values* to be perceived in the political life, and these beliefs can have important *emotional dimensions*«(Almond & Verba, 1965: 516).

Trust in Parties

Trust, as related to politics in modern societies, is a most ambiguous and disputable category.[99] The empirical findings of the initial stage of

99 The 1999 collected data from the IEA Civic Education Study of 14-year-olds to examine trust on three levels—trust in institutions, with which individuals have little, or no daily contact (those delegated as representatives in institutions, such as the national legislature), trust in institutions with whose representatives individuals interact frequently (schools), and trust in other people. The findings are vivid

democracy in Bulgaria are not less a reflection of the chaotic break of the old structures. But even more of the crisis of a *system of values*, that has cultivated for decades mistrust to politics and its instruments of coercive power. Parties are still grasped as products of some »conspiracy theory», or sphere of most corruptive interests, and less as political institution in favor of society. The rapid *proliferation* and *fragmentation* (nearly 300 parties registered) has contributed to this rapid devaluation of the political system in transition. The changing context of international politics has had an additional impact on the shaping new political infrastructure in this country too. It is not less a result of a politically sobered public with growing pragmatic expectation at the »output« of the political process. The table below reflects trust in parties as expressed by representative sample of Bulgarians enquired at the *initial stage of transition* to market society and democracy. As far as it identifies the »cores« and »peripheries« in support of major political parties it is of certain interest for the political scholar in the field of comparative research. We offer those data therefore as registered in May 1991 by the independent Center for the Study of Democracy:

Table 1

Trust towards bigger political parties and formations in Bulgaria
(Initial stage of transition to democracy)
% of enquired

	Nov. '90	Dec. '90	Jan. '91	April ' 91	May '91	Average
BSP (Socialist party)	21–22	20–22	18–23	23–26	22–24	21–23
UDF (Democratic union)	33–41	24–38	20–32	23–28	28–30	25–34
BZNS(Agrarian party)	8–32	6–12	7–12	9–14	10–37	8–19
MRF(Ethnic Turks party)	6–14	4–6	2–4	4–5	6–17	4–9

Source: Center for the Study of Democracy, 1991, Archive

reflection of a most disputable pattern(s) of evaluation of political orientations in complex societies, moreover in emerging democracies in Eastern Europe. Those three levels of trust are compared in five democracies whose levels of political stability not only vary (Bulgaria, Chile, Colombia, England and the United States). Formal indicators of democratic development (R. Rose) are taken out of totally different cultural contexts and backgrounds. This makes findings less relevant to the Balkan countries (and some other countries »in transition«). See: Trust in Government-Related Institutions and Civic Engagement among Adolescents CIRCLE Working Paper 17. August 2004.

Table 2

Electoral »cores«of bigger political parties and formations in Bulgaria
(Initial stage of transition to democracy)
% of enquired

	Jan. '91	April ' 91	May '91	Average
BSP(Socialist party)	18	21	18	19
UDF (Democratic union)	20	19	20	20
BZNS(Agrarian party)	6	7	8	7
MRF(Ethnic Turks party)	2	3	5	3

Source: Center for the Study of Democracy, 1991,Archive

The idea of identifying »cores«, »center« and »periphery« of the party electorates has clearly positioned 2 »compact« political blocks – the one of the Bulgarian socialist party (BSP) and The Movement for Rights and Freedoms (MRF). Both of them had smaller peripheries (3–4 % of the national electorate for each of them). The largest periphery had the Union of Democratic Forces (UDF) – 6–10%. The block of the Agrarian party played the role of some symbolic center. Thus over 1/3 of the Bulgarian electorate has been referred to the »zone of the periphery«, defined (labeled) as »alienated«. Most experts admitted that a *»last minute«* vote (10–15 %) might have a decisive effect on the final votes of what looked as a vote of »all against one«. Few experts agreed that a situational change might influence the outcome of what looked more of a *»civil combat«* than proper democratic competition. As the share of those, who did not vote, rose up to 57 % a decade later, it became obvious that formal indicators of measuring a total loss of trust in the political systems of a Balkan type, are as limited as useless.

A more explicit reflection of trust in parties (in so far they have moved on the »left«/«right« scale in the years of transition, offered few measurement of the *political identification of the electorate*. Their empirical configuration nearly 17 years after the change is presented below:

POLITICAL IDENTITY (LEFT-CENTER-RIGHT)

	Left	Rather Left	Center	Rather Right	Right	Non resp.
January 2004	22	12	31	9	11	15
November 2004	16	11	38	9	9	17
April 2005	**22**	**11**	**32**	**11**	**9**	**15**

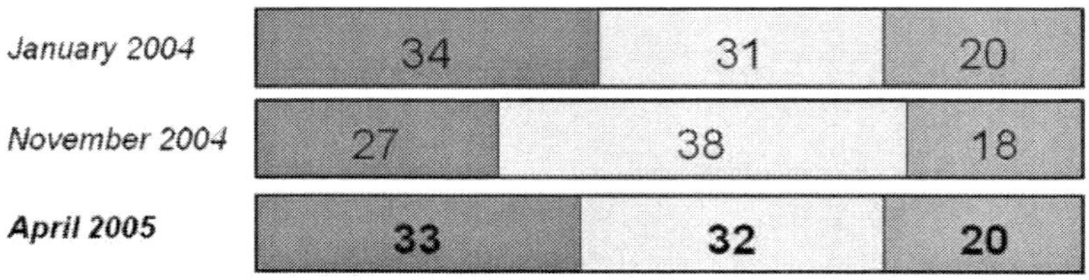

Source: RSS, ASSA-M, January 2004, November 2004, April 2005

ACCA-M
www.assa-m.com

Source: ASSA–M Archives

As disputable as »ratings« of different political parties (moreover politicians) could be, they give a notion of the *rapidly declining trust in most parties* of the »turbulent« movement to democracy. »Left« and »right« (liberal/ conservative) scales lost on meaning, as platforms of most parties in this country merged. The data below illustrates the shift in this respect, as a less nationalist (in the traditional sense), but a more radically opposing »populist cohort«(Attack) entered the political scene.

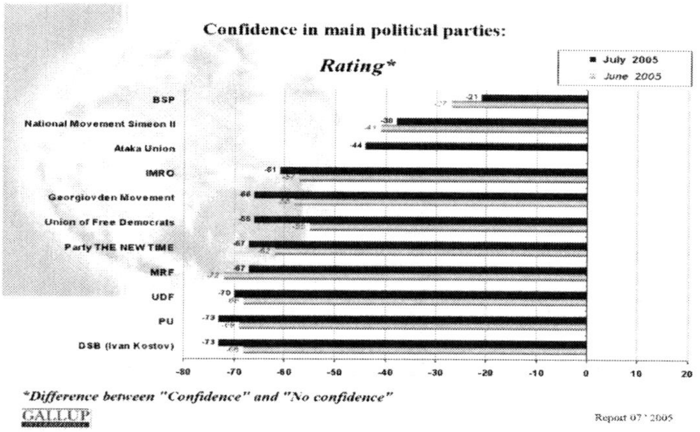

Source: BBS Gallup International
(On platforms of major political parties in Bulgaria see Attachment 7)

The data available reflects «milder« shapes of a vigorously propelled trend of mobilizing significant segments of the Bulgarian electorate, who feel »excluded« from immediate democratic participation. This has in its own way contributed to a most painful »blow«, which the »right« wing parties had to suffer in the autumn of 2006. (See Appendix, Presidential elections 2006).

TO WHICH of the political parties do you SYMPATHIZE?

/open question, with a possibility of up to two answers, controlled by the observations of the interviewer/

	November 2004	*April 2005*	*June 2006*	*October 2006*	***January 2007***
CB (BSP)	24	30	24	26	**21-23**
MRF	4.9	4.7	5.7	5	**5***
NMSS	10	15	5	3-6	**2-3**
CEDB (BB)	–	–	11	5-7	**9-12**
Ataka	–	–	5	4-8	**6-9**
UFD	2.6	1.8	0.5	0.3	**0.2**
UDF	10	8	7	6-12	**4-6**
DSB	1.2	3.7	5	2.5	**1-2**
Small parties	5	11	2	2	**2**
Do not sympathize	43	31	35	37	**42**
Non response	1.7	0.6	0.8	0.5	**0.9**

* *Without reporting the probable votes from Turkey /turks with bulganan citizenship/, who in the elections for eurodeputies /May 2007/ most likely will be 60-100 000 valid votes*

Sources: NRS of ASSA-M, January 2004, November 2004, April 2005, June and Oct. 2006, January 2007
Age 18-70 years; two-level random sample by electoral sections and lists;
Size of the realized sample – 1 200 persons.

ACCA-M
www.assa-m.com

The neo-liberal strategies of the Democrats for Strong Bulgaria (DSB) seem less acceptable at present The center-oriented »coalition« (BSP, National Movement Simeon II, MRF) at present in rule, seems still to feed on the EC entry and some rest-positive orientation of voters in this respect, tolerating its obvious failures in a socially misbalanced reform. On Dec. 3, 2006, right at the threshold of Bulgarian EC entry, an alternative »right-center« Party (GERB) – has been founded. The Citizens for European Development of Bulgaria – as they preferred to call themselves- still have to add to an uncertain democracy, as most of them contributed in the field of Bulgarian sport, and even for the emerging entrepreneur sphere. The political seasons ahead might bring more shifts, but a process of *»recycling«* of the old/new political elite, which has more to loose than to gain from a sobered Bulgarian political mind seems already propelled.

Trust in Institutions

The curve of trust in the institutions in a way follows the one of couple of economic crisis in this country in the years of transition. Still a no lesser invisible change of the political orientations seems to have had an impact on this. A more systematic analysis of the results from recent social surveys would show that institutional trust is influenced more by affective operating media and less by outcomes of real politics. The »anger against politicians« reflects thus some radicalism of the political culture. It is a result of illusive paternalist expectations considering the institutions as only generators of a subjectively experienced change. Low levels of institutional trust are not less a public response to the traditional style[100] of non-transparency, as related to their activity, and a broadly used »centralism« in the process of decision-making.

For decades on the institutions in this country have been mere instruments of totalitarian power. They have cultivated less of some proper rationalism (Weber) but rather a deeply rooted voluntarism. Couple of reform waves spilled onto the rocks of corporate and partisanship interests. This explains the low »threshold« of trust in most institutions in this country, which have. The latter have a long way to go, as related to transforming into democratic instruments and structures that serve (and less steer) the public interests. This process reflects the level of political emancipation of the Bulgarian citizens, as participant actor in real politics.

As 34% of Bulgarians in the early days of the democratic change shared no trust in *The Great National Assembly*, over 40% claimed they do not trust their *local authorities of government* (see graphic below: Confidence in institutions).

100 Within the Anglo-Saxon and continental political tradition until recently two major political styles have shaped: »ideological« and »pragmatic«. The first is relevant to the »Weltanshaungsparteien« type and relates to a deeper affective involvement into explicitly expressed political values, which do not refer only to political issues, but are linked to other spheres of l life as well. This hierarchy of values is based on the so called »premises« of first rank meaning. The pragmatic style, from another side, refers to judgements based mostly on »personal gains«. Thus the difference between »opened« and »closed« value systems, or such which stress on »expressive« behaviours and those that focus on »instrumental political behaviour« have been defined.(S. Verba). In the Bulgarian case we have enough arguments to consider that a diffusive (non systematically mixed) type of political style has shaped in the decades after 1989. The latter results as some fusion between a culture of collective social solidarity (as inherited from the past) and a shaping new culture of competitive entrepreneurship, operational in wider global context. This is relevant to other ex-socialist countries however, but as well as Italy, Spain or even Greece. The »pragmatic« political style is relevant to a still narrow segment of the political elite in Bulgaria. What counts most is that the spread of the traditional ideological political style in this country and the adoption of some type of pragmatism as in other European countries is in progress. See: P. Georgiev, Balgarskata politcheska kultura, K&M, Sofia, 2000.

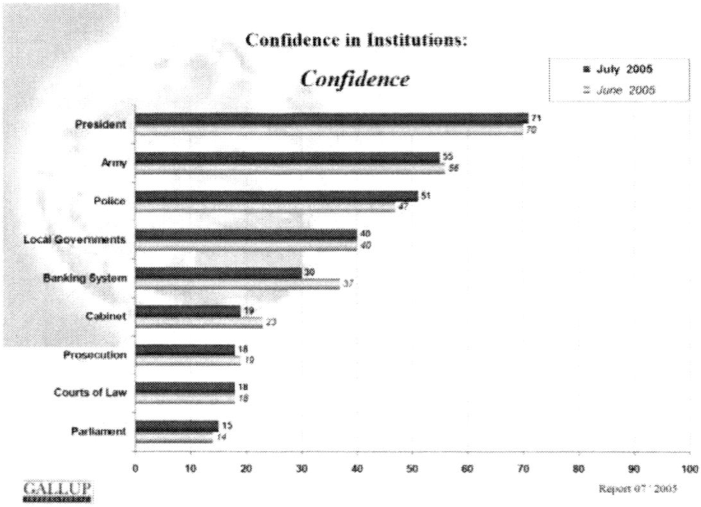

Source: BBS Gallup International

Over 30% of the Bulgarians at the start of the transition declared »no trust« in *any state institution* (1991). This »input« of the political system in crisis became most problematic indeed.

Positive attitudes have been expressed only as related to *government* (+43% – 20%), which more likely reflects a higher grade of etatist expectations and less realistic notions of the reform.

> »The *Bulgarian army* seemed the only institution acceptable, as trusted by 67% of all respondents (10% – no trust). There were all reasons to believe that this not only reflects a deep crisis of the political system, but also could threaten the social peace .«[101]

Still the »revolutionary« pressures of the street, as propelling the process of democratic transition engaged less consistent party »cores«. Most institutions managed to recover from the initial rapid decline of both status and meaning. Common sense, as resting on some inertia of the past, turned traditional conformism into reasonable (if not fully rational) political

101 See: Proportions of chaos in figures. Bulgarians facing the crisis. In Culture daily,Nr.23, June 7, 1991 (Proporzii na haosa v zifri.Balgarite pred lizeto na krizata., Nr.23, 7 Jni., 1991.

behaviors. The violence of the street had less support, as scenes of TV studios occupied, setting on fire of party and governmental offices, etc. »happened«, but more or less virtually. This had a most disputed effect, as related to some »second breath« of re-determined post-totalitarian institutions. The latter became less possible as the process of democratization accelerated.

Presidency, Parliament and Government

Trust in the »three whales« of the political object varied, as correlating with the *rapid shifts* of political preferences of the Bulgarian electorate. Number of surveys between 1990–91 indicated *trust in the Presidency* (between 40–46% among the ranks of UDF (Democrats), while only 10% of this »blue cohort« trusted The *Great National Assembly* (6% had no trust in it at all).

Slightly higher levels of »trust« among voters of UDF (7–16,4%) enjoyed the first non-communist government (D. Popov). This became obvious first after the fall of the government of the Socialists, ahead of A. Lukanov.

Between 16–17% of the followers of Socialists (BSP) trusted the Great National Assembly, 13–19% the Government, while only 3,3 had trust in the Presidency. Thus a kind of *»reddish« skepticism*, as related to the institutions and their role in the process of real democratization, became explicit. It fluctuated from 20–30 % of all enquired adherents of the Socialists in the early years of transition. A *»chart of non-approval«* reflecting mistrust to most Bulgarian institutions by the end of 1990 and the beginning of 1991 is empirically presented below. It may be of interest to the European scholars, as it reflects an *overwhelming anomie* in the days of transition. Another reason why the idea of »upgrading« of the institutional structures in this country seems still less relevant as in other Eastern European countries It seems even less acceptable as Bulgaria has joined the EC.

Table. 3

Trust in Bulgarian institutions

Have no trust in (%)	Dec. '90	Jan.'91
No syndicate organization	30,4	32,1
No state institution	22.5	26,2
No political organization	23,8	25,4
No political leader	14,6	17,0
Will not take part in elections	17,6	22,3

Source: Center for the Study of Democracy

This leads to the following hypothesis:

The political alienation at the very start of the economic reform in Bulgaria might explain an irreversibly *missed chance* of the political culture in this country to involve and participate more actively in the complex democratic change.

The trend reflects a dominating pattern of behavior, as reflecting the *fragmentation,* but no less a most perplexed political mind, less aware of basic instruments of real democratic government.

Thus the *gap* between the »people« and their notorious »organs of political power«, as stated by penetrating surveys from that period[102] was widely opened, to reach new depths and find new shapes at present.

A tendency of *»sedimentation«* of the initial passions of total denial has been reflected first in the empirical results, as offered by the National center for public opinion research in 1990–91:

Table 4

»What is your attitude as related to the work of The Great National Assembly?«

% of enquired

	Nov./Dec. '90		Jan/Mach '91	
Approve	10,9	24,4	35,0	44,0
Do not approve	71,7	62,1	52,4	-
No impressions	7,8	13,5	12,7	-
Can not judge	9,6	.	.	.

Source: National center for public opinion research (NCIOM).

102 This survey has been conducted on the base of standardized interviews (n = 2021, over 18 years old), as the representative sample reflected basic social and demographic characteristics of the structure of the Bulgarian society by the end of 1990. The stochastic falure of the data is in the intervals of 5–10%. The previous surveys conducted with the same methodical instruments which makes the result comparable with those from Jan, 1991. See: Mass consciousness and political moods in Jan. 1991, Sociological problems (Quarterly), Nr.3, 1991, p. 109.

Table 5

»What is your attitude, as related to the work of the Presidency?«
% of enquired

	Nov./Dec '90		Jan./ March '91	
Approve	72,2	60,5	61,4	63,0
Do nit approve	13,4	20,2	22,1	-
No impressions	14,4	19.2	16,5	

Source: National center for public opinion research (NCIOM).

Table 6

»What is your attitude, as related to the work of the government?«
% of enquired

	Nov./Dec '90		Jan./ March '91	
Approve	31,7	28,7	46,5	57,0
Do nit approve	55,9	48,3	18,3	-
No impressions	12,,4	22,9	35,3	-

Source: National center for public opinion research (NCIOM).

The *internal dynamics* of those shifts in the political orientation, as related to the institutions are not less interesting, concerning an *ad hoc* change of political structures in transition:

1. *Trust in Parliament* (36 and 37 Genuine National Assembly), as measured by BBS Gallup International« from 36% in Jan. 1993 dropped to a »critical minimum« of 12% by the end of the same year. Mistrust towards this institution dominated during most of 1995. Slight »upheaval« has been observed immediately after the parliamentary and local elections (1994), but it stayed in the limits of 55–46% of all enquired during 1995. The attitude of the »blue« and »red« cohorts (Democrats v/s Post-communist) was opposite. While nearly 50% of the »red« electorate trusted the National Assembly, this was relevant to only 15% of the »blue«. The latter adhered to deep mistrust as related to the work of the Parliament, dominated at that time by a majority

of the Socialists. The »red« electorate performed higher levels of trust to those institutions (50–45%).

2. *Trust in the Presidency* (defined rather dualistically by the concepts of »the President« and »The Presidency«) seems not less consistent. It varied from 51–39% of the adherents of the UDF (Democrats) through most of 1995. While 3 years earlier (1992) 88% of the »blue« cohort strongly supported the President, a year after (1993) less than 50% did so. A turning point was President Z.Zhelev's appeal for a national agreement and his idea of the need to restructure the political space. The shared trust to his personality dropped dramatically short after this. Thus by the end of 1995 less than 50% of the Bulgarian voters had trust in »their« President, whereby 1/3 of the all enquired hesitated on his role of correct arbitrary on the political reality.

Outputs:

At the Presidential elections of Oct–Nov. 1996 in favor of Petar Stoyanov, candidate of the UDF (Democrats) – nominated after primaries – voted 2 502 517 (59,73%) Bulgarians.

In favor of Prof. Ivan Marazov (candidate of the Left block) – voted 1 687 241 (40,27%).

The »tandem« of UDF (Union of Democratic Forces) and the United Democratic Forces mobilized – at the secondary elections – 612 692 votes.

The Coalition for Bulgaria (Leftists) was supported by 529 088 voters

(See Attachments for more details)

The painfully evolution to a balanced attitude towards the Presidency as guarantee of *peaceful transition* was less influenced by hypothetic »models« of an »imperial«, »symbolically week«, »above-party balanced«, or even »corporative« etc. type of Presidency.[103] All those »ideal types« proved less relevant to a participant-subjective culture that has shaped long before 1989 in this country. The cognitive scope of the majority of the electorate in this country seemed »personality centered«. President of »all Bulgarians« has been the most acceptable mantra of latest voting campaigns, whereby a »non-militant«(even though paternalist) role of the President is given merit. Recent empirical surveys reflect a relatively *sustainable structure of institutional trust* in Bulgaria 17 years after the change. Bulgarians seem still confronted though with the demand to discover and invent more efficient forms of public control over »their« institutions. This is a real challenge for the shaping new participant culture in this country.

---

103 D.Kjuranov, Iv.Krustev, Politicheskotonastojaste (The political present): 1995–1996, Sofia, 1996.

The Army

The Bulgarian army enjoys higher trust than any other institution ever since the change after 1989. As it passed through several critical turning points in a process of reform and modernization (»next-door« war in ex-Yugoslavia) it managed to keep aside from political rivalries. This has contributed most for its status of guarantee of peace in internal and external national aspect. A traditionally positive (and rather sentimentally bound) attitude of most Bulgarians, as related to »their army«, has deeper roots in the Bulgarian political culture. The memories of couple of wars (victory at all battlefields, but diplomatic failures and »*daggers in the back*«) still nourish the patriotic Bulgarian heart. The Bulgarian army has contributed for the territorial integrity of this country, and played for decades on even the role of a significant socializing institution. This relates to sort of a »melting« pot of ethnic, educational and cultural differences (obligatory military service until 2007) in this society. Most of the ratings in the period of transition position the Bulgarian army on top of all scales – 70–75% of all Bulgarians from 1993 to present trust »their army«. The Bulgarian Army is facing at present new responsibilities as member of NATO. It counts as reliable factor of stability in South Europe.

The Police

The attitude to this institution is determined by a rather *ambivalent pattern* of mistrust, as related to the boom of criminal activity, widely spread corruption, abuse of human rights etc. As recent surveys show, the police seems to recover from a rather perplexed status of *ad hoc reform*, as it gets actively involved in new responsibilities in the war against terrorism, securing the internal order of a democratic society and state. While in 1993 nearly 39% of the »red« electorate trusted these institutions, only 34% of the adherents of the »blue« democratic idea had trust in it. The decline of trust culminated in 1995, whereby every second Bulgarian enquired, had no trust in the police at all.[104] The very notion of positive attitude of Bulgarians to »their police« is influenced by its old image as instrument for violations on the civic mind in the years of totalitarian rule. This institution still inherits much of the old style and manners irrelevant to democratic society. This has sharpened the sensitivity of the public eye to misuse of power, corruption, etc. What counts most are appeals for more »transparency« of this institution, and a growing civic awareness that public pressure and control over this institution have to be propelled. In one way or another the Bulgarian police is

---

104 BBS Gallup International, Public opinion in Bulgaria, Annual report, Sofia, 1995, p. 20–23.

still to undergo a process f reforms, related to its new role and responsibilities in wider European context.

The Justice

The *Law in Courts* and *The Prosecution* have been among the most disputed institutions in the years of Bulgarian transition. One reason for this is the lack of credit given to those independent centers of power. As corruption, misuse of power, delayed justice allocation, abuse of human rights, or even a »shadow-system« schemes in support of organized crime, have turned to be not only »rumors« but backed by facts – the reform of those institutions became a real »hurdle« on the Bulgarian road to EC membership. In so far the political culture support the demand of *radical reform* and the abolishment of what is called »a state in the state«, it seems that »trust in law and justice« has still a long road to go. A generally opposed pattern of behavior is the illegal privatization, which has enriched oligarch corporative structures, as they grasped control over whole segments of the Bulgarian social infrastructure. From 1995 to 1998 trust in Law in courts and the Prosecution dropped to less than 25%, no matter the »color« of political preferences of all Bulgarians enquired. Decisive changes are still expected, as to restore a deeply rooted Bulgarian notion of social justice, which seems to has suffered most through decades of transition to democracy and proper market economy.

National Identity

The national identity, or to which political unit an individual feels that he belongs to and how deep and fulfilled this identification is, determines significant features of each national political culture. To what extend a certain nation has a clearly defined ego- *satisfied identity* is most important for »its« politics. The problem of the national identity, unity and loyalty, could displace and even make pointless such processes, as the democratization and the social reform, as most authors from Almont and Verba to present have stressed. The history of *»split nations«*, such as the Italian, or the German (until recently), not to mention the colonial states, are an explicit example.[105]

---

105 In conditions of »crisis of the identity« the individual is inclined to take part in acts directed to creation or redefining of his identity. This could vary from aggressions against other nations to regular expressions of nationalist feelings and behaviors as L. Pye points out. This could arise, or fully clear off *»multiple loyalties«* – as related to »sub-national«, »parochial-traditionalist«, or regionalist and separatist tendencies. See: Political Culture and Political Development, L.W.Pye, S.Verba (Eds.) Princeton Univ.Press, 1965, p. 531–532.

The Bulgarian has cultivated a sense of equality to other nations and an accented feeling of national dignity ever since the National revival. The source of these values are rather in his industrious self-awareness though, than in the idea to dominate over others.[106] In this sense the Bulgarian national identity rests not so much on the notion of some »total«, »great«, or even »entire« national entity, but is rather a consequence of number of dramatic *»crisis of identity«*. The latter relate to irrevocably lost traditional Bulgarian areas, as Thrace and Macedonia, the feeling of *»crash of the national ideal«* and, what we have defined as, *»a catastrophic matrix«* in the political culture of this nation.

Into its modern social, historical and social-psychological dimensions, the Bulgarian national identity is to be related more to a pragmatically, than religiously determined course, as is the case of India, or even Russia up to the 1917.

The integration of other people and nations in the Bulgarian national entity is rather a bitter fruit of formal- administrative, contradicting »acts«, than an evolutionally maturing and deeply conscious cultural- integration processes. As newest data (unconfirmed) shows approximately 7 million Bulgarians live outside the territory of Bulgaria. They are concentrated mainly in Macedonia (1.4 million), in Greece (250 000 million), the Povolozjie region in Russia (3 million). The *Bulgarian diaspora* in Canada, USA, Spain, Belgium , Germany, UK and even the Republic of South Africa, (after 1989) is a phenomena still to be studied. It reflects the demand of redefining national and collective identities in a global world.

In one way or another the process of re-shaping of the Bulgarian national identity, as of most ex-communist countries is crucial both for those nations in transition, as well as for Europe in a rapidly changing new global cultural context (Lepsiuis, 2004) Bulgarians seem rather »split« as related to the boundaries of their country, which is characteristic for other Balkan nations and people as well. The empirical data from »The Balkan monitor« give a clear notion of this tendency.

---

106 The Bulgarian historian M.Madjarov witnessed in this respect: »When the Turks from the near to Koprovshtitza villages came shopping in the city…to sell their agricultural product and faced our well dressed *abadjii* (masters of hand made clothes) , who stood and talk to them in high Turkish language, they became humble and even started to show themselves in a better light. But when they entered the nice and well maintained houses in Koprivshitza, while loaded with their cabbage, they literary had to loose their »self confidence. See M. Madjarov, Memoires, Sofia, 1958, p. 120–121.

Table 7
What do you think for the present boundaries of your country?
(In% from the population)

	Bulgaria	Macedoni	Rumania	Turkey
Fully acceptable	32	34	34	61
Unacceptable but nothing could be changed already	30	30	23	14
Unacceptable but it isn't the time this question to be put	15	14	26	8
Unacceptable and now is the time this question to be put	4	9	4	5
Other	1	2	-	-
Do not know	9	11	12	10

Source: BBS Gallup International, Balkan monitor (1996/7)

An important aspect of the national identity is the national self-awareness and satisfaction of belonging of a certain nation. The identification with most symbols of the nation and the state seems in a way »suppressed « for the Bulgarian. Even soul compatriots reject to deny their Bulgarian nationality, though, but their national identification doesn't seem a source of a special »pride« (as related to USA, or UK political culture). In his patriotism the Bulgarian is rather more similar to the Italian. He remains as him aside from some enthusiastic readiness to dedicate or sacrifice. Bulgarians have been related to some »latent« (and harder) patriotism of the Germans. This gave reasons to some authors to consider them as »*Prussians of the Balkans*«.

Trust in the Compatriot

As far as the national identity is related to some »*vertical*« notion of identity – the other important component of the political culture refers to a »*horizontal identification with the compatriot*«. It concerns a »feeling of integration«, which the individuals has to other people, members of the political system».[107] The Bulgarian could not be characterized as

107 Around 3 million *volzki* Bulgarians (from the region of Volga, Russia) have identified themselves at present as descendants of the Bulgarian nation. According the information of an independent Bulgarian press, (1998) nearly 300,000 people in Kazan (the Crimean peninsula) have applied in court for recognition of their Bulgarian citizenship. Other 150,000 already have Bulgarian passports. The re-defining of the Bulgarian national identity in a new global context is growing on demand . See: »Protection and spiritual uniting of the Bulgarians around the world«, Sofia 1998; P. Ganchev, »Towards a Bulgarian

disintegrated, even though he often gives an expression of a kind of mistrust to his surrounding. This rarely turns into open hostility though. One of the factors for this is the social nature of the Bulgarian family and the character of the Bulgarian paternalism, the deeply rooted traditions of regional- social communal life. The values of mutual respect and recognition, as well as a most amazing *tolerance towards others* (no matter of their religion, or nationality) have been nourished for ages. This seems a most positive experience in a culturally most uncertain world.

The limit of this *»civil – cooperative«* spirit of the Bulgarian are more strict, however, as compared to other people and nations. A Bulgarian rarely is inclined to spread »outside his rug« (in the sense of overestimating his material status). His life view gravitates closer to the narrow circle of his family, neighborhood, or closer friends. Antagonism to the compatriot with higher status is explicitly expressed, however, and this in a most vigorous »temper« against the richer, the well off, less however against »the strong men of the day«. This attitude (which some anthropologists relate to most Balkan people) is rarely a source of some »social radicalism«, as empirical surveys prove:

Table 8

The incomes of the richest people in Bulgaria must not exceed more than 3 times the incomes of the poor ones:

(in % of the population)

	Bulgaria	Macedonia	Rumania	Turkey
Yes	56	67	33	50
No	24	26	38	31
Hesitation	20	7	20	20

Source: BBS Gallup International, Ibid.

Bulgarians are rather sensitive to issues as »origin of capital«. This is often a reason for moral accusations expressed even towards »relatives«. Nearly 40 out of 100 (in an interview after 1989) do believe that it really matters if the capital is »dirty« or »clean«. Most Bulgarians comply however that it is of greater importance for what purposes this capital is being used. 30 out of 100 Bulgarians, agree on this, while 49 out of 100 in the first years of the transition, believed that it is »necessary that capitals are to be nationalized from all who became rich during the last 5 years«. The presented empirical

philosophy of history, Sofia, 1999; here quoted from Unpublished manuscript, Institute for philosophical research, Sofia, 1998.

data below reflects this unfriendly climate, in which independent business has to operate on the Balkans.[108]

Table 9

Do you consider it as necessary that the capitals of people who became rich during the last 5 years should be nationalized?[109]

(in % from the population)

	Bulgaria	Macedonia	Rumania	Turkey
Yes	49	55	34	29
No	24	30	51	40
Hesitate	27	15	15	31

Source: BBS Gallup International.

The Church

The Bulgarian Orthodox church is to be related to some limited, if not by deeply *»alienated parochialism«*, as element of a systematically interrupted traditional Bulgarian political culture. Having covered a most complicated and contradictive path of it's own consolidation in different stages of the state development, the Bulgarian Orthodox Church played an indirect role in the social life of this country for the last 45 years. This national institution was not indifferent to the democratic change and gave its significant contribution for a peaceful transition after 1989. At the same time it paid the high cost of *separatist trends* within it's own ranks. This has been reflected in couple of inside crisis, expressed in splitting and dissent.

The Bulgarian Orthodox church has the support of approximately 40 out of every 100 Bulgarian citizens enquired (1998). This attitude is not influenced much by the political orientations and preferences. As we can witness nearly 40 out of every 100 voters of the Bulgarian Socialist Party and nearly 50 out of 100 from the Democratic opposition in Bulgaria explicitly express certain dedication to the values of the Bulgarian Orthodox Church.

Whether and how much the role of this institution in the building of a proper democratic civic society in Bulgaria will raise to the demand of the present day, corresponding to it's thousands year role of a traditional pillar of this nation, is still a question of the future. The tendency of »returns« to the values of Christianity in the present Bulgarian society after 1989 is consistent. Even though religious values don't have such an accented impact as in most civic cultures in the West. The table below gives a clear picture of

---

108 BBS Gallup International, Political and Economic Index, 1995, p. 248.

109 Ibid, p. 250.

the religious structure of the Bulgarian population and its dynamics in the last 90 years, or so:

Bulgarian Population / Confession and Year of Census

Confession	1910	1920	1926	1934	1946	1992	2001
	Number (in thousands)						
Total	4337513	4846971	5478741	6077939	7029349	8487317	7928901
Eastern. Orthodox	3643918	4062097	4569074	5128890	5967992	7274592	6552751
Muslim	602 078	690 734	789 296	821 298	938 418	1110295	966 978
Catholic	32 150	34 72	40 347	45 704	–	53 074	43 811
Protestant	6 335	5 617	6 735	8 371	–	21878	42 308
Jewish	40 067	43 232	46 431	48 398	43 335	2 580	653
Armenian-Gregorian	12 259	10 848	25 402	23 476	–	9 672	6 500
Other (not indicated)	706	371	1 456	1 802	79 604	15 226	7 784
Not identified	–	–	–	–	–	–	308 116
	Structure –%						
Total	100.0	100.0	100.0	100.0	100.0	100.0	100.0
Eastern–Orthodox	84.0	83.8	83.4	84.4	84.9	85.7	82.6
Muslim	13.9	14.3	14.4	13.5	13.3	13.1	12.2
Catholic	0.7	0.7	0.7	0.8	–	0.6	0.6
Protestant	0.1	0.1	0.1	0.1	–	0.3	0.5
Jewish	0.9	0.9	0.8	0.8	0.6	0.0	0.0
Armenian–Gregorian–	0.3	0.2	0.5	0.4	–	0.1	0.1
Other (not indicated)	0.0	0.0	0.0	0.0	1.1	0.2	0.1
Not identified	–	–	–	–	–	–	3.9

Source: Bulgaria Human Development Report 1996

The Family

Among the institutional generators of political culture, the Bulgarian family has a special place and own function. Having passed through many challenges concerning the urbanization of this country for the last 40–50 years, it seemed until recently a »secondary« factor for political socialization. The initiative in this respect has been left mainly to the school and the system for education, which traditionally conservative character is not liable to doubt even after 1989. The Bulgarian family played a kind of supplementary role into a still centrally regulated system of education. The latter is orientated to a social–homogeneous society, dominated by collective values, though the emerging of private schools in the recent years might well change this mix in the next decades to come. Most social researches prove that the family bares significant qualitative changes even long before 1989. So in the early 80s not more than 2/ 3rd from the Bulgarian families were »*nuclear*« (as 1/ 3rd live together with their parents.) The husband is most often defined as »the head of the family« for about 74 percent from the interviewed by representative social surveys. For 16.7 percent such a role isn't recognized, as they declare that both partners mutually decide on important matters and even discuss them together with their children.[110]

The traditional democratic values of the Bulgarian family, described by Ivan Hadjiiski until the WWII have less in common with the dynamic of the modernization. The tendencies to a social homogeneity of the Bulgarian society at the postwar decades, has been replaced by »a forced« migration from villages to towns during the 60 and 70s. The contemporary Bulgarian family is to be characterized with high *educational homogeneity*. Happiness and chances for realization of the personality in society is a value priority and moral resource for successful married life. From the 70s until now a tendency of some idealization of marriages motives are to be witnessed. The character of present family communication is rather *›socialized‹ than religious.* This reflects a common European trend into which the equality of the Bulgarian woman as a partner is explicitly expressed. The traditional Bulgarian family is not to be considered as authoritarian (as in the case of South Italy for example). The child is recognized as object of educational influence, though. It doesn't enjoy the independence and freedom as in other western countries, being very often a mere »executor« of the advices and sheer will of his parents.

> »More than 58 percent of the interviewed Bulgarian teenagers and young people witness on attempts of their parents to impose their free will and opinion, while only 13.2 declare that their parents treat them in an authoritarian way, being not really interested of their own personal

---

110 See: Savremennoto Balgarsko semejstvo, (Ed). Prof. Ch. Kjuranov, (The contemporary Bulgarian family) , Nauka i izkustvo, Sofia, 1987, p. 351–385.

> points of view. Meanwhile nearly 45 percent of the enquired from families with children between 10 and 18 share that their parents consult with them on matters, but in spite of this impose their will. As far as this generational cohort is now between 36 and 45 years old we could accept that their early socialization inherits elements of some traditionally embedded authoritarian mentality. This doesn't change the democratic character of the Bulgarian family, which operates as a dominating pattern though.«[111]

The contemporary Bulgarian family has rather an »*open*« social-collective, than some individualistic-egocentric character, which is typical for other European cultures. In nearly 1//3rd from the Bulgarian families, the spouses take part in discussing on problems of social life. In more than 30 percent of the families enquired such kind of conversations are common. The facts are more discern as related to different social groups and correlate with the level of education. Public interest and cooperation are expressed more rarely in such group's [3]. From the table below one can draw his picture of communicating on social (and political) issues, as in the years of totalitarism even:

More than half of the families object of the social research until 1989 have been involved in forms of social activity in the social organizations. Men receive less support by women in their social activity though. Political interests remain outside the family, as traditions rendered indirect influence on the political socialization of the growing up generation. The type of a family of two working spouses, who mutually support each other in their social realization, dominates. The factor analysis discovered biggest satisfaction from marriage life in this type of families. Traditional alienation l seemed still typical for the Bulgarian family until 1989. .

> »Some post materialistic (Ingelhart) values definitely had an impact on the younger Bulgarian generation. Even long before 1989, an intensifying interest to autonomy, postponing of getting married, a kind of hedonism and increased mobility (if not some drifting style of life) could be witnessed. The empirical evidence, which we dispose, are more limited, or not enough representative, to judge on possible developments of an activist role of the Bulgarian family, as related to affirmation of democratic values and the shaping new political culture. It is of less risk to claim though that civic values will widen their impact and scope of influence in the decades to come .«[112]

The reproduction of the political class in Bulgaria in which a new elite is being recruited inevitably follows a family tradition involvements into government and politics. This doesn't mean, that the »*nepotism*«, which had

---

111 Ibid.

112 Plamen Geogiev, Balgarskata politicheska kutura, (The Bulgarian politcal culture), K & M, Sofia, p. 310–313.

its place in the political life of the country for the last 45 years (and to a certain extend still has some impact) is to be excluded. As this society involves in the system of proper competitive democratic and civic society, we could expect, that its political culture will go beyond sheer nepotistic political involvements. Even though the Bulgarian family is to be considerable as basic factor for political socialization and a milestone of the shaping new civic culture.

Ethnic Tolerance

Bulgaria is a conglomerate of most diverse ethnic and ethno-social groups, integrated to a different extend into the system of a *one nation state*. Enduring ages of living together and diffusion of different cultures, the bigger ethnic groups in Bulgaria (Turks, Gypsies, Jews, Armenians and others) played insignificant role in the political life until 1989[1]. The present constitution proclaims the right of each Bulgarian citizen to make use and learn his mother's language , together with the compulsory learning of the Bulgarian language (§ 36). In § 56 the right of everyone to develop »his culture« in accordance with his ethnical belonging is clearly proclaimed. The last one is acknowledged and guaranteed by the law.

In the political life of Bulgaria, which is based on the principals (§ 11, al. 1) the creation of parties on ethnical basis has been prohibited. This is considered by some authors for the objective obstruction of the idea of integrating the minorities into the political and government system[2]. Others give more credit to social, educational, professional, qualification and other factors, which impede the full realization of this complex process[3]. In the present constitution new texts, as related to forbidding decriminalization and implementing the principle of the UNESCO declaration from 1966, claiming that that each culture has its worthiness and value, have been included.Not earlier than 1999, though the Bulgarian Parliament ratified the frame convention for defense of minorities of EU, as it explicitly demonstrated a common civilization approach to the idea of their full integration in the democratic society. Bulgaria deserves the approval of the democratic world as country with a relatively steady ethnic tolerance. This turned into crucial problem on the background of couple of ethnic wars in ex–Yugoslavia after 1989.

> »The Movement of Rights and Freedom as represented in couple of Parliaments since 1991 on is considered to be the only »Ethnic Turk« party within the political system of this country but in a wider context as well. It has contributed for the ethnic peace in its own way, and played the role of a balance in critical phases of the democratic development in this country. Other ethnic groups have parliament representations in particular and participate mostly through cultural, or educational and syndicate forms of democratic involvement. With exception of few cases

in the last 7–8 years, the ethnic situation in Bulgaria is to be characterized as steady if not necessarily unloaded with tentions. Most of them have social character (unemployment, law levels of education, miserable living conditions especially among the Roma etc). The results from representative demoskopic surveys confirm this .« [113]

A »bird view« over the *ethnic attitudes* in 4 neighboring Balkan countries wittiness their restrictive character, as compared to the Bulgarian case. This concerns tolerance towards using other language, except the official one in one's contacts with the public institutions (the army, the municipality, the lower court, the school, the radio and TV). Restrictive attitudes are rather more explicit in Bulgaria, while ethnic attitudes in Macedonia seem considerably more tolerant. More restrictive but rarely repressive attitudes are expressed against the Roma, than to the Ethnic Turk minority in Bulgaria.

The highest of tolerance is given to the right of minorities to confess freely their religion. This reflects long lasting traditions of tolerant and peaceful coexistence of both Orthodox Christians and Muslims in Bulgaria. Ethnic prejudices and xenophobia do not blur the present citizen, less even is this relevant to the younger generations? Bulgarians do not feel threatened much by the existence of *»ethnic parties«* and even »got used to« this as the MRF and VMRO(Bulgarian-Macedonian patriotic movement) contributed for a shaping culture of pragmatically nation-oriented »political players« no matter of their ethnic origin. Bulgarians have a clear notion of their cultural responsibility in a wider Balkan and diverse European context. They are highly sensitive to nationalistic or ethnic feeling that could interfere with the traditional peaceful co-existence at both sides of the Balkan.

113 Plamen Georgiev, Etnichesko raznoobrazie i sozialni naprezhenij v Severoiztochna Balgaria (Ethnic Diversity and social tentions in North Eastern Bulgaria, in: (Ed.) Prof. P. Ganchev. Soctalni konfliktu v possozialisticheskite straini v uslovijata na globalizazjata I regionalizatsiata (Social Conflicts in the post-socialist countries in the aspects of Globalization and Regionalizaton), Free University of Varna, 2004 p. 153–163.

Table 10

Do you think that the people from the minorities in our country should have rights 4 (in % of enquired)

Yes/ no / don't know	Bulgaria			Macedonia			Romania			Turkey		
to talk their language	77	15	8	8	12	5	46	50	4	59	30	11
to confess thier religion	87	8	5	93	5	2	93	5	2	63	26	11
to have schools where the education to be on their language	24	63	13	52	38	10	66	32	2	33	52	15
to have a radio and TV in their language	19	68	13	60	32	8	60	31	9	29	56	15
to have their parties	32	54	14	59	33	8	39	52	9	26	60	14
to separate in in autonomous areas	3	88	9	19	75	6	4	89	7	14	70	16
to separate and form independent states	4	88	8	6	83	11	2	92	6	10	77	13

Source: BBS Gallup international, Balkan monitor, 1997

The Media

The appearing of independent media and the manifestation of some *»4rth power«* after 1989 rendered certain impact on the public opinion and the formation of the Bulgarian political culture. The tendencies of higher trust to the electronic media reflect the transition to pluralistic information society and the specific role of the new information technologies in this process. Highest rating enjoyed the Bulgarian radio (2/3rd of the enquired), as followed by the Bulgarian TV, (60–65 out of 100 enquired gave preference to it). Trust in the independent presses immediately after 1989 reflected positive attitude shared by ¼ and 1/3 of the Bulgarian citizens. In the last decade trust in the party press has progressively declined – 40 percent of the electorate by the end of 1995 and even less to present.

The notion that *»there is a censorship over the national media«,* remains a lasting belief. This conviction share about 1/3 from the enquired Bulgarian citizens. The debates on the clauses of »the law for electronic media« (1996), the most uncertain role of public control in the information branch and other factors, reflect a rather »keen« competitive pattern of media-market performance. It is influenced more by production of political »signs and symbols«, as propelling democracy in a rationally persuasive way.

> »For a period of 76 years, censorship dominates over the periodical Bulgarian press in the run of 42 years. Bulgaria passed through 25 years of direct police censorship, 110 years of some forms of »preliminary control«, and 7 years of most severe military censorship. During the rest of the time the legal normative acts have to some extend supported the development of democratically acceptable base for functioning of the press.«[114]

During the last decade a growing »sensitivity« to pluralism has shaped. Among more educated, but also broader circles of the present Bulgarian society, journalism doesn't enjoy much trust, less even moral credit. The grounds for this are the open partisanship of the press, operating as »shadow« actor in elections after 1989, its manipulative style, or even direct interventions in the private life, appraisal of neo-liberal reforms and even schemes of illegal privatization (including the media market).

One can add here the traditional readiness of part of the journalist guilt at this side »to go after the winner«, the incorrect style of public polemics, etc. The »cynic« attitude to the media and what »the press« has to say – reflects a trend of pragmatic shifts in the public interests. Still a competent, well aware of democratic values and its new responsibility media network is still to be developed in this country and in a wider European context. Rationale and objective political persuasion is to be considered volatile. This has a negative impact on the shaping of a proper civic culture in this country.

Political Participation and Civic Competence

The traditional interest of Bulgarians to politics has been vividly expressed in different regimes even though political participation is not to be characterized with high civic competency. There are many historical, social and psychological reasons for this. A *quasi–political public* has traditionally

---

114 Plamen Georgiev, Balgarskata politicheska kultura (The Bulgarian political Culture) , K & M, Sofia, p. 317–19.

reproduced most colorful patterns of »participating parochialism«, mixed with rather perplexed notions of politics, as compared with civic activity, typical for advanced democratic societies. The contradictive political context and spontaneous »political impulses« of participation, have been channeled until 1989 mainly in official social and political organizations. A general shift to patterns of individual and not so much »collective« involvement and orientation to political parties and movements, as well as local groups of interests is in progress. The role of NGOs is less acknowledged though in the process of political decision-making. The »state« seems still both source and actor of significant social change.

The diminishing interest in political issues, which most demoscopic surveys register in the last decade, is motivated by an inevitably sobering pragmatism, as well as sequential crisis in the political interaction of the individual with his immediate political object. The disappointment from politicians (of all featherings), the deficit of trust in institutions, the feeling of isolation from the levers of significant political change, the impotency of most regional communities (especially in small towns and villages) to influence governmental politics, reconfirm traditionally alienated, »non-atavistic« patterns and forms of political participation.

What is claimed here has been reflected in many public opinion surveys in Bulgaria, dedicated to political *»anomie«* in this country.[115] Though this trend seems still to prevail it cannot be considered as typical, especially as new hopes and sense of new civic status within the wider European context are gaining after the accession of this country into EC.

115 This survey of ASSA-M under the scientific guide of Dr. M. Mirchev is a part of a bigger international project dedicated to the comparative research of *anomia* in countries as China, Australia, South Africa, Malaisia and others. It was coordinated by the Academy of Switzerland(Prof. P. Ateslander). Data is representative for the population of Bulgaria aged 18 to 70 years, totally 5,8 million people. The sample (/Dr. Boris Chakalov)/ has been controlled by 8 socio-demographic markers as: size of population of residence place, age, sex, education, labour status, family status, social group, ethnicity, plus 3 additional: self-estimation of material status, political orientation and religious belonging. See J. Vladimirov, Iv. Katzarski, T. Boyadjiev, M. Badjakov, Balgaria v kraga na anomiata, Sofia, 1998 p. 190–199.

Table 11

Many people are not interested in politics. What is the reason according to you?[116]

	doesn't depend on me	passive, inert	disappointed by politicians	disappointed by everyting
Populated place				
Sofia	6.0	22.1	34,7	37.2
Big city	8.8	19	45.0	34.4
Small town	12.7	13.9	47.3	26.1
Village	7.0	16.8	42,0	34.2
Social group				
Private business	9.6	19.2	46,6	24.7
Intelligentsia	6.8	15.5	46,6	31.7
Staff	7.9	13.9	44,4	33.8
Workers	9.4	16,1	40,7	33.8
Farmers	8.4	15,9	41.1	34.6
Ethnicity				
Bulgarians	8.4	14,8	44.0	32.9
Bulgarian–Muslims	5.3	158	57,9	21.1
Turks	14.5	17.1	44,7	23.7
Roma (Gypsies)	4.7	30.2	9,3	55.0

Source: ASSA Public opinion research agency, Archives.

The traditional patterns of political participation contributed in no lesser extend for a re-confirmed *centrist model of government* in this society after 1989. The latter has hindered the individual to grasp more rationale and effective forms for competent civic participance. The table below reflects typical forms for political participation, as co-related to factors as residence place, education, social status, age and ethnicity. The empirical data is not discern from other conventional forms of political participation, as civic competence remains within the limits of *»moderate alienation«* relevant to other European democratic systems.

116 Ibid. For more details see ASSA, Archives.

Table 12

Could you influence somehow the forming of the government politics and taking of decisions?[117] (in % of enquired)

		yes, by voting	yes– by protest action	no, since I don't trust anyone	no, it doesn't depend on me
Political sympathy					
UDF (Democratic forces)		47	6	7	40
BSP (Socialists)		39	1	7	53
DPS (Ethnic Turkish party)	30	11	13	46	
Euroleft (Social democrats)	50	5	9	36	
BBB (Business block)		46	10	8	36
Other		35	9	26	30
Do not sympathize		19	4	17	60
Education					
Basic		22	3	11	64
Secondary		35	7	12	46
Professional	37	5	12	46	
Higher		46	6	11	37
Social group					
Farmers		21	0	6	73
Workers		30	3	13	54
Staff	41	6	12	41	
Inteleienzia		45	9	9	37
Private business		46	6	10	38
Ethnicity					
Bulgarians		37	5	11	47
Bulgarian Muslims		26	0	21	53
Turks		25	4	11	60
Gypsies		2	5	23	70
Age					
18–20		28	11	9	52
21–30		36	6	13	45
31–40		44	6	11	39
41–50		31	4	11	54
51–60		40	2	13	45
61–70		27	2	10	6

Source: ASSA Public opinion research agency, Archives.

117 Ibid.

Chapter 3: Between Scylla and Charybdis of Participant Political Cultures

We shall present here the final results from a broader complex study of the Bulgarian political culture in the framework of Almond and Verba's theory (Georgiev, 2000). The idea is to initiate further cooperation in the field of comparative studies of Balkan political cultures. This, however, in a wider European and global context and not so much from the point of view of a *differentia specifica*, on which both prejudice and nationalism traditionally feed at this side. As we believe the imperative of Europe and a kind of new universalism both shape the political cultures of South Eastern Europe in a new way. This confronts political sciences with the demand to grasp the changing features of national (and other) identities on the Balkans, as more than a traditional »boundary«, »backyard«, less even »buffering« cultures in a risky world. The process of democratic transition is a challenge for those nations, but goes beyond the limits of sheer democracy promotion in a global world. It involves other nations into new networks of shifting interests and coexistence in a world of growing responsibilities. The prevention of a possible clash of civilizations involves most Balkan nations and especially Bulgaria into new frameworks of interaction. This turns the political cultures of the region into a significant factor of a new European integrity.

***

The first question we have to answer here, as far as it implicitly arises from this study, is where is the constellation of the Bulgarian political culture to be situated in the traditional framework of Almond's and Verba's theory (as presented in the 5 democracies and their cases). In so far this classical study has been an empirical snapshot of the Cold war period; we will use its typology to describe only general features of the Bulgarian political culture, as most closely related to the European (continental) type of civic cultures. As our study has shown the Bulgarian political culture in its complex entity seems more than mere »deviation« from its common European roots. It has shaped »unique«, but not less »compatible« forms, which link it with the constellations of other European political cultures as well. Let us discuss this briefly here.

The Italian political culture: It seems to us that the Bulgarian political culture relates most closely to substantial features of the Italian political culture as the strongly expressed alienation of the subject from its political object. As the Italians, Bulgarians are not to be characterized with a »high« grade of patriotism (as might be the case of US political culture). We are even more alien to the moderate political partisanship of the British, or the American subjects. Bulgarians, as Italians, do not involve as readily into social a political activity and are even less inclined to this. A kind of introvert orientation has always dominated our political mind. Bulgarians react more explicitly to situations of unexpected social risks, though. They seem less steered in their political behaviour by the traditional paternalism of the Italians. We still prefer to pay tribute to it, however. The *fragmentation* and *isolation* from political life are common features both of the Italian and the Bulgarian political culture. As one of the leaders of the Italian national liberation movement claimed 100 years ago « Having made Italy, we have to create Italians as well«– Bulgarians could only add: »God created us Bulgarians indeed, but we were always unlucky with our rulers.« Still Bulgarians seem less depressed by painful outputs of the nation building of the 19th century, as compared to the Italian *Risogrimento.* No split in the mentality of the Bulgarian North and South is to be witnessed , as in he case of the Bulgarian political culture.

The German political culture: The Bulgarian political culture has been influenced by a »*traumatic history*« as is the case of Germany, which most scholars refer to. It inherits an own *»catastrophic mix«,* as related to a *fragmented subjectivism* (as an »output« of the 1912,1913 and 1919 most devastating wars). The Bulgarian political culture is an »aspiring« one, as the German has been often defined. The political activity within it is less passive and formalized though. Less than Germans, Bulgarians seem ready to join political organizations (or even NGOs). Most often we still prefer to »have nothing to do with politics«. As Germans, though, Bulgarians have cultivated a rather extreme *cynicism to politics.* It is less related to their rationally balanced pragmatism, though, and is often expressed in most emotional way. The general political orientation of Bulgarians (as in the case of the German political culture) is the one of the *subject,* and less of the participant. As a »rule« Bulgarians are often unsatisfied with their government – which seems less typical for the Germans. We are more attached to the symbolic signs, but less to the real structures of our political system. The political hostility between the two major parties is openly expressed among us. Bulgarians seem less driven by some »conservative-liberal« scale of political opposition. The notion of some traditional confrontation between »rich« *(chorbadjii)* and ordinary working class people prevails among us.

The UK political culture: There seem to be fewer similarities between the Bulgarian and the UK political culture. This relates mostly to the participant role of the citizen. Less is the Bulgarian, as the subject of the British crown, inclined to take part in immediate political life, except in crucial moments threatening his existence. The expressing of political interest and his political competence are less sophisticated than in the case of the UK. The Bulgarian political culture is to a lesser extend a result of »excluding« patterns of political involvement, and some systematic diffusion of its subject and parochial elements, as is the case of Britain. Bulgarians are less to be characterized as respecting independent authorities. This shaky balance is achieved in more »robust«, and even coercive way, at this side of the Balkan. Respect is shared mostly for professional achievements. As the British though, the Bulgarian subjects rely more on his state (less on some possible monarchism) to steer their social life, and own political participation even.

The American political culture: Bulgarians have always been tempted (but less inspired) by some radical shift in their position of »ignored citizenship« as some brave soldiers of the American War of Independence. Their participation has contributed less to a systematically cultivated loyalty to their government, or »fathers of the nation«. The Bulgarian traditionalism has less supported political cooperation with the co-patriot. Non–formal groups had rarely an impact on real political life. An Eastern type of oppressive administration has shaped a rather fatalist (or servitude) pattern of system involvement. The political partisanship of the Bulgarian is more vigorously and emotionally expressed. This might be the reason why it rarely results in consistent patterns of political engagement. The balance between traditional, subject and participant roles is rarely achieved. A *dominating subjectivism* has prevailed and hindered rationale participant orientations. The cooperation with the co–patriot at this side is loaded with a notorious individualism, which hinders open political communication.

The Mexican (Latin American) political culture: The Bulgarian political culture seems rather closely related with the »*alienation and aspiration*« of the Mexican type of political culture. It is very much so inconsistent, as concerning some common patterns of orientation with its political objects. Still Bulgarians expect more (but rely less) on their government, though they rarely blame it publicly. As the Mexican citizen, the Bulgarian one seems most sensitive to *equal treatment* by »his« administration, or the police, especially as concerning the abuse of individual rights and freedoms. The latter are often swapped for some »sultan« type of protectionism by the »strong of the day«. Bulgarians are less fascinated by the idea of some »*presidencialisimo*«, as in the case of Mexico, however. They are more influenced by the leadership personality, than this institutional type of leadership. Bulgarians are less inclined to express their national pride. Revolutions of »permanent« type never occurred at this side. We have had series of uprisings, but less of the vigorous Mexican type. This has shaped a rather »floating«, hardly to be propelled openly political activity of Bulgarians. Corruption is another bridging link between the Mexican and the Bulgarian political culture. It is not so much a result from the »extractive« forms of capitalism that have eroded most Latin-American countries and their political cultures, though. Still the polarization between »rich« and »poor«, the miserable situation of some ethnic groups (Roma).), has shaped patterns of Latino–American model of political behaviour in the years of transition in Bulgaria. This is less likely to be tolerated once Bulgaria has joined EC and the state recovers from an initial perplexity and uncertainty as related to proper democratic performance.

To brief here: As an intermittent type of political culture, the Bulgarian one has passed through 3 forms of political life – *monarchy, republic* and an authoritarian rule of some *»Balkan despotism«*, related to the years of communism. The latter, as we believe, is a deviation, as disputable, as it is, from the »authentic totalitarism« (H. Arendt). Few studies have dared to penetrate deeper in the social nature of this culture inherited. It has in spite of that shaped certain forms and patterns of civic orientations and behaviour, as we have illustrated so far. What we need now is a broader universal outlook aimed to network the present Bulgarian society with a rapidly changing world and its complexity. This means to draw a wider political and cultural perspective, as far as a new/old European nation shape this complexity in an own sovereign way. We offer such an attempt in the fragments to follow.

From »People's Government« to »Mixed« Political Culture

The years of transition in Bulgaria after the fall of the Zhivkow regime (1989) result at the *»output«* of the political process less as some inevitable »reverse« to older historical forms and patterns of political life. Say capitalism, as mentioned in a »subtle« and theoretically most uncertain debate in this country. What we believe is taking place is a painful emergence of a *new political culture in transition*. Its participant forms and patterns – interrupted in the longer run of the development of this nation, give a *new meaning* to political life and change the way in which parties are supported indeed.

This painfully shaping culture (as most cultures of the Balkans) could not be rationalized, as a mere negation of an »older culture«, (or even couple of »subcultures«), that has proliferated in this society in the last 50 years or so. Talking about national cultures, we have to remind that they do not change according weeks schedules. Therefore, it will be more correct to define the output of this process as a saturating »mix« of an »old-new« Bulgarian *»traditionalism«, »subjectivism« and »citizenship«*, as institutional ingredients, that shape the real political culture of any other nation.

That this culture inherits a civic potential, and undertakes autonomous role in the system of contemporary Bulgarian society, might seem still doubtful. One reason for this is the shaky stand of theory on democratic and social change. This has been reflected in a way not only by recent demoscopic surveys at this side. It could be drawn out from a wider complex analysis of the *»quasi«–forms of participation* in the political life of this country, as in most Balkan countries after 1990.

What drives the process of significant social (and political change) are the shaping elements of a *complex society* operating through more or less typical forms and patterns of a »mixed« political culture in Bulgaria, as we could witness. The result of this process, as we claim, depends on the extend to which traditional and new values merge to cope successfully with each other for relatively longer periods of time. This is to be regarded as the structural base of a shaping *new collective identity of this nation* (but also other Balkan nations), as disputable as they seem in the framework of a still shaping new political architecture of the Balkans. .

Let us put ahead some arguments in favour of those participant patterns of political orientations and behaviour in the case of Bulgaria after 1989, minding the limits of space and time. But also a well known »cognitive dissonance«, which still binds Balkan people to a world of wishful thinking and prejudice.

First: Both patterns (models) of political orientation and interaction with the political object in their *»liberal-democratic«* and/or *»conservative«*, i.e. *»left«–»right«* alternatives, undergo an apparent fiasco in this country, as we face the realities. Nearly two decades after the democratic turn over, a sobering citizenship seems well aware that those two fundamental patterns of social and political change (at least in their domestic performance) are not capable to overcome the confrontations. Less have they contributed for meaningful forms of civic life, which Bulgarians, inheriting thousand years of states craft tradition have rationalized in their own way? The transition to »multiple identities« in a global world, as disputed, or rejected by the idea of an inevitable end of the national state, seems less realistic.

Second: The reasons for this misfortunate output, should not be looked for in other direction, but in the underestimating and ignoring of the objective *traditional, subjective* and *civic elements* of an already shaped Bulgarian culture of a new »mixed« type. There still doubt that this constellation in progress could guarantee the autonomous reproduction of proper democratic values and structure in this country. The key to the balance of this culture has it roots in this society that go back much deeper than 1989. Its typical culturally reconfirmed forms and patterns, offer enough potential for an active democratic participation in the complex development of this nation. This gives us reasons to admit that this participant culture, even as ignored, or pushed aside could not be postponed, less even manipulated for much longer.

Third: The *»peoples-government«*, confirmed as typical form of political life in the long run of an unsystematically structured Bulgarian political culture from the mid of XX c. to present, is in search and to a certain extend finds its adequate forms of real participation. This process, as we believe, seems possible only within a system of a »mixed« political culture, i.e. one of a *civic type.* Its autonomous functions are not to be rationalized in the context of a *»quasi« pluralistic system*, which has been offered by a most disputable and ego-cantered political elite. What seems even more important is the lack of real interaction of the individual with »his« institutions. This *»uninvolved engagement«*, as we could witness, is even less relevant to a set of formalized functions of a »system in transition«.

Fourth: The driving force of this new and significant cultural change is the generated civic culture of this nation in the longer historical run. The latter rejects the idea of some sequential »discrete«, less even *forced attempts* to restore older, trivialized forms of political participation. Major values that integrate the political object are those of tolerant coexistence within »mixed« forms of economic, political and cultural life in the system of the national state. This is an objective sociological fact, which could not be substituted by other »codes«, i.e. »models«, less even cultural »paraphrases«, as offered on the political market.

Fifth: This driving force is not be grasped fully in its traditional »class«, »milieu«, less even »mass« aspects. It is an emanation of a traditionally alienated but *self aspiring national culture*, as it strives to more efficient forms of immediate participation in the political life. The latter are based on individual patterns of political behaviour. They could develop successfully however only in collective, *autonomous forms and structures* coherent with a new political system of this country. This civic culture could unfold its creativity only within an *activist model of political participation*, consistent with its national spirit.

What has been claimed above is reflected in the context of the national but also a general Euro-*centric orientation* of this nation (as well as other Balkan nations). This trend, as we believe, in an imperative of a new age. How are its aims to be fulfilled is the first question still to be answered. The *»blood, sweat and tears«* price offered to some Balkans nations, seemed most unacceptable for Bulgarians. In search of more rational, peaceful forms of transition, the traditional political alienation might still turn into real political participation. But only when the involved *»so far«* step aside (even *not that »far«*) from the mainstream of proper democratic change propelled in a wider European and global context.

Shifting Euro-Bulgarian identity: The Spring 2005 Euro barometer survey was conducted in a particularly eventful environment for Bulgaria and its integration into the European Union. The interviews, carried out between the 17th and the 31 st of May, were soon after the Bulgarian Parliament ratified the Treaty for the Accession of Bulgaria into the EU and coincided with the launch of the parliamentary election campaign. In the EU itself, this period was marked by the difficult debates on the EU Constitution and the budget of the Union beyond 2007.

To understand the views of the citizens in the 25 EU Member States and the Accession and Candidate Countries on key issues in the debate on European integration, the 63.4 wave of the Euro barometer included special questions on the Treaty on the European Constitution and EU Enlargement, main results of which are briefed here.

BBSS Gallup International, using a representative national sample of 1018 people, aged 15 and over, has collected the data related to Bulgaria. The national analysis draws a picture of public opinion in Bulgaria on the eve of the EU accession. It is also compared with the views of the citizens, recorded in:

- The EU Member States, including both the old (EU15) and the new (EU10);
- The other EU accession country, Romania;
- The two EU Candidate Countries – Croatia and Turkey;
- Other countries with similar views.

Where relevant, the analysis also draws comparisons with public opinion in France and the Netherlands, whose citizens have become more sensitive to the issues of EU integration during the period of research. The particular focus of these comparisons is to show the opinion of the »average Bulgarian« versus the average European citizen. It also shows the trends in Bulgarian and European public opinion as compared to the previous Euro barometer survey [118] and takes a closer look at the view of the young people on key issues for the future of Europe and the European Union.

Bulgarians and the European Union

Bulgaria counts among the countries for which the EU has the most positive image (60%), after Ireland (68%), Romania (67%) and Italy (64%). This percentage has decreased by 3 points in the last half-year, without, significant increase in negative attitudes, however, which remain at a 9% low (EU25 – 19%). Some of the »very positive« opinions have been transformed into »fairly positive« (+3 points), shaping a more realistic image of the EU in Bulgaria

The EU membership of Bulgaria has been perceived as something good by 54% of the citizens surveyed and this figure coincides with public opinion in the EU25. While remaining significant, this support has decreased by 5 points over the last half year in scope. The share of neutral positions (30%) has increased by 4 percentage points, while the negative opinions remain almost unchanged (+1 point) at a 7% low. A large majority of Bulgarian citizens believe that the EU membership will increase the economic (64%)

118 See Standard Eurobarometer 62.0, Autumn 2004, published in February 2005 : www.europa.eu.int/comm/public_opinion/archives/eb/eb62/eb62_en.htm

and the political stability (57%) of their country, as well as their personal security (64%).

Bulgarians have become more self-critical, but more realistic regarding their awareness and knowledge of the EU.

According to their self-assessment (using a scale of 1 to 10, where 1–4 means »know nothing at all« and 7–10 »know a great deal«) they know less about the EU than the average European, while six moths earlier it appeared that they knew more. Their current average score is 4.1 (EU25 – 4.5), while before it was 4.5 (EU25 – 4.3). More precisely:

– Nearly one-quarter (23%) of Bulgarian citizens consider they know nothing at all about the EU (marks 1–2 on the scale)

– Nearly half of them (47%) know very little (marks 3 to 5)

– Less than one-fifth (17%) are well informed (marks 6–8)

– 4% consider themselves as very knowledgeable (marks 8–10)

– The share of those who cannot judge on this remains unchanged at 8%

In general, seven out of ten Bulgarian citizens say they know nothing at all, or very little about the EU. Demographic analysis show that those who consider themselves least informed are also those who do not perceive the EU membership as something good for them and for their country. These are mainly elderly and retired people, those from the rural areas, least educated, unemployed, as well as some managers and some of the most highly educated.

The reality of this self-assessment is largely confirmed by the results of a knowledge test included in the standard Euro barometer questionnaire. The Bulgarian poll on the whole scores better than six months before but had the lowest scores in the entire survey. One quarter of those interviewed (26%) provide correct answers to the general questions about the EU and its institutions (EU25 – 41%), nearly one-fifth (18%) are wrong (EU25 – 33%) and the highest of all countries, more than half of the Bulgarian poll (56%) does not offer any answers at all (EU5 – 26%)

Increasing interest in information about the EU. The Euro barometer survey has registered a sharp decrease (7 percentage points) in the share of those who never seek information about the EU. It is now 9% and remains lower than the EU average (10%). This may be explained by the increase (+6 points) of the role of informal communication (discussions with relatives, friends and colleagues) as a source for information on the EU, which was the case for nearly one-third of the Bulgarian respondents (32%). Television has increased its role (+2 points) as the preferred information source on the EU (77%) for Bulgarians (EU25–70%). It is followed by the radio (34%) (EU25–32%) and discussions with relatives, friends and colleagues, which now rank third and have become, even more important as an information source than the press (29%). This is evidence that issues related to the EU have become part of the daily life of Bulgarian citizen.

Media coverage of the EU. The Bulgarian poll is generally positive regarding the amount of information on the EU provided by the national press, radio and TV, but to a lesser degree than the public in the EU25. 45% of Bulgarian citizens consider they get sufficient news and information on the EU from television, 37% – from the press and 35% from the radio. For half of those interviewed in the Member States, the main source of news on the EU is the press (50%) (13 points higher than in Bulgaria), followed closely by television (48%) and the radio (41%).

Only around one-third of Bulgarian respondents, however trust the media for providing them with objective information about the EU. Television is mostly over-positive for at least four out of ten interviewed (42%); slightly more than a third of them find it objective (34%) and one-fifth do not take any position. The results for both radio and the press are very similar, with 31% considering their information about the EU objective, slightly less (27% for the radio and 29% for the press) overly positive and the highest percentage of the poll (39% for the radio and 37% for the press) without any opinion. The results for Bulgaria are characteristic for all countries outside the EU, while EU citizens, even in the most Euro-skeptic countries, think that the media and especially television provides them with objective information on the EU.

The EU triggers positive feelings. Both in the EU and in Bulgaria the main feelings associated with the EU are hope (for every six out of ten respondents, EU–25 – 44%) and trust (for every fourth respondent, EU 25 – 22%). Enthusiasm, which was third on the Bulgarian list six months before, has diminished by half (–7 points) (8%) and has been replaced by anxiety, shared by 15% of the Bulgarian respondents and 20% of those in the EU. Bulgarian feelings towards the EU coincide largely with those of the average European citizen. They are more intensive (expressed in higher percentages) if positive and less intensive in the negative spectrum.

For Bulgarians, the EU means mainly freedom to travel, study and work anywhere in the EU and economic prosperity, e.g. a personal solution to the two most important issues for the country, according to public opinion, unemployment and the economic situation. Although to a lesser degree than before, the EU is associated only with positive opportunities: freedom to travel, study and work anywhere in the EU (45%), economic prosperity (38%), peace (34%) and social protection (29%).

For a quarter of those polled, it also means democracy, and for one-fifth – cultural diversity (18%), as well as a stronger say in world politics (18%), and the euro (15%).

Negative associations, such as unemployment (11%), bureaucracy (8%) and wasting money (6%) have also diminished and continue to rank last.

Fears regarding European integration remain lower than in the EU. Trends in the development of public opinion month's show that Bulgarians, as well as Romanians, have already started to feel some of the typical enlargement blows on the eve of the EU accession. More than half of Bulgarian respondents (52%) fear difficulties for their farmers (10 percentage points more than six months before), which is 25 points less than similar fears in Hungary and other agricultural countries among the EU Member States. Every second Bulgarian citizen is concerned that their country may have to contribute more than it can receive from the EU budget. This stands at 12 points lower than the EU average (62%). Other fears, such as the increase in drug trafficking and international crime (49%) are not typical for at least half of the Bulgarian citizens.

Strengthening the European identity of Bulgarians. As a result of a positive trend (10 points) three-quarters of Bulgarians now feel more attached to Europe. This is higher than the average for the EU, where two-thirds of citizens share the same view.

Bulgarians are increasingly dissatisfied with national democracy and increasingly satisfied with European democracy. While the majority of EU citizens are satisfied with the functioning of democracy in their countries (53%), only one-fifth of Bulgarian respondents share the same opinion regarding their national democratic system. Over the last half year, satisfaction has decreased by 2 points, to top further feelings of dissatisfaction, expressed now by three-quarters (76%) of the poll. Similar trends dominate public opinion in some of the EU10, particularly Latvia and Hungary (10 percentage points) and in neighboring Greece, where dissatisfaction is up by 14 points. Bulgarian satisfaction with EU democracy is twice as high (46%) as satisfaction with national democracy (20%). Nearly four out of 10 Bulgarians surveyed do not express any opinion regarding satisfaction/dissatisfaction with EU democracy. Almost the same share (41%) say they do not understand how the EU functions.

Bulgarian institutions face a crisis of confidence. The low level of trust, recorded in the previous Euro barometer survey, has stayed the same for most of the national political institutions. Some of the »don't knows« have been transformed into negative opinions, resulting in a 10 point increase in mistrust in the national Parliament (81%), a 6 point increase in political parties (83%), a 7 point increase in national government (70%) and a 5 point higher mistrust in the Bulgarian justice system (70%). Whereas in the EU, one in two citizens says he/she trusts their national justice system, Bulgarians appear to trust least their national legal system (20%) of all the countries surveyed by the Euro barometer.

Trust of Bulgarians in the EU remains high. Although it has decreased by 2 points, trust in the EU in Bulgaria (56%) remains higher than the EU average (44%) and in most of the EU Member States. Due to a strong decrease in trust in the EU institutions, half of the Bulgarian poll does not have confidence in them.

Trust in the European Court of Justice (most probably confused previously with the European Court of Human Rights) has fallen by 13 points (40%), trust in the European Parliament – by 11 points (46%) and trust in the European Commission – by 9 points (41%). This corresponds with the general mood of Europeans, following the negative referenda results in France and The Netherlands, where trust in the European Commission has fallen by 6 points (EU25 – 46%), while trust in the European Parliament remains at 52%, following a decrease of 11 points.

Trust in the EU institutions depends on awareness about them and the perception of their role in European integration. Most Bulgarians have heard of the European Commission (62%), with nearly the same percentage (59%) considering that it plays an important role in the life of the EU and 41% tending to trust it. In Bulgaria, as in the EU, the European Parliament is most well known and trusted by citizens: 71% have heard of it, 65% think it plays an important role and 46% tend to trust it. It is also noteworthy that in Bulgaria the most trusted EU institution following the Parliament is the European Central Bank (44%) with three points higher than the European Commission (41%).

Climate of Bulgarian public opinion – between pessimism and optimism. The survey showed that, of all the countries polled, Bulgarians and Romanians are the most dissatisfied with their quality of life. This opinion is shared by 70% of the Bulgarians and 55% of the Romanians polled, an upward trend of 4 percentage points.

Pessimistic expectations of life in near future: Looking ahead, at least half of EU25 and Bulgarian citizens do not expect any changes in their standard of living over the next year. While for the EU citizens (51%) this means the prospect for personal satisfaction, for 56% of the Bulgarian poll it means the opposite – continued dissatisfaction with the way of life. The share of such opinions in Bulgaria has increased by seven percentage points. In Bulgaria, as in the new Member States, citizens have higher expectations regarding the forthcoming improvements in the public sphere, while in the EU15 citizens are more positive regarding the improvements in their personal situation. One fifth (22%) of Bulgarians surveyed see improvements in the quality of their life, 17% – in the country's economic situation and 16% in the financial situation of their households; 15% are optimistic about the country's employment situation, while those expecting improvements in their personal job situation stand at 2 percentage points lower (13%).

Unemployment and economic situation continue to be citizens' main concerns in both the EU and Bulgaria. Nearly six out of ten (57%) Bulgarian respondents consider unemployment, and four out of ten, the economic situation as the most important issues facing their country. For the EU25 these figures are 50% and 27% respectively. Over the last six months, these concerns have decreased by 3 percentage points regarding unemployment, and increased by 4 percentage points, regarding the economic situation in Bulgaria.

Bulgarians believe that EU plays a positive role in solving these issues: Nearly four out of ten Bulgarians polled (39%) feel that the EU can help the fight against unemployment and nearly half of those polled (48%) believe the EU could help improve the economic situation. 65% think the EU plays a positive role in fighting terrorism and crime (63%), as well as in defense and foreign policy (52%). Regarding social policies, such as housing, healthcare and education, the EU is mainly seen as playing neither a positive nor negative role. Only one-fifth of respondents are convinced of the positive role of the EU, as regards rising prices/inflation and taxation.

EU accession is related to reforms, which require public support and citizens' participation. The results of the Euro barometer survey show that, unlike for the citizens in some of the new Member States, such as Slovakia and Latvia, in Bulgaria for the majority of those polled (52%) the term ›reform‹ has a positive meaning (59% in the EU25). For one-third of Bulgarian respondents and for fewer citizens than that in the EU 25 (29%) it has a negative meaning.

The majority of *Expectations related to the future of Bulgarian EU membership:*

For personal life: the Bulgarian Euro barometer respondents expect that during the next five years, when Bulgaria operates as member of the EU, the Union will play a much bigger role in their everyday lives (54%). Moreover, this is perceived positively, since more Bulgarians (up by 12 percentage points) would like the EU to play an important role in their everyday lives (66%) – to a much higher degree (+15 points) than EU citizens (49%). This could be explained by the positive role, which is assigned to the EU for solving the major problems facing Bulgaria (unemployment and the economic situation). It is also indicated by the fact that Bulgarians, compared with other countries' citizens, are among the least optimistic about their personal situation improving over the next five years (BG–28%, EU25–42%).

For the country: Six out of ten Bulgarians questioned believed that their country would take advantage of its future EU membership. This optimism has become more moderate in the course of the last six months observed (–3 points). However, it compares with the high level of confidence in the new Member States that followed the first year of EU membership when their countries have been able to benefit from it (EU10 59%). Bulgarians are equally optimistic as EU citizens regarding the economic situation in their countries in five years' time (56%). 45% of them also believe that as a result of EU membership their country will become more influential in the EU; 31% take the opposite view and a quarter are hesitant to express any opinion.

For the European Union: A large majority of Bulgarians is in favor of the developments towards a European Political Union (73%), and a European Constitution (64%). When it comes to the Treaty on the Constitution, it appears that nearly half of them (47%) have never heard of it, 50% have heard of it, but know very little about it, and only 4% consider they know enough about what it is about. Support for the Constitution demonstrated by the Bulgarian poll (46%) is close to the EU average (48%). 55% of Bulgarian respondents say they would support the EU Constitution because they see in it an opportunity to advance further the European integration process. Four out of ten interviewed see in it more democratic opportunities and the strengthening of European institutions. Among its disadvantages, half of them point out the danger of losing national sovereignty, as well as the lack of information (44%) and the complexity of the text (22%).

The desire for more information is strongly reflected in the Bulgarian opinion on the key priorities for the future of the EU. A growing number of Bulgarians (+6 points) – close to the EU average (BG–17%, EU25–19%) – consider that getting closer to European citizens by providing them with more information about the EU policies and institutions should be a priority for the EU.

The Bulgarian and EU preference for retaining and advancing further the EU social model is also well reflected in the current public opinion poll. Both Bulgarian and EU respondents consider that the first priority for the EU should be the fight against unemployment and social exclusion. This percentage is higher for Bulgaria (69%) than for the EU25 (44%).

Alongside their Balkan neighbors, and mainly Greece and Turkey, Bulgarian citizens believe strongly that in the next five years the European Union will achieve its goal of becoming the most competitive economy in the world (63%), while the general moods in the EU are rather negative (35% »yes«, 54% »no«).

The most optimistic regarding the European Union and its role for Bulgarians' future are young people, aged 15–24. They have stronger beliefs than half a year ago (+4 points) that Bulgaria will benefit from its EU membership (75%) and show stronger support for Bulgarian membership (+5 points) than the average Bulgarian (85%).

Bulgarians and EU Enlargement: One in two EU citizen's supports Bulgarian accession to the EU. This is due mainly to the strong support in the new Member States (70%) and the opinions of the young generation, whose support is 6 percentage points higher than the EU average.

Support in the EU15 is 45% and has increased, over the last years 2 by 7 points. Among the EU Member States, support is strongest in Poland (75%) and lowest in Austria (21% – »for«, 68% – »against«). The results of the survey show that Bulgarians and Romanians show mutual and the highest support for each other's EU membership (80% Romanian support for

Bulgarian membership and 75% Bulgarian support for Romanian membership).

Bulgarians are quite supportive of EU enlargement to their Balkan neighbors: Bulgarian opinions about future enlargements of the EU coincide largely with those of EU citizens. Possible enlargements towards EFTA countries and especially Switzerland (BG and EU25 – 78%) and Norway (BG– 76%, EU25 – 78%) top the list.

Bulgarians are also more supportive of a EU future for their Balkan neighbors than EU citizens. Their support for a future enlargement towards Turkey (45%) is over 10 points higher than the EU average (32%), but slightly lower than the average for the new Member States (48%). There is also a very high support for a possible enlargement towards FYRO Macedonia (64%), Croatia (61%), Bosnia and Herzegovina (55%) and neighboring Serbia and Montenegro (60%).

To summaries, the key message from this Euro barometer report is that, Bulgarian citizens have become less pessimistic in national terms and more realistic in their Euro-optimism and Europe's role in the future of their country.

Synopsis of a »Last Catch« Accession

– The 2005 parliamentary election in Bulgaria ended eight years of opposition for the Bulgarian Socialist Party, which as part of Coalition for Bulgaria received 34.17% of the vote (82 seats), but failed to ensure an overall majority.

– Seven parties and coalitions – managed to carve out parliamentary presence resulting in the most fragmented and variegated configuration since the beginning of the transition period with no obvious model for a stable coalition government.

– One surprise from the election was the breakthrough of an anti-establishment formation in the face of Coalition Attack, which gained a high level of support and positioned itself as the fourth largest parliamentary group in the 40th National Assembly.

– A second surprise was the doubling of the number of votes for the Movement for Rights and Freedoms, which achieved the best election result since the party was formed.

– Overall, the election result worked in favor of small parties, which gained votes at the expense of Coalition for Bulgaria and National Movement Simeon II.

– The turnout of 55.7% was the lowest in parliamentary elections since 1990 irrespective of measures that aimed to enhance the degree of participation such as the introduction of an election draw; increasing the number of voting sections abroad and staging expensive media orchestrated election campaigns.

– The highlight of the campaign was a shift in the energies of the parties with frequent, professionally designed commercials on national TV stations, which accentuated the party's major strengths and election pledges.

– Europe was not a salient issue in the election campaign of any party including those with marginal chances for parliamentary presence and more populist appeals such as New Time, Democrats for Strong Bulgaria, Coalition People's Union and National Union Attack.

Political background: Since the 2001 parliamentary elections Bulgarian party politics has been enlivened by the unexpected return of the ex Bulgarian king in exile – Simeon Saxe Coburg Gotha in the role of a prime minister after his party (National Movement Simeon the Second – NMSS) won the battle for hearts and minds, one seat short of an absolute majority.

Even prior to Simeon's victory at the polls in 2001, political commentators were skeptical of his most ambitious program, which was long on promises and short on details of how to fulfill them. The Bulgarian public was won by a paradox pattern of mass persuasion using the regal charisma and optimistically cast of an exotic vote for National Movement Simeon the Second, believing that this time their hopes for better life were finally in safe hands. The following four years in office was testing time for Simeon who struggled to meet his pre-election pledges in full and saw the popularity of National Movement Simeon II shrunk by a third at the end of the first year in power. This trend persisted in the remaining three years and days prior to the June 2005 general elections the party was capable of mobilizing just 20.6% of the vote.

This substantial drop in support can be explained with the inability of Simeon to live up to three of his major pledges:

– Firstly, he came to power promising a robust economic reform which to transform the lives of ordinary people for the better in only 800 days. Although, an economic program was implemented indeed, which had a positive effect on the level of trade, foreign investment and unemployment, the benefits failed to filter down to the older and less educated strata of the population, particularly pensioners and those on minimum wage. In addition, there were alarming gaps in the implementation of the health reform. This was coupled with the lack of action in modernizing the educational system and failing to address the issue of the low remuneration that teachers and lecturers continued to receive.

– The second failing of Simeon was his failure to uproot corruption, which neutralized his original claim to pursue high morality in politics. He was the first to receive criticisms for the restitution of vast plots of woodland and properties that presumably formed part of his inheritance, but which many believed were returned by the courts to him because of his high position and ability to influence the institutional and legal structures. His ministers were also not immune to scandal. Many of the privatization packages that the government approved, such as the deals for the Bulgarian tobacco company »Bulgartabak«, the Bulgarian Telephone Company (BTK) and the »Trakia« highway concession scheme, were suspected of enriching the pockets of the political elite and were often criticized for that by the opposition circles. Simeon's decision to apply for the restitution of the highest mountain peak in Bulgaria – Mousala provoked anger and suspicion in many citizens who insisted the peak was part of the national heritage.

– Most obviously, Simeon's government did not succeed in transforming the legal system to secure convictions of career criminals involved in international drug trade who were regularly shooting each other on the streets of Sofia and other major cities in broad daylight, creating concerns for the European Commission in regards to the forthcoming EU membership of Bulgaria. Last but not least, the ex-monarch's authoritarian style of leadership is, in part, responsible for the erosion of trust that the party suffered in the public domain. It became Simeon's trademark to restrain from commenting on the events of the day in front of the cameras as any prime minister is expected to do, opting instead for the folklore phrase that comments on the subject would be made: »*When the right time comes*!« In many people's eyes that sort of behavior was seen as arrogant, dismissive and alienating and usually understood through the prism of his privileged upbringing.

To his credit Simeon II was extremely successful outside Bulgaria in advancing Bulgarian foreign policy, NATO and EU membership. Bulgaria became a member of NATO in 2004 and in April 2005 signed the accession treaty with the European Union on the basis of the expectation of full membership in 2007. On that note, according to a survey published in the Information. Bulletin of National Movement Simeon the Second in 2005 27% of the people were of the opinion that the government has managed to improve the international image of the country and ultimately nowadays Bulgaria is more popular among investors and desired as a partner on the European scene.[119]

In the last four years National Movement Simeon II governed in coalition with Movement for Rights and Freedoms, (Ethnic-Turks minority party) present in Bulgarian politics since 1990. When the coalition government was originally announced after the 2001 elections the majority of Bulgarians were disappointed that the »king« appointed Movement for Rights and Freedoms instead of the United Democratic Forces as its coalition partner, for there was

119 Survey commissioned by the National Centre for the Research of Public Opinion in March 2005. Source: NDSV Informatsionen Buletin (NMSS Information Bulletin),No.4, 2005, pp.5.

a widespread mistrust towards Movement for Rights and Freedoms due to its record of previously rocking the boat of both Socialist and Democratic governments. At best the analysts predicted an unstable coalition in which the »politically inexperienced« Simeon was forced into making concessions for the benefits of the Turks. At worst analysts envisaged an early election in a few years time. As it happened the NMSS–MRF coalition seemed not such a bad deal after all. From the very beginning the leader of Movement for Rights and Freedoms – Ahmed Dogan made the usual request for his party to receive 3 of the ministerial chairs of the agricultural and forestry sector, which is most closely linked to the livelihood of its electorate. He was particularly supportive of social programs on the list of National Movement Simeon II that were expected to benefit primarily the Bulgarian Turks. In relation to foreign policy Dogan remained firm on European membership and did not give in to the Socialist proposition to pull out the Bulgarian military personnel from Iraq in due course.

At the 2005 general elections Movement for Rights and Freedoms was predicted to take its traditional 7.6% of the vote, although from the party's point of view the decision of the other minority party »Evroroma« to appear independently in this election, as well as the introduction of an integrated ballot paper (for a first time), were issues that could mark its prospective electoral performance. Evroroma in particular had a powerful potential to divert the young minority supporters away from Movement for Rights and Freedoms.

Apart from National Movement Simeon the Second and Movement for Rights and Freedoms, the titans of the bi-polar model in Bulgaria – Coalition for Bulgaria and United Democratic Forces – were also certain of entering the 40 th National Assembly. The Bulgarian Socialist party dominated the Coalition for Bulgaria, as a successor party of the Bulgarian Communists. The party won the first democratic elections in 1990 and returned briefly to power in 1994 with the Videnov administration, which lasted two years and plunged the country into a deep economic crisis. Since then Bulgarian Socialist Party (later Coalition for Bulgaria) has remained in opposition firstly to a United Democratic Forces government in 1997 and then to a NMSS–MFR–led coalition in 2001. At the last election Coalition for Bulgaria mobilized just 17% of the vote, which amounted to its hard-core electoral base. In the subsequent four years it successfully climbed its way up to a confident 36% support rate in the days before the general election in 2005 and was tipped by most sociological agencies to emerge as the winner in the forthcoming contest (although short of an absolute majority).

The formula of its success depended primarily on its ability to persuade voters of the reformed nature of the Socialist party, which was helped by the successful presidency of the Bulgarian Socialist Party candidate Georgi Parvanov after the 2001 presidential elections in Bulgaria. The new, all-inclusive image was further emphasized with the young face of Sergei Stanishev, a 38 year-old bureaucrat, who was appointed as a Bulgarian Socialist Party leader after Parvanov vacated the post. Bulgarian Socialist Party took the necessary steps to ensure it satisfied the criteria for becoming a full member of the Socialist International (in late 2003), which in a way legitimized its claims for being a contemporary liberal formation.

In contrast to socialists, the political right in the face of United Democratic Forces (UDF), Democrats for Strong Bulgaria, National People's Union, Union of Free Democrats and party Radicals, remained unconsolidated. This can be seen in the reduction of support for the UDF from 18% in 2001 to an expected 9.9% in the 2005 elections. United Democratic Forces is the only party on the right before 2005 that was represented in parliament and all the other parties of the right have subsequently emerged from it. Originally UDF was formed as the democratic, market-orientated opposition in Bulgaria to the communist system. It was in government twice: for a first time between 1991 and 1992 with the Dimitrov administration and again between 1997 and 2001 with the Kostov cabinet, which was the first Bulgarian government in modern times to complete a full term in office. After the fall of Kostov, the UDF leadership could not agree on the line of politics and the party split into many fractions, each formed around a different leader.

Outside the above four parties the pre-election prognosis speculated on the possibility of four additional parties and coalitions joining the main players in the next parliament, making it the most kaleidoscopic to date. All of them buzzed around the 4% threshold mark, so there was no guarantee that any of them would pass the trustworthiness check on Election Day. With the highest percentage in the polls (5.8%) from the hopefuls were Democrats for Strong Bulgaria, the right wing party of the ex-prime minister Ivan Kostov. Its main difference to United Democratic Forces (main) was its ideological leaning towards anti-communism, which was reflected, in its aggressive rhetoric against the socialist party. Second on the list was New Time with 5.5% of the vote which is a splinter party from National Movement Simeon the Second, organized around that part of the party machine which was unhappy about Simeon's authoritarian style of leadership and presented itself as a new leadership alternative to otherwise identical policy choices. Thirdly, Bulgarian People's Union with 4.2%, is a complicated venture of three smaller formations: the Agrarians with Anastasia Moser, the right wing party of the Sofia mayor Stefan Sofianski – »Union of Free Democrats« and the nationalist party – »Revolutionary Internal Macedonian Organization« with Krassimir Karakachanov. Finally, no one really expected with modest 3.9% the first anti-establishment party in Bulgaria. Coalition Attack appeared on the Bulgarian scene two months before the general election presenting a program which was in opposition to every political consensus that has been agreed over the years: participation in the Iraq war, EU accession agreements, the sale of land to foreigners to name but a few.

Coalition for Bulgaria is the party that attracted most votes at the 2005 election and secured 82 seats. However, this tentative victory failed to match the inflated pre-election prognosis for anywhere between 89 and 118 seats, depending on which polling agency one preferred to believe in the last minute warm up prior to the election results. The fact that the coalition did not manage to win an absolute majority was not a setback in itself, because the party was prepared to form the next government in a coalition with Movement for Rights and Freedoms. These original plans were complicated after the election, when the worse-than-expected performance of Coalition for Bulgaria effectively placed the party in a position to require the cooperation of two, rather than one coalition partner, most probably from the political center, as the joint votes of Coalition for Bulgaria and Movement for Rights and Freedoms were short of reaching the 120 seat majority.

Second, in terms of voter preference, came National Movement Simeon II with 53 seats, which, at first sight, appeared to be a dishearteningly bad result for a governing party to score. In the 17 years of democratic history the Bulgarian public has never re-elected a government in office, so coming second at this election was not such a bad news for National Movement Simeon the Second. In fact the party did marginally better than the pools suggested in the election week, some giving it as few as 49 seats in the next parliament. The National Movement Simeon the Second emerged from the election with a refreshed bargaining power.

Thirdly, the impressive performance of Movement for Rights and Freedoms which gained 34 seats and moved in rank to third political power in parliament did not match the polling forecasts which, at their most optimistic, interpreted the potential of the movement to be around 25 seats. With the ability of hindsight it seems that the sudden appearance of Union Attack on the political landscape has acted as a mobilizing factor for the Movement for Rights and Freedoms electorate, who were afraid that anti-ethnic forces might outdo their representation in parliament.

It was the unexpected victory of Union Attack to secure 21 seats that laced the newspaper headlines in the morning after the election. Attack's breakthrough is a result of a punitive vote against the established political class in the face of the Bulgarian Socialists and the centrist National Movement Simeon the Second.

On the whole, United Democratic Forces suffered the biggest decline in support and did not live up to the pre-election scenario of 26 seats, settling instead at the 20–seat benchmark. From a positive perspective, they kept their position of being the biggest political power on the right, but to make their voice heard at the next parliament they need to coordinate their efforts with the other two parties – Democrats for Strong Bulgaria and Bulgarian People's Union.

Finally, Democrats for Strong Bulgaria and Bulgarian People's Union succeeded in their determination to get into next parliament and both parties came out stronger than expected prior to the vote. However, as in the case with United Democratic Forces all parties on the right need to work in cooperation to repair some of the damage done to the political right by this very fragmented representation.

Europe and the Election Campaign:

– At the 2005 general elections in Bulgaria the campaign started on a false note with the controversial announcement of the National Movement Simeon the Second government that it intended to boost turnout rates by spending four million leva (2 millions Euro) on an election draw, open to everyone who voted at the general election. This initiative was cleverly adopted with the intention to lure the active proportion of voters to the polls, as it is within this group that National Movement Simeon the Second's electorate can be usually located.

– The idea was immediately denounced as *undemocratic* by all other parties and most strongly by Coalition for Bulgaria, which saw it as a threat to their own electoral success. Even the EU was puzzled by what position to take on the draw, but eventually half-heartedly approved the idea, providing it was based on political consensus and public approval.

– Another aspect of the campaign was the professionally designed TV commercials that emphasized the party's strong points and election pledges a dozen times a day. For a first time the battle for the public vote was being fought to such a great extent from the marketing departments of party offices and PR agencies across the country, which outperformed each other with extravagant ideas, aimed at making their clients popular and liked.

– Coalition for Bulgaria led a tolerant, balanced and active campaign with emphasis on voter contact, touring, speeches and locally organized party celebrations with traditional dances and tons of promotion materials. At the other extreme National Movement Simeon II adopted a lackluster approach to the election, which well matched the silence of its leader throughout the active campaigning period.

– On the right, Democrats for Strong Bulgaria and United Democratic Forces were keen to rehearse their standard approach of mobilizing street rallies which inspired support in the post-communist days, but which have since outlived their winsomeness. The biggest rally with 20,000 people was organized by DSB one week before the election in Sofia, while United Democratic Forces were visibly less successful with never more than a few hundred people in sight.

– Movement for Rights and Freedoms busied themselves with active campaigning, using their time-honored tactic of offering ›inducements‹ to their electorate in the form of anything that is worth mentioning: sacks of coal, meat balls and other traditional delicacy, free trips from Turkey and 10 leva notes were some of the most well circulated incentives.

– Finally, Attack's campaign emanated from the platforms of hastily organized and racially incited, nationalist, demonstrations and rallies, as well as from the comfort of TV screens in the evening bulletin »Ataka« (Attack) on the satellite station – SKAT.

It is surprising, in view of the Bulgarian EU membership in 2007, that the topic of Europe rarely came in the debates and when it was thrown at the party candidates, they often failed to exploit it to their benefit by differentiating their position from that of competitors.

– Overall, there was a sense of political consensus and urgency to finalize the necessary reforms to transform the legal system on time and raise the level of public awareness in relation to Europe. Outside the trajectory of consensus remained only the question of renegotiating with the EU the closure of the nuclear reactors in Kozlouduy. The variation of opinion was mainly between the mainstream political class and Union Attack with the latter proposing to review sections of the accession treaty that did not appear to uphold the national interest with direct reference to the above issues.

– Europe was often high jacked in the process of the campaign as a populist front by National Movement Simeon II and Democrats for Strong Bulgaria, to discredit the ability of the Socialist party to finalize the accession process.

For example, in this spirit the Bulgarian ex-foreign minister Solomon Passy (National Movement Simeon II) famously remarked that the public was at a crossroad to decide: »either BSP or EC«.

Outputs and future prospects:

The 2005 elections in Bulgaria produced a very splintered result, which is difficult to regard as victory. Weeks after the elections it became unclear whether it will succeed to find coalition partners and utilize the vote. The political class managed however to get differences under control and demonstrated the ability to realize the Bulgarian bid for EU membership in 2007.

Negotiations between the three main parties – Coalition for Bulgaria, National Movement Simeon II and Movement for Rights and Freedoms, took weeks, and even though a coalition of the three seemed most unlikely to emerge, as the party leaders seemed uncompromising in regards to the prime ministerial position – it »happened«. When in September 2006 the European Commission prepared the evaluation report on the country's progress the »bumpy road« of Bulgarian EC Accession seemed straighter than expected.

A wide coalition with five center-right parties – National Movement Simeon the Second, Movement for Rights and Freedoms, United Democratic Forces, DSB and BPU – turned an unrealistic scenario, which could not accommodate most diverse interests, less even secure stability, in the long turn. Thus the modus of »three man in a boat« (not counting the dogs) appeared to be most acceptable.

The forthcoming 2007 local elections hide a new potential of political bargaining. Populism and nationalism might add new problems of the ruling system. The political culture in this country seems however already propelled to a new pragmatic European gravity. It will no doubt push actively a »quasi-democracy« in the direction of significant social change, as well to more political responsibility.

Adjusting Quasi–Democracies on the Balkans Towards Innovative Studies of Comparative Political Cultures

1. It is often claimed that collapse of the totalitarian regimes in Eastern Europe after 1989 added to a third wave« of democratization. Proper democratic *achievements* in number of countries of transition, however, still remain a most disputable matter. One reason for this seems the stand of democratic theory. The latter has rather chased rapid developments, but has less contributed for the rationalization a »zigzag«, and painful democratic change in the East. In their recent book »Post-communism and the Theory of Democracy«, Richard Anderson Jr., M. Steven Fish, Philip Roeder, and Stephen Hanson[120] argue that most widely accepted theories of democracy fall short when confronted with the evidence of post-communist cases:

> »On one hand, classic political science studies claiming to identify the »prerequisites« of democracy, whether they emphasize the importance of industrialization, wealth, pre–existing democratic traditions, or vibrant civic culture, simply don't explain the pattern of distribution of democracies, semi-democracies, and autocracies now found in the post-communist region. On the other hand, early predictions of a smooth democratic »transition«, resulting from elite pacts and a careful »crafting« of formal democratic institutions, which tended to downplay the importance of totalitarian institutional and social legacies, have proven equally unhelpful in making sense of broad outcomes thus far. In short, the progress of democracy in the post-communist region presents a more mixed picture than originally anticipated by either pessimistic sociological or optimistic institutional analysts«. (Hanson, 2001)

Whether individually, nationally, constitutionally, or ethnic and »multi-culturally« designed, most models of democracy and their cumulative indexes fail to grasp immanent societal change, relevant to the complex and controversial system transformation in Eastern Europe. Some comparative

120 Stephen E. Hanson is Professor at the University of Washington, associate professor of political science, and the director of the Russian, East European, and Central Asian Studies Program of the Jackson School of International Studies.

assessments have brought even new misunderstanding. As S. Smooha points out in a profound critical overview:[121]

> »The main weakness of the model (liberal) is, however, is its over-demanding and unrealistic normative conception of democracy. A regime that is not civic in nature and does not provide full equality to all citizens and ethnic groups is deemed non-democratic. Public and elite commitment to democracy, universal suffrage, fair elections, free media, and full and effective use of means of democratic, non-violent struggle by non-dominant groups, to name just a few of the components of democracy, are treated as trivial and deceptive. This myopic view misses the essence of regimes that are characterized by an inherent contradiction between democratic and non-democratic tendencies but also by incremental change, flexibility and relative stability .«(Smooha, 2001)

FIGURE 1
SEMI-LIBERAL, ILLIBERAL, AND LIBERAL DEMOCRACIES AS PERCENTAGE OF ELECTORAL DEMOCRACIES (2001)

	Liberal democracy		*Semi-liberal democracy*		*Illiberal democracy*	
	%	Total	%	Total	%	Total
Worldwide	58.3	70	20.8	25	20.8	25
Europe (without post-communist states)	95.9	23	4.1	1	–	–
Post-communist Europe and CIS	50.0	9	16.7	3	33.3	6
Africa	28.6	6	23.8	5	47.6	10
Asia	23.1	3	38.5	5	38.5	5
South Pacific	66.7	8	25.0	3	8.3	1
South America (including Central America and West India)	63.3	19	26.7	8	10.0	3
North America	100	2	–	–	–	–

Sources: Classification and calculation according to Larry Diamond, *Developing Democracy. Toward Consolidation* (Baltimore, MD and London: Johns Hopkins University Press, 1999), pp.279f. *Freedom House* (Internet: httpw://www. freedomhouse.org/research/freeworld/2000, accessed on 3 May

121 European Centre for Minority Issues (ECMI), Working paper 13,

2001); Aili Piano and Arch Puddington, ›The Freedom House Survey Gains Offset Losses‹, *Journal of Democracy*, Vol.12, No.1 (2001), pp. 87–93, esp. pp. 90f.

The figure shows that considerable percentage of the states Freedom House lists, as *electoral democracies* are not liberal, constitutional democracies. In 2001, only 58.3 per cent of all electoral democracies could be called liberal. As Wolfgang Merkel critically argues – the differentiation of liberal, semi-liberal, and illiberal democracies, is also based on a theoretically unrefined and problematic measure for democracy. Karatnicky and Diamond simply use numerical thresholds provided by the *civil rights scale* – one of the two measurement scales used by Freedom House. Any regime scoring 1 or 2 points on this 7-point-scale counts in this assessment as a liberal democracy. A regime with a score of 2.5–3 counts as semi-liberal, while everything that figures below 3.5 counts as an illiberal democracy. This neither justifies these arbitrary thresholds theoretically, nor does it define the terms liberal and illiberal democracy as conceptually based on a root concept of liberal democracy. This is surprising, given the depth of the theoretical debate on democracy. Freedom House data, as Merkel concludes are sufficient for trend reports and the development of first hypotheses, but for *in-depth comparative analyses* with a small sample, they are not refined enough. (Merkel, 2001)

2. What seems even more disturbing is the impotence of most global oriented comparative assessment frameworks to reflect (and in a way avoid) a rapid *loss of meaning* of democratic functioning in number of countries in transition. »Opposing« dichotomy ranking scales often blur a realistic view of democratic achievements, as painfully suffered in most of those national cases. Instead »quasi-effects of facade democracies are often promoted. The exclusion of whole segments of societies in transition from real and proper democratic involvement has a devastating effect both on the populations of those countries and in a wider global context.

»These models are all in a sense *quasi-democratic*: they copy many features of Government constitutions (representation, voting rights, debating rights) but there is one crucial difference. In a democracy, these rights are handed out to a selected group; in the case of quasi-democracy, those who can be bothered to claim them, claim these rights. Technologically mediated political discussion, bottom-up e-democracy and online polling are the same. They are quasi-democratic, but only quasi because they rely on people caring sufficiently to get involved. The absence of the silent majority is not felt in any way. They are (a new term here!) *auto-representative.* Their voice speaks only for itself. In a democratic society, however, voices come together and become something else entirely, which is the nature of genuine representation. Any true democracy has to be, in a fundamental sense, representative not simply vocal« (Davis, 2005).

This reflects, as we believe, a new paradigm that has shaped in Eastern Europe nearly two decades after the fall of the Berlin wall: comparative studies have to reconsider political cultures in most societies in transition in a new theoretical and political context. In a nutshell, as we believe, they have to involve political cultures much more explicitly as factor of significant democratic progress. The malfunctioning of the »hard-« and »software« democratic increase in many »new democracies« (rather generously called so) is not to be considered as product of their internal contradictive nature. Less seem they caused by most »fragile« and uncertain civic cultures. As we can witness, at this side of the Balkans, they are more likely hampered, by quasi-effects of politically propelled façade democracies, as related to the initial phase of transition in a wider European context. While societies situated nearer to advanced democracies (Central Europe) could perform better in this process, »periphery«, or quasi-democratic »enclaves«, lost their initial democratic momentum. There is less doubt that this reality is to be changed. This is not to be achieved, however, by sheer remote control social engineering, derived from the experience of the near past. Many Eastern European political cultures in their overriding national capacity have already bridged the gap of their chaotic transition(s) and more or less successfully upgrade their life strategies on European democratic pillars. Most countries in Southern Europe (Bulgaria and Romania as conditional EC newcomers) seem to be facing another »lag« of delayed reforms. This is not a new round of political and cultural deprivation. The rapidly changing political climate, as related to growing democratic pressure on governments at this side is more than symptomatic. People have »learned« simple, but still effective strategies to reach democratic aims through patterns of civic pressure on the system. There is less doubt that political science has to go beyond the static frameworks of »stands of democracies«, and rationalize a specific internal dynamics of real democratic progress in the countries in this region. *Debalkanizing the Balkans* seems the key phrase of this new strategy, which has to upgrade what some consider »dwarf states« on the Balkans and integrate their changing national and cultural identities in a new European political context. This is easier to articulate but still problematic in many ways. Even though it is an inevitable challenge of European politics in a wider context.

3. A set of »*meta cultural structures*« has emerged in the era of transition in South Europe, as we could witness. Generally speaking those structures are not bound to the notion of the state, or even the republic, as »chief executive« and carrier of patrimonial tradition. They hang less even to a still living totalitarian tradition of governance and its authoritative styled regimes, which made »good use« of the initial inertia of the past to launch capitalism »enforced from above«. This happened in a radically changed global context (marked by the fall of the Berlin wall). The emerged meta-structures have to

be rationalized as respond to a *new paradigm*, which has shifted from the idea of »radical« to »negotiable transition«. Those structures feed on their *own sources of power*. They generate new fields of influence and dominance. They invent and abolish »rules of the game« in a most sensational and opportunist way. Their voluntarism, inspired by some pervert theory of chaos, turns whole segments of societies and even cultural aerials into »dark holes«. The latter are out of reach of market obsessed media and deeply perplexed forms of public control. This influences both the »in« and the »output« of the system. It raises immense problems for the population in those countries in transition, moreover for the democratic world.

Political cultures in most countries of South Eastern Europe, however seem not to comply with the aims of a *»democracy for the few«*. They are less even inspired by the idea of some *polyarchy* (Dahl), steered by most egocentric national »elites«, or the ultimate free market forces. Liberal values have a diminishing chance to grass-root, less even successfully flourish in the environment of »competitive scarcity«, which has even deepened at this side in the years of transition. As vague as civic cultures in those countries appear to be, their capacity to challenge the mainstream of coercive networks control over public domains is not to be underestimated. As far as money is not considered as substitute of democratic politics, the discontent among the citizens in most Balkan countries is growing. This is a shift to a new civic consciousness and democratic awareness. The problem is that most of the cultures on the Balkans inherit a traditional antagonism related not only to there near communist past. They »kill« decent in their own naïve and rather enthusiastic way. They are less bound to the values of individual worthiness. Their »social solidarity« is a hybrid of the old »structured collectivism« and most volatile communitarian structures that emerged in marginal segments of the system in transition. The latter gives birth to populism of a new cloning, which may turn open protest »waves« into most destructive tsunamis. The appeals for the »strong hand« are more than symptomatic. Quasi-democracy can generate only authoritarian regimes, even though they appear to be so sophisticated and European friendly.

4. What we define here as *»quasi-democracies«* (relevant to the Balkans) refers to specific patterns of voting behavior, election procedures, and pseudo–democratic institutional functioning, that have shaped in the years of transition. This steered process of quasi-system transition has generated an own »critical mass« of corporate bound and illegally controlled public domains of power. The latter have deviated most societies at this side from basic requisites of liberal democracy. They have shaped a culture of »arrogant denial«, to differ from a »repressive tolerance« (Fetcher). Resting on a voluntarism of some irrational (asocial) kind, this culture feeds on dualistic (relativist) values, irrelevant to the »embedded« norms of a democracy. Its »operators« perform in different fields and under different

conditions. Though they behave in many respects like ordinary *»quasi–particles«* (in terms of modern physics) they have highly unusual properties. To brief here only but a few:

– Qasi-democracies perform in the frameworks of parliamentary systems, this occurs however only expressively;

– They act through own networks of influence, which are not (necessarily) institutionally bound;

– They inspire the emerging of NGOs, and/or even steer »grass roots« movements in their own public support;

– They are hardly to be identified by conventional variables of representative democracy, as they feed on direct forms of influence.

– They lack the »mass« of proper politics, as generator of significant and desired social change;

– Still their »fields« control societal change and even propel it into desired directions (media and PR techniques);

– Quasi-democracies relate to public life in »twisted« patterns (beyond mere asymmetry).

– In their deeper sociological sense (Weber) they spring from cognitive structures, which are irrelevant to the democratic mind.

We might better rationalize this phenomenon by 2 major premises:

a) Quasi-democracies (as quasi-particles) can be regarded as admixtures of negatively charged electrons (patterns of individual behavior) and positively charged holes (social domains);

b) An equal mix yields a quasi-particle (specific behavior) that is electrically (politically) neutral – yet it still carries spin one-half, just like an ordinary electron (political behavior).

The idea of studding quasi-democracies using analogues of modern physics might still look too vague, in so far it does not involve empirically proved (yet) evidence of occasionally observed »side effects« of a system in transition. Some of those quasi-effects however, became clear under certain conditions. September 11, 2001 inspired new global political purposes. Quasi-democracies at this side appeared to gain a new momentum from this new field of political bargaining. The demand of new coalitions in global strategic plan, the changing balance of powers, the economic, environmental etc. risks, have in a way propelled a »double standard« of proper democratic assessment. Some of the new democracies (New Europe) were even encouraged in their quasi-democratic performances and rapid structural change. This relates to military expenditures, neo–liberal policy, irrelevant to the devastated economic situation in most Balkan countries, promotion of a national elite of disputable cultural capacity, support of oppressive measures of »security« and abuse of human rights. Civic cultures have been in a way ignored (or totally excluded) from real democratic involvement, as they are pushed back into the realm of apathy and resignation.

5. Quasi-democracies are not to be grasped as generators of a *new meaning* of democracy (no matter liberal or of other types defined so far). Untouchable elites, oligarch groupings, non-transparent institutions, organized crime, infiltrating law and order, corrupted courts of justice, para-corporative settings etc., could only illustrate, but less explain the deviating structural effects by trivial models and assessment schemes. A more innovative approach is in demand, concerning controversies of religious, cultural, political, economic etc. complexities at this side of the Balkans, and in a wider European context. It is obvious that a sufficient definition of democracy has to go beyond sheer *democratic electoralism*. Not only procedures but also the goals behind democratic elections have to be fulfilled. For democratic elections to be *›meaningful‹*, not only does the selection process of the governing elite have to be democratically fair. There also has to be an institutional guarantee that the democratically elected representatives rule by democratic and constitutional principles in the period between elections. The rapid loss of meaning of democratic structures results not so much of traditional patterns of alienation, but restriction of proper participation, less adequate to the system of transition. Those effects spring from the lack of capacity of such systems to emancipate political cultures and involve them into the process of real democratic functioning. Considering some premises of Merkel's theory of »embedded and defective democracies), (as related to South Eastern Europe) we might get a clearer notion of such »quasi-democratic« performances in regional and even wider social context.

> »An embedded, liberal democracy – so Merkel, consists of five partial regimes: a democratic electoral regime (A), political rights of participation (B), civil rights (C), horizontal accountability (D), and the guarantee that the effective power to govern lies in the hands of democratically elected representatives (E). These five partial regimes show that our concept of democracy goes beyond the definitions put forth by Downs, Huntington, Przeworski, and even Robert Dahl's concept of polyarchy. Still, the concept is ›realistic‹, in that it is based exclusively on the *institutional architecture* of a democracy and does not use *outputs* or *outcomes* as defining characteristics of a constitutional democracy. Our understanding of democracy therefore lies between the ones put forth by Joseph Schumpeter and Hermann Heller. A welfare state, fair distribution of economic goods, or even ›social justice‹ may be desired policy results of the democratic processes of decision-making, but they are not its defining elements.«(Merkel, 2001)

Neither of the above mentioned 4 premises seem fulfilled in the case of the »new democracies" in South Eastern Europe. Or more correctly – most of them only *appear* to be such. As referred to the »neglected« output of a prolonged and most teasing »system transition", they draw another picture:

A) Electoral regimes, regulated by disharmonious laws on political parties and diverse electoral systems, are widely used as instrument of coercive power in »night-over« adjustments of electoral regulations in favor of ruling majorities;

B) The »subsystem« (regime) of political rights and participation operates in a not less problematic way. Most of the constitutional rights stay written; they are unknown both as contents and meaning to the majority of the citizens.

C) Civil rights are not less a problem-generating source, as the scarcity of existence in the quasi-transition shaped new economic, social and cultural dependencies. This has restricted basic individual and collective rights and freedoms.

D) The variable of »horizontal accountability« is even less predictable in the situation of permanent »institutional wars«. The media progressively add to the erosion of their status and meaning. Governments can only react by inventing parallel structures (agencies, intermediary state-pubic operators, etc.) as old hierarchies (networks) produce instability.

As far as guarantees that power lies in the »right hands« of representatives that are democratically elected is concerned, patterns of political voluntarism packed as »alternatives« are even more spread. Beliefs that a »third party«, or an »outside« arbitrary control (EC institutions) might change the situation prevail. In so far this process flows in less transparent bureaucracy patterns, euro skepticism rises. It could be easily propelled into »feedback« pressure on European institutions in favor of subsidizing the social and political deficits at this side. A new field of bargaining, as relate to the European constitution is shaping as well. This gives the chance of a »second breath« for quasi-democracies on the Balkans. All this bounds the »new democracies« in South Eastern Europe to some »cultural conservatism«, which is another obstacle for deeper European integrity. The answer to it has been less inspired by the idea of upgrading some fair forms of governance and more or less acceptable social existence, but more likely by the idea to abolish »the whole«. This has an additional »exhaustive impact« on young democracies at this side.

7. The flow of democratization, as we could witness, has created a wide spectrum of forms of democratic regimes, but blurred the boundaries between democracy and non-democracy: »The recent global wave of democratization has presented scholars with the challenge of dealing with a great diversity of post-authoritarian regimes«[122]. The challenge to comparative studies in the field stems from the deviation of some of the regimes from the democracies practiced in progressive industrial societies. Many researchers cope with this by adding adjectives to democracy. This »strategy« contributes less to increase the analytical differentiation and maintain of conceptual validity, but

---

122 Collier, David/Levitsky, Steven, 1997: Democracy with Adjectives: Conceptual Innovation in Comparative Research, in: World Politics. (April), 49/2: 430–451.

without conceptual stretching. Digressing from the classical western types of democracy is believed to achieve this. It seems less applicable to many Eastern countries in transition, however. Another approach is related to the use of »diminished adjectives. For instance, the type »restrictive democracy« is given to regimes that prevent certain political parties from participating in elections and violates the right of every party to aspire for power. Next »witty trick« of that kind is the avoiding of a simplistic dichotomy »democracy-non-democracy« and the recognition of the »mixed« and/or »hybrid« nature of many new and renewed regimes. Can all this help to grasp real democratic achievements in societies in transition, which aspire to some form of democracy in their own way?

A relatively innovative way to cope with the transition to an era of multiplicity of democratic regimes seems the focus on the dimension of *quality* of democracy. Democratic regimes that meet the minimal and procedural definition differ considerably in the degree of their quality, however. Endorsing this position, Etzioni-Halevy explains[123] why: »Democratic procedures are not enough. Such procedures produce democracy, but procedures alone cannot produce a high quality of democracy«. The quality of democracy may be reflected in general consensus on democratic procedures, equality of civil and political rights, legitimacy of all votes, political tolerance, the exclusivity of parliamentary laws, reduction of class inequality, ease of mobility to political elites, political representation of all population groups and effective struggle of deprived groups.

In addition to quality, democracies differ also in degree of their stability and efficiency. Stable democracy prevails in times of rapid change and deep crisis. Instability can stem from unsettled internal conflicts. Efficient democracy makes it possible to regulate conflicts between population groups peacefully. What can quasi-democracies do is another aspect of this never-ending discourse. It seems to us that the involving of political cultures, as both variable and factor of significant and desired democratic change might give a new push. Let is discuss this briefly from another methodological point of view.

8. One of the most influential developments that have affected our concepts of interacting is the Fermi Liquid Theory of Landau. It postulates that there exist »quasi/particles« with the same quantum numbers as non-interacting particles, even though the particles may be strongly interacting. 3 Another key development is the »Random Phase Approximation«, which provides a theoretical basis for description of systems that appear to obey Fermi Liquid Theory. (The arguments depend upon agreement with

123 Etzioni-Halevy, Eva (1999),'Èlites, Inequality and the Quality of Democracy in Ultramodern Society, International Review of Sociology, Vol. 9, Nr.2, 239–250

experiment and with the few exact calculations that have been done.)[124] This allows us to draw the following typology that we find useful to rationalize quasi-democratic systems in operational plan:

I Non-interacting systems
A. Well-defined independent particle states and Fermi surface
B. Many-body excitations are sum of independent particle excitations

II. Wakly interacting excitations
A. This is a theory of excitations (not the ground state)
We assume here that
– Independent particle excitations are weakly interacting (phenomenological aspects)
– Internal and external factors lead to excitations (defined for democracy potential near the one of established democracies)
– Width (inverse lifetime) of such systems is proportional to $(E - E_F)^2$
– concern of research (argument) is a simple phase space
– Operational problem to be tackled is the invention of parameters for measurement of effective mass of quasi-democratic systems (as in the case of Fermi liquid parameters)
– A most important political effect appears to be the renormalized susceptibilities of such quasi-democratic systems
B. Phase transition can occur only when interactions are sufficiently strong (vibrant civic cultures of activist participant type).

III Theory of Interacting systems (sophisticated methodological steps and approaches that might be of use)
A. Reminder of second quantization notation
B. Hamiltonian for interacting electron gas
C. Hartree
– Ignore interactions (except for an average effective potential)
D. Hartree-Fock
– Interactions to first order, wave functions to zero order
– Reasonable ground state energies
– Disaster for excitations near Fermi Energy – due to long range Coulomb interaction
E. Beyond Hartree-Fock-Correlation
– Divergence of straightforward perturbation theory
– Gell-Mann and Brueckner showed how diagrams could be summed

124 Important References: »Landau Fermi Liquid Theory« Abrikosov, Gorkov, and Dzyaloshinski; Mahan; Jones and March, sec. 2.9.

IV Random Phase Approximation (RPA)
- A. Interactions screened – physically motivated selected summation of diagrams
- B. Frequency and wave vector dependent screening – described by dielectric function
- C. Modifies Hartree-Fock in a way that qualitatively leads to Fermi liquid type behavior for excitations near the Fermi energy – in agreement with experiment
- D. Improved ground state energy compared to Hartree Fock

Using the premises of this theory in the framework of Almond and Verba's, we might be able to extend the innovative scope of comparative analysis of political cultures. Improved complex understanding of democratic performance in systems in transition, as they emerge and/or fade away in a changing context (situational & semantic approach) seems to us a must of modern comparative research. This has to be perceived from a different point of view and find its relevant empirical assessment. Political cultures are first to be emancipated in a given social context and only then assessed as integral variable of real democratic progress. In so far they rest on different values and norms, but in one way or another support (by immanent common and specific patterns) the functioning of democratic institutions, those complex entities are to be considered as specific networks of interference. The assessment models have to be free and open to evaluation done by the very carriers of democratic change. Such a »populist« approach appears to be not only fruitful, according to recent innovative studies in the field, but adds to our idea of detecting »quasi-democratic« effects in any system in transition. Finding adequate methods for there »adjustment« to normal fields of interaction is what is practically at stake. Let us brief on such a project, in so far it involves civic cultures as integrative marker of substantial democratic change.

9. In 2002, International IDEA published two major reports on their State of Democracy project in association with Kluwer Law International. The first of these was *The International IDEA Handbook on Democracy Assessment.* It sets out the methodology; provides a database of sources; lists international standards and best practice for comparative purposes; describes processes for stakeholder and other consultative legitimating, the use of opinion polling, and techniques for validation, publicity and dissemination. The second volume, *The State of Democracy: Democracy Assessments in Eight Nations Around The World*, provides a summary of the eight assessments;[125] builds a comparative set of both qualitative and quantitative indicators; and draws a

125 The methodology has been applied in Africa Australia, Ireland, the Philippines, Mongolia, and South Asia on a comparative basis.

series of comparative conclusions.[126] The framework is founded on a fundamental set of democratic principles and mediating values. It explicitly draws two fundamental principles of democracy:

(1) *Popular control over public decision making and decision makers*, and

(2) Equality of respect and voice between citizens in the exercise of that control.

Seven mediating values have been invented in addition in the framework as 1) participation, 2) authorization, 3) representation, 4) accountability, 5) transparency, 6) responsiveness, and 7) solidarity.

As one can witness the framework is based on a broader conception of democracy that includes institutional features and rights, going beyond the mere protection of civil and political liberties, including economic and social rights of citizenship. The democratic principles and mediating values have been used to construct four main pillars of the assessment framework, each of which has a series of sub-categories (see Table 1). Each of the sub-categories has an overarching question and a series of ›search‹ questions (a total of (94) for which qualitative and quantitative indicators can be assembled by the research team (see Appendix 7).

The use of these questions marks out the second major difference between the State of Democracy framework and other assessments of democracy. The approach in this case does not aim to provide an aggregate ›score‹ for a country, nor does it seek to rank order democratic experiences between countries. Rather, the framework recognises that democracy is a *multifaceted affair* and seeks to build a democratic ›performance profile‹ that shows the possible tradeoffs between different mediating values.

Table 1. Main pillars and subcategories in the State of democracy framework of IDEA

Main Pillars	*Sub–Categories*
Citizenship, Law, and Rights	Nationhood and citizenship The rule of law and access to justice Civil and political rights Economic and social rights
Representative and Accountable Government	Free and fair elections Democratic role of political parties Government effectiveness and

126 Experts associated with the State of democracy project have met in international conferences in London in June 2004, in Essex in December 2005, and in Fukuoka in July 2006. In conjunction with the Human Rights Centre at the University of Essex, IDEA is currently revising the *Handbook* and is developing a state of democracy website.

	accountability Civilian control of the military and police Minimizing corruption
Civil Society and Popular Participation	Media in a democratic society Political participation Government responsiveness Decentralization
Democracy Beyond the State	International dimensions of democracy

Source: International IDEA Stand of Democracy project

The original set of pilot studies [127] provided evidence that this framework can be applied to old, new, and restored democracies. The original studies showed that there are a number of notable democratic achievements that can be made early during a period of transition and consolidation. In all the countries, a broadly agreed constitution with a bill of rights was available; some established ombudsmen and/or a public defender present; the holding of free elections and universal suffrage; the revival of local government; and the protection of basic freedoms, such as party association, press, speech, and assembly was also present. Effective inclusion of minorities and women's participation have been reported to be much more difficult, though, as well as equal access to justice and protection of the right to life, meaningful inner-party democracy, control of executives, reduction in private influence and private interests in the public sphere, and a significant role for opposition parties. As the assessment reports conclude there still remains a gap, significant in some countries, between the establishment of the *procedural dimensions of democracy* and the *full protection of citizen and human rights,* including economic and social rights.

This gap between the institutional and rights dimensions of democracy has been described as comprising a distinct ›illiberal‹ sub-type of democracy. IDEA's general orientation towards democracy as *ongoing and evolving process* seems as realistic as innovative since it entirely expects that the assessment of the quality of democracy require necessarily a *multi-dimensional appro*ach. This seems a most promising way to provide a more nuance and contextually specific democratic performance profile of different countries and their political cultures, used as integrative indicator of significant but also desired societal change.

10. In the particular circumstances of today's Bulgaria all this would mean not only the finalization of some imaginary »deconstruction of totalitarism«. The transition to proper democracy means moreover an intensification of the

127 In Bangladesh, El Salvador, Italy, Kenya, Malawi, New Zealand, Peru and South Korea.

modernization process, opening up to the world, the establishment of the autonomy of the individual, encouraging personal social initiative, civic responsibility, pluralism and tolerance. Last but not least – the process of democratization is most closely related to the creation and enlargement of guarantees for human rights. The scope of effective guarantees for the rights of man (political, civic, social, economic) is a main indicator of the democratic nature of any advanced society. In this sense, the transition to democracy leads to a society aimed by the majority of the people at society of liberty, justice, and human rights. This is possible only if the democratization does not transgress human rights, if it is carried out within bounds that do not threaten to destruct social links that do not lead to the falling apart and atomization of the community.

The stability of the transition depends further on a multitude of factors: the effectiveness of democratic institutions, the degree of entry into the social tissue of democratic mechanisms and procedures, the scope of support for democratic changes. The stability of democratic change depends above all, however, on a wider and deeper social consensus around the underlying principles of proper *democracy* and *real market economy*. The degree of this consensus cannot be measured by sheer »level of societal tolerance« (to other opinions, to social and class differences, to the involvements and moreover sacrifices needed). It has to involve (on theoretical and operational level) the specific culture of *societal constructive capacity* of both individuals and social groups, committed to real democracy and their capability to unveil and dethrone its quasi-forms along the vertical and horizontal dimensions of society. These socio–psychological »cross–cuttings« of the new democracies and in a wider European context, is, as we believe, a new field of future in depth comparative studies, still to be conquered and empirically proved. It may be a significant contribution for the shaping new European integrity.

Conclusion: Civic Society and Modern Nationalism

The alternative driving force of representative democracy in Bulgaria after 1989 seems the one of immediate participation of the individual in the political life. It is realized by more or less typical patterns of civic interaction, i.e. sanctions at the very *»output«*, but not so much at the *»input«* of the political system. Appearing only ostensibly as passive at the »input«, this culture inherits in a way some of the values of »peoples governance », as shaped in the years passed. But not necessarily organizing, subordinating, less even stressing on worn out »cognitive maps« and ideological platforms.

This new shaping culture is less inspired by the idea of some *»cybernetic governor«*, determining the »highway« of the development of a modern society at this side. The present situation in Bulgaria reflects, as we believe, not so much objective regularities of some general political process, grasped *an sich selbst.* What appears more relevant to us is a process of *self-actualisation of a national ego* generating some typical elements of a complex society. A decisive factor within this system is the quality of the »mix« of amalgamated and successfully diffusing values and behavioural patterns in the system of social and political life.

We face here the inevitable question: »what is to be expected beyond?« Is it a new circle of *poliarchy,* defined as »continuing responsiveness of the government to the preferences of its citizens, considered as political equals« (Dahl), or something else? It is less probable that the scarce resources of this country might inspire another experiment, concentrating on the level of the national state, i.e. on the verge of another forced attempt to overcome an «*era of post-scarcity*«, which most respectful scientist believe will characterize the global world in XX century (Giddens: 1990) What seems more likely is an attempt to change the position of the national state, among others, in the system of the shaping new global order.

Those efforts are not up to the potential of the institutions or the political system only. They will have to cope with *new forms of local organizations* submerging from »below« and such, as intensively proliferating on international level. Most authors, engaged seriously with post–modernism in a global context, express less doubt that such forms of democratic participation will spread more intensively. They will have greater influence on governments and institutions in different political systems. Those civic forms could take the shapes of pressure *movements* to democratic participation at work, in local associations and even transitional groupings. Insofar such questions refer to relations between different states; there is less doubt that movements of this kind will be regulated in the system of the new global order.

Even so the idea of a world government, to regulate conflicts and direct the general coordinating efforts, is defined as a realistic utopia. This idea inspired its authors, engaged with the first phase of the globalisation. Initially underestimated, the idea of the *sovereign autonomy of the national state* seems a well aware sin of modern politics. This is where a new cultural temptation for many Balkan nations hides, but as well a new political chance still to be grasped.

In an age of global integration and transformation of economic and social-political structures, where vigorous competition of different cultures is taking place, Bulgaria (as other Balkan countries) could respond to tendencies and challenges of ethnic and cultural disintegration and fragmentation in the region with an energetic politics of a new *modern nationalism.* The latter could open new perspectives for a modern state in the future, to differentiate from the nationalism of previous epochs, when the factors of globalisation were missing, or did not go in such an intensive process of political integration, bound to a common system of international relations. This new world order emerging keeps in mind the objective and regular character of such process, the inevitable perspective that societies from *closed local type*, as based on their traditional cultures, will have to integrate in the global world. Its structures are no doubt programmed technologically and democratically by more advanced western societies.

Modern nationalism seems the road to this integration, not as much as some »westernising« of developing societies, as a precondition for their technological, economic and political modernization. But more likely in the recreation and modernization of their national cultures, their active implementation in the system of world's cultures, as a motivating factor for complex development. What is at stake, therefore, is not a return »back to history«, less even some detention of the historical process, but by stepping on the fundament of history, to grasp the impulses of a new Spirit, as we head into this venture: global cultural, economic and democratic modernization.

In this way, without loosing identity and dignity, which matters especially to Balkan nations and people, we might be successfully integrated into a complex European and global entity as *whole cultural nuclei.* The national state has to play a decisive role in this new political architecture, where the state of closed local-space type, or the »non–West«, finds the ideology of self–maintenance, by changing its functions. To participate successfully in this new system, such states have to surpass traditional attitudes, binding political behaviour into the »matrix« of authoritarian, sheer administrative regulation, moreover total control on its citizens. They have to adopt the role of a chief–arbitraries, coordinators, and strategists of their social activity.

This seems the only rational way to integrate the autonomous economic subjects of any post-communist society in the new *complex system* of a rapidly changing world, the informational institutions and the world wide informational networks. Thus guaranteeing a dynamic stability of the society and its natural environment, as well the integration of all social groups, institutions and organizations. Key factors on which the state of the modern nationalism has to be based are the development of education, culture and material prosperity of its citizens. It has to generate and offer to them forecasts of their future, as well as reliable strategies for successful adaptation to the radically changing social environment.

Based on such aims and factors only, the policy of the state of modern nationalism might count on the support of the emerging civic society in this country, as well as in most countries of South Eastern Europe. As we could witness, these cultures already work for their liberty and prosperity, which means for a new dignity. The rest, as we have learned from our »Balkan past« (and even more from the present), might well turn into another utopia.

witness, these cultures already work for their liberty and prosperity, which means for a new dignity. The rest, as we have learned from our »Balkan past« (and even more from the present), might well turn into another utopia.

Literature

ANGELOV, Dimitar, Istoria na Vizantia 1204–1453. (History of Byzantium) III, Nauka i izkusvo, Sofia, 1976.

ARENDT, Hanna, Totalitarismat, (Totalitarism). Sofia, Panorama, 1993.

BELEZITI, Balgari, Ocherzi v 7 t.(Prominent Bulgarians. Essays in 7 Bd.) Sofia, 1979.

BANKOV, Angel, Razvitie Na filosofskata misal v Balgaria, (Development of philosophical thought in Bulgaria), Nauka i izkustvo, Sofia, 1966.

VENEDIKOV, Jordan, Soziologichskite predizborni prouchvanija mezdu serioznoto i opasnoto, (Sociological polls between the serious and the dangerous), Sofia, 1994.

VLADIMIROV, Zh, IV. KATZARSKI, T. TODOROV, M. BADJAKOV. Balgaria v kragovete Na anomiata (Bulgaria in the circle of anomie), Sofia, 1998.

GANCHEV, Petko, Kam filosofiata na balgarskata istoria (Towards the Philosophy of Bulgarian History), Sofia, 1998.

GENCHEV, Nikolai, Balgarskata kultura. XV–IX v. – Bulgarian Culture), Sofia Univ. press, Sofia 1988.

GENCHEV, Nikolai, Balgarskoto Vazrazdane (The Bulgarian Revival, 4 th revised Ed.), Sofia, 1995.

GENCHEV, Nikolai, Balgarskata vazrodenska inteligenzia (The Bulgarian Inteligenzia of the Revival), Sofia, 1988.

GEORGIEV, K. Plamen, Dvulikijat Janus ili dilemite na Lipmanovata teoria za obstestvenoto mnenie (The double faced Janus and the dilemma of Lipmann's theory of public opinion), Savremenna jurnalistika, Nr.4, 1987, 187–195.

GEORGIEV, K. Plamen, Evropejskata politiceska kultura (The European political culture) – Soziologicheski problemi, Nr.3, 1991.

GEORGIEV, K. Plamen, Balgarskata politicheka kultura v »defizit« ili »promjana« (The Bulgarian Political Culture in »deficit« or in »change«) – Godishnik na Varnenskija svoboden Universitet (Issues of the FU of Varna) Bd.I, Varna, 1997.

GEORGIEV, K. Plamen, Spiralata na »balgarskoto malchanie«. (The Spiral of »Bulgarian silence«), Godishnik na Varnenskija svoboden universitet (Issues of the FU of Varna), Bd.I, 1988.

GEORGIEV, K. Plamen, Balgarskata politicheska kultura (The Bulgarian Political Culture), K & M, Sofia , 2000.

GEORGIEV, K. Plamen, Soziologia. Osnovni ponjatia I savremenni teorii (Sociology. Basic concepts and contemporary theories), Idea, St. Zagora, 2006.

GRUEV, Stefan, Korona to trani. Tzaruvaneto Na Boris III 1918–1943 (A crown of thorns. The reign of Boris III), Bulgarski pisatel, Sofia, 1991.

GALABOV, Konstantin, Chovekat na kavala. Chovekat na Ribnia bukvar. Chovekat na Balkana. (The man of the shepherds flute. The man of the Fisher primary. The man of the Balkan), Iztok, I, Nr.15, Sofia, 1926.

DOBREV, Petar, Proizhod na prabalgarite, (Origin of the proto–Bulgarians) Sofia, 1993.

DOBREV, Petar, Neobjasnenoto i neobiknovenoto v rannata balgarska istoria (The unexplained and the peculiar in the early history of Bulgarians), Izdatelstvo »V.Nedkov«, Sofia, 1993.

DOBREV, Petar, Istoria na balgarskata darzavnost (po nai starite tzarski I tzarkovni letopisi)–(History of Bulgarian states–craft (according oldest King's and Church chronicles), Slavena, Varna, 1995.

DIMITROV, Ilcho Iv, Epoha 1885. Istoricheski ocherk za saedinenieto na Severna i Juzna Balgaria, (Epoch 1885. A Historical study on the unification of North and South Bulgaria), Sofia, 1995.

DIMITROV, Strashimir, Kr. Manchev, Istoria na balkanskite narodi (History of the Balkan people), Sofia, 1971.

DRAGANOV, Mincho, Psichologia na balgarskia seljanin. (Psychology of the Bulgarian peasant), Sofia, 1963.

DRAGANOV, Mincho, Koga vsastnost e sazdadena balgarskata darzava? (When was the Bulgarian state found actually?), Slavika, Sofia, 1994.

DJIDROV, Petar, Partii I partizanstvo.Archiv za stopanska i sozialna politika 1926, kn.4.(Parties and partisanship. Archive of economic and social policy), in: T. Nedelcheva (Ed.) Narodopsihologia i politika (People psychology and politics), Sofia, 1966.

DNESHNOTO balgarsko semejstvo (Coll.) (Ed.) Ch.Kjuranov (The contemporary Bulgarian family), Nauka i izkustvo, Sofia, 1966.

ZHELEV, Zhelju, Fashizmat (totalitarnata darzava).Fashism (the totalitarian state), Sofia, 1990.

ZHECHEV, Toncho, Balgarsjijat Velikden ili strastite balgarski (The Bulgarian Eastern or the Bulgarian passions), G.Danov, Plovdiv, 1990.

ELENKOV, Iv., R.Daskalov (izd.) Zasto sme takiva? V tarsene na balgarskata identichnost,(Why are we like this? In search of the Bulgarian identity), Prosveta, Sofia, 1994.

ISTORIA na Balgaria v 14 t., (History of Bulgaria in 14 Bd.) Balgarska akademia na naukite (Bulgarian academy of sciences), Sofia, 1979.

IKONOMOV, Todor, Memoari. (Memoirs), Balgarski pisatel, Sofia, 1973.

IRECHEK, Konstantin, Balgarskoto knjazestvo, (The Bulgarian Principality), Sofia, 1897.

KARVELOV, Ljuben, Sachinenija. (Collected works), Sofia, 1966.

KOSEV, Konstantin, N. Zechev, D. Dojnov. Istoria na Aprilskoto vastanie 1876(History of the April Insurrection 1876.), Sofia University press, 1996.

LALKOV, Milcho, Balkanskoto nazionalno osvoboditelno dvizenie prez XIX v. – 1804–1878. (The Balkan National liberation Movement in the XIX c.), Sofia, 1982.

Levski, Vasil, Dokumentalno nasledstvo. (Documentary heritage), Nauka i izkustvo, Sofia, 1973.

MADJAROV, Mihail, Spomeni (Memmoirs), Sofia, 1968.

MACHIAVELLI, N., Izbrani sachinenija (Collected works), Nauka i izkustvo, Sofia, 1987.

MARKOV, Georgi, Balgaria v Balkanskia sajuz sreshtu osmanskata imperia 1912–1913, (Bulgaria in the Balkan union against the Ottoman empire), Nauka i izkustvo, 1989.

MILEV, Geo, Balgarskijat naord dnes (The Bulgarian people today), Vezni, Nr.3, 1921

MICHALCHEV, Dimitar, Za roljata na sluchainostta i na velikite ljude v istorijata (On the role of chance and prominent personalities in history), Filosofski pregled, XIII, 5–6, Sofia, 1941.

MUTAFCHIEV, Petar, Kam filosofiata na balgarskata istoria. Vizantizmat v srednovekovna Balgaria (Towards the philosophy of Bulgarian history. Byzantism in Bulgaria of the middle centuries), Filosofski pregled, 3, Nr.2, Sofia, 1933.

MUTAFCHIEV, Petar, Pop Bogomil i Sveti Ivan Rilski. Duhat na otrizanieto v nashata istoria (Priest Bogomil and Saint Ivan Rilski. The Spirit of Denial in our history). Filosofski pregled, 4, Nr.2, 1934.

PANTEV, Andrej, Balgarskiat April 1876 v Anglia i SAST (The Bulgarian April 1876 in England and USA), Sofia, 1996.

PANOV, Todor, Psihologia na balgarskia narod (Psychology of the Bulgarian people), Tarnovo, 1992.

PENEV, Bojan, Istoria na novata balgarska literature. T.III. Balgarskata literatura prez vtorata polovina na XIX v. (History of the new Bulgarian literatre. Bd.III. The Bulgarian literature in the second half of the XIX c.), Balgarski pisatel, Sofia, 1977.

PETRO, Nikolai, O konzepzii politicheskoj kulturoj ili osnovnaja oshibka sovetologii (Rus.) –(On the concept of political culture or the basic mistake of Soviet studies), Polis, I, Moskva 1998.

SEMOV, Marko, Narodopsihologia. Balgarinat i vastta (Peoples psychology. Bulgarian and Power), Slavena, Varna, 1995.

SEMOV, Marko, Narodopsichologia. Razmisli varhu napisanoto i nenapisanoto za balgarskata narodopsihologia i nazionalen harakter (Peoples psychology. Thinking over the written and unwritten on the Bulgarian peoples psychology and our national character). Bd.I, Slavena, Varna 1995.

STOJANOV, Zahari, Zapiski po balgarskite vastania (Notes on the Bulgarian Insurrections), Balgarski pisatel, Sofia, 1976.

STRASHIMOROV, Anton, Nashiat narod. (Our people), Sofia, 1925.

STRASHIMOROV, Dimitar, Istoria na Aprilskoto vastanie. T.I, II, III. (History of the April insurrection – 1st original copy Edition), Plovdiv, 1907

TANEV, Todor, Predgovor kam G.Almond I S.Verba. Grazdanskata kultura, (Introduction to the Bulgarian translation of G.Almond and S.Verba's Civic Culture), Sofia, 1998.

TURLAKOV, Marko, Harakter i disziplina (Character and discipline), St.Zagora, 1929

FOTEV, Georgi, Sozialna realnost i vaobrazenie. Soziologichesko izsledvane varhu renesansa (Social reality and imagination. A Sociological study on the Renaissance), Idea, St.Zagora, 1996.

HADJISKI, Ivan, Optimistichna teoria za balgarskia narod. Sachinenija v 2 t. (Red.) Nesho Davidov i Efrem Karamfilov (An Optimistic Theory of the Bulgarian people), (Eds.) N.Davidov and E. Karamfilov, Balgarski pastel, Sofia, 1974.

SHISHMANOV, Ivan, Izbrani sachinenia, t.I, Balgarskoto Vazrazdane (Collected works. Bd. I. The Bulgarian Revival), Balgarska akademia na naukite, Sofia, 1965.

SHEITANOV, Najden, Duhat na otrizanieto u balgarina (The Spirit of denial in the Bulgarian), Filosofski pregled, Nr.2, 1933.

SHEITANOV, Najden, Balgarskiat svetogled (The Bulgarian life view). Prosveta, 8,Nr.4, 1942.

ALMOND, G.S. Verba.1963: The Civic Culture. Political Attitudes and Democracy in Five Nations, Princeton University Press.

ALMOND, G. 1980: The Intellectual History of the Civic Culture Concept. – In: Almond, G.A. S. Verba (Eds.). The Civic Culture Revisited, Boston.

ALLPORT, G.W. 1979: Attitudes in the History of Social Psychology in: Attitudes, N.Warren & M.Jahoda (Eds.), New York: Penguin Books.

AXT, H. –J. 2002. Malta. In: Jahrbuch der Europaischen Integration, 2001/2.W. Wiedenfeld und W.Wessels, Bonn.

ARON, Reymond.1977: Main Currents in Sociological Thought (1) COMTE, Montesquieu, Marx, and Tocqueville. (2) Pareto, Weber, Dürkheim, London: Penguin Books.

BAUER, H., H.M. Kepplinger, K. Reumann (Hrsg.). 1981: Öffentliche Meinung und Sozialer Wandel, Opladen.

BELL, Daniel, The End of Ideology.1981: On the Exhaustion of Political Ideas in the Fifties, New York: Free Press.

BEETHAM, David (Ed.). 1994: Defining and Measuring Democracy, London.

BERG–SCHLOSSER, Dirk.1972: Politische Kultur.Eine Neue Dimension Politikwissenschaftlicher Analyse, München: Ernst Vögel Verlag.

BEYME, Klaus von. 1984: Die Politische Theorien der Gegenwart. Ümcneh–Zürich: R.Piper & Co Verlag.

BEYME, Klaus von. 1994: Systemwechsel in Osteuropa, Frankfurt.

BUEL, W. 1970: Evolution und Revolution, München.

CANETTI, Elias. 1985: Masse und Macht, Frankfurt am Mein: Fischer Verlag.

CLIFFORD, Geertz.1964: Ideology as Cultural System – in: Apter D.E. (Ed.) Ideology and Discontent. New York: The Free Press.

CONNOLY, W.E. 1988: Political Theory and Modernity, Oxford.

DAHL, Robert A. 1971: Polyarchy. New Haven.

DAHL, Robert A. 1989: Democracy and its Critics. New Haven/London.

DAHL, Robert A. 1994: A Democratic Dilemma: System Effectiveness versus Citizen Participation, in: Political Science Quarterly, 109/1: 23–34.

DAHRENDORF, Ralf. 1964: Recent Changes in the Class Structure of European Societies, Dedalus, Winter.

DAHRENDORF, Ralf. 1983: Die Chancen der Krise. Über die Zukunft der Liberalismus.Stuttgart: Deutsche Verlags–Anstalt.

DAVIDSON, W. 1965: Public Opinion: Introduction. In: International Encyclopedia of the Social Sciences. Ed. D.L. Shills, New York.

DEUTSCH, K.W. 1970: Politics and Government, Boston.

DIAMOND; Larry al. (Eds.). 1997: Consolidating the Third Wave Democracies, Baltimore/London.

FOTEV, Georgi. 2005: Ethnicity, Religion and Politics, Sofia, Pensoft.

FUKUYAMA, Francis. 1995: The Primacy of Culture, in: Journal of Democracy, 6/1: 7–14.

GEORGIEV, Plamen K. 1988: Elias Canetts Werk »Masse und Macht« – eine Reflexion des Humanismus und philosophishen Inuition – Im: Canettis Masse und Macht oder die Aufgaben des Gegenwärtigen Denkens, Wien: Bundesverlag.

GRAUMANN, C. F., S. Moscovici (Eds.). 1987: Changing Concepts of Conspiracy. Springer Series in Social Psychology. New York–Heidelberg.

GEYER, Dieter. 1989:Perestrojka und die sowietische Geschichte.Geschichte und Gesellschaft, Göttingen, Heft 3.

GIBBINS, John R. (Ed.) 1989: Contemporary Political Culture. Politics in Postmodern Age, London: Sage Publications.

GIDDENS, Anthony. 1991: The Consequences of Modernity. Cambridge: Polity Press.

GLAZER, Nathan. 1983: Ethnic Dilemmas (1964–1982), Harvard University Press.

GLENNY, Misha. 2000: The Balkans 1804–1999. Nationalism, War and the Great Powers, London, Granta Books.

HABERMAS, J. 1976: Zur Rekonstruktion des Historischen Materialismus. Frankfurt, Surkamp.

HAUG, Wolfgang F. 1989: Gorbatschow: Versuch über den Zusammenhang seiner Gedanken, Hamburg, Argument –Verlag.

HÖSCH, Edgar. 1988: Geschichte der Balkanlander: Von der Fruhzeit bis zur Gegenwart. München, C.H.Beck.

HUNINGTON, Samuel P. 1997: The Clash of Civilizations. New York.

ISMAYR, Wolfgang (Hrsg.) 2002: Die politischen Systeme Osteuropas, Opladen: Leske+Budrich.

JESSOP, Bob. 1990: State Theory. Putting Capitalist States in their Place. Pens. State University Press.

KAPLAN, M.A. 1967: System Theory in: J.C.Charlesworth (Ed.) Contemporary Political Analysis, New York.

KAVANAGH, Dennis. 1980: Political Science and Political Behavior. The Decline of the Civic–Culture in Almond and Verba, London.

KORNHAUSER, William. 1959: The Politics of Mass Society, Glencoe.

KORNHAUSER, William. 1968: Mass Society and Democratic Order – in: F.Lindenfeld (Ed.) Reader in Political Sociology. New York: Funk & Wagnalls.

LAPALOMBARA, Joseph. 1965: Italy. Fragmentation, Isolation, Alienation – in: L.W.Pye, S.Verba (Eds.) Political Culture and Political Development, PU.

LEPENIES, von W. 1989: Europa als geistige Lebensform.Ein Pledoyer für witschafliche Einigung und kulturelle Vershiedenheit. Die Zeit, 27 Okt.

LEPSIUS, M. Rainer, (2003):Institutionelle Entkopplung, europäische Integration und Identitätsbildungin: Jutta Allmendinger (Hrsg.), Entstaatlichung und soziale Sicherheit. Verhandlungen des 31. Kongresses der Deutschen Gesellschaft für Soziologie in Leipzig 2002, Teil 1, Opladen: Leske + Budrich, S. 516–522.

LIPSET, Seymour M.1963: Political Man. The Social Bases of Politics, Heinemann.

LUHMAN, N. 1970: Soziologische Auflärung, Köln/Opladen. Westdeutscher Verlag.

LUTTBERG, N.R. Michael M. Gant. The Failure of Liberal–Conservative Ideology as a Cognitive Structure. In: Public Opinion Quarterly, Vol.49: 80–93.

MALINOWSKI, Bronislav. 1951: Die Dynamik der Kulturwandels.Wien: Humblot Verlag.

MARX, Karl. 1951: Zur Kritik der Politische Ökonomie. Berlin: Dietz Verlag.

MELUCHI, Alberto. 1989: Nomads of the Present. Social Movements and Individual Needs in Contemporary Society. London: Hutchinson Radius.

MERKEL, Wolfgang.1999: Systemtransformation, Opladen.

MERKEL, Wolfgang / Hans–Jürgen Puhle / Aurel Croissant / Peter Thiery. 2006: Defekte Demokratie Band 2: Regionalanalysen, Wiesbaden: VS Verlag für Sozialwissenschaften.

NEUMANN, Elisabeth Noelle. (Ed.). 1981: The German Public Opinion Polls 1967–80. Institut für Demoscopie Allensbach, Greenwood Press.

NEUMANN, Elisabeth Noelle, 1993: The Spiral of Silence. Public Opinion – our Social Skin. Second Ed. Univ. of Chicago Press: Chicago–London.

NEUMANN, Elisabeth Noelle, Renate Köcher.1987: Die Verletzte Nazion.Über den Versuch den Deutschen, ihren Character zu ändern, Stuttgart.

OFFE, Claus, 1994: Die ›demokratische Revolution› in Osteuropa – eine neue Bewährungsprobe der Demokratietheorie, in: Ders.: Der Tunnel am Ende des Lichts. Frankfurt is Main/ u. New York.

ORTEGA Y GASET, J. 1956: Der Aufstand der Massen, Reinbek.

PATEMAN, Carol. 1980: The Civic Culture: A Philosophic Critique in Almond and Verba, London.

PATRICK, G.M. 1984: Political Culture in: Sartori, G.(Ed.) Social Science Concepts: A systemic Analysis, London: Sage.

PYE, Lucian W., Sydney Verba. (Eds.). 1965: Political Culture and Political Development, Princeton University Press.

PYE, Lucian W. 1990: Political Science and the Crisis of Authoritarianism, in: American Political Science Review, 84: p. 3–1.

REICHEL, P. (Hrsg.).1984: Politsche Kultur in Westeuropa. Frankfurt am Mein

SCHMIDT, Manfred. 1995: Demokratietheorien, Opladen.

SENGHASS, D. 1982: Von Europa lernen. Entwicklunggeschichtliche Betrachtungen, Frankfurt am Mein.

SPIRO, H.J. 1967: An Evaluation of System Theory – in: J.C.Charlesworth (Ed.) Contemporary Political Analysis. New York.

STEFANI, Winifried. 1989: Pluralistische Demokratie. Opladen.

TOCQUEVILLE, A.1963: Democracy in America, New York.

TOCQUEVILLE, A. 1968: Despotism in Democratic Nations – in: Reader in Political Sociology, F. Lindenfeld (Ed.), New York, p. 180–206.

VALENTIN, Veit. 1979: Geschichte der Deutschen (1 Aufl.), Köln:Verlag Kiepenheuer & Witsch.

TUCKER, R.C. 1987: Political Culture and Leadership in Soviet Russia: From Lenin to Gorbachev, Brighton, Wheatsheaf.

WEBER, Max. 1973: Soziologische Universalgeschichliche Analysen. Politik (Mit einer Einleitung von E.baumgarten, (Hrsg.) Johannes Winkelmann), Alfred Kröner Verlag. 5 Aufl., Stuttgart.

WEBET, Max.2006: Wirtschaft ind Gesellschaft, Volmedia.

WELCH, Stephan. 1987: Issues in the Study of Political Culture – British Journal of Political Science. 17(4).

WELCH, Stephan.1993: The Concept of Political Culture, New York: St. Martin Press

WILSON, R.W. 1992: Comparative Ideologies: Rethinking Political Culture, Cambridge Univ. Press

ZAKARIA, Fareed. 1997: The rise of Illiberal Democracy, in: Foreign Affairs, Nov./Dec.: 22–43.

Appendix

1. Elections and Political Situation

Results of Bulgarian latest (25 June 2005) parliamentary elections: It was expected that the Coalition for Bulgaria, led by the Bulgarian Socialist Party (BSP), will win the elections and indeed it became the biggest political group with 82 seats in the new Parliament.

The sudden appearance and popularity of a new political player, the nationalist movement »Attack«, with 22 seats, has taken some of the hardcore voters of all traditional parties.

The predominantly Turkish Movement for Rights and Freedoms (MRF) almost doubled its support and obtained 33 parliamentary seats.

The rightist Union of Democratic Forces (UDF) led by former first diplomat Nadezda Mihaylova again lost the elections ending up with 20 members of parliament, while former PM Ivan Kostov, who split from the UDF to create a new party – Democrats for Strong Bulgaria (DSB), received 17 MPs.

In the end, 7 political groups entered the Parliament, which is a pluralism record in this country, as it started on its democratic reforms in 1989.

These were the sixth parliamentary elections since the end of Communism and the second in a row to be called on a regular basis, after the four–year term of the government. Turnout was 55,8%, a new lowest level since the start of the transition period.

Party/Coalition	% of votes	seats
Coalition for Bulgaria	34,2	82
National Movement Simeon II	21,9	52
Movement for Rights and Freedoms	13,7	33
National Movement Attack	9,0	22
United Democratic Forces	8,4	20
Democrats for Strong Bulgaria	7,0	17
Bulgarian People's Union	5,7	14
TOTAL	100%	240

– Coalition for Bulgaria incorporates Bulgarian Socialist Party, Party of Bulgarian Social Democrats, Political Movement Social Democrats, Bulgarian Agrarian People's Union »Aleksander Stambolijski«, Civil Union »Roma«, Movement for Social Humanism, Green Party of Bulgaria, Bulgarian Communist Party

– Coalition Union Attack consists of National Movement for the Salvation of the Fatherland, Bulgarian National Patriotic Party, Union of Patriotic Forces and Militaries of the Defense Reserve

– Union of Democratic Forces includes Union of Democratic Forces, Democratic party, Bulgarian Agrarian People's Union, National Democratic Party, George's Day Movement, BZNS National Union, Movement for an equal public model

– Bulgarian People's Union is a coalition of Bulgarian Agrarian People's Union – People's Union, Internal Macedonian Revolutionary Organization, and Union of Free Democrats

Source: Bulgaria Update, 05 May 2006

2. Corruption and Organized Crime

Corruption and organized crime, coupled with ineffective judicial system, counted as major stumbling blocks on the way of Bulgaria joining the European Union.

According to a report of the Coalition 2000 – an initiative of Bulgarian non–governmental organizations aimed at combating corruption – customs officers, police officers, and judges are the most corrupt professions in Bulgaria. Prosecutors, lawyers, ministers, and tax officers were also among those professions listed.

According to a March 2006 report by the independent Center for the Study of Democracy (CSD) in Bulgaria, while in the 1990s corruption occurred mainly in misappropriation of funds and bribes, associated with privatization deals, the current cases are found in public tender management, EU fund distribution and VAT fraud.

The corruption perception index of Transparency International places the country far below other European countries, on 55th place.

Despite the persistent European criticism on organized crime in Bulgaria, both governmental and independent sources allow more positive notes. Street criminality, for example, was below the EU average in 2004.

Source; Bulgaria Update, 05 May 2006

3. Economic Stand and Perspectives

Despite the progress made in the run up to the accession to the EC, high unemployment and a relatively low standard of living continue to face Bulgarians in daily life.

According the Human Development Index of the United Nations Bulgaria takes position 55, out of 177. This index measures achievements in terms of life expectancy, educational attainment and adjusted real income.

Despite continuing economic hardships, Bulgaria has a promising financial stability and averages 4% economic growth since 2000.

The country has been able to attract serious foreign direct investments as well.

Source: Bulgaria update, 05.May 2006

4. The Bulgarian Transition in brief:

The wave of East European democratization caught Bulgaria fully in 1990; as Zhelyu Zhelev of the United Democratic Front was named the first post war non–communist prime minister.

The 1990s saw constant public unrest and a series of shaky coalition governments and grave economic crises, as Bulgaria attempted to establish a free–enterprise system.

In 2000 Simeon Saxe–Coburg–Gotha, son of Boris III returned to Bulgaria and established a new party, which won the parliamentary elections of 2001. Simeon, who formed a broad political coalition, was named prime minister, a position he retained until August 2005.

In the early 2000s, the government underwent a series of no–confidence crises and continued economic uncertainty, but economic growth resumed, and foreign relations generally improved.

Bulgaria joined the North Atlantic Treaty Organization (NATO) in 2004.

Bulgaria concluded negotiations for membership in the European Union (EU) in 2004 and its parliament ratified the accession treaty in 2005

The prospect of entry into the EU in 2007 stimulated a variety of domestic reforms and stabilized a broad coalition government that included both of Bulgaria's largest parties under Prime Minister Sergey Stanishev.

New legislation in 2005 and 2006 focused on reforming the judiciary and reducing the crime rate.

Source: Library of Congress – Federal Research Division
Country Profile: Bulgaria, October 2006

5. Major Political Parties in Bulgaria

Social Democratic Parties Bulgarian Socialist Party (BSP) Party leader: Sergey Stanishev. Website: www.bsp.bg

The BSP is the leading governmental party. It is a full member of the Socialist International and of the Party of European Socialists. BSP is the former leading Bulgarian Communist Party, which emerged in 1919 from the Bulgarian Social Democratic Party (founded in 1891). In 2000 this party made a significant break with the past by changing its former negative attitude towards NATO membership into a positive stance. Active NATO relations should, however, not lead to deterioration of bilateral relations with any third country, Russia included. The BSP possesses well–organized party–structures inherited from the past. The party has 230.000 members. Despite being the main governmental party, the BSP is still struggling to regain trust from the voters after the unsuccessful period in government in the 90's.

Bulgarian Social Democratic Party (BSDP) Petar Agov www.bsdp.info

BSDP was founded in 1891 and re–established in 1989. For the 1997 elections it joined the United Democratic Forces. At its party congress in September 1997 a sharp conflict arose between a group that wished even closer cooperation with the UDF, and others who demanded a distinct social democratic line. The latter emerged dominant. Another split–off from the party (in 1997), led by Jordan Nihrizov won a court case about the legal right to the name BSDP. This BSDP, led by Nihrizov joined the UDF coalition. The BSDP claims to have 15,000 members, but an estimate of 5,000 seems more accurate. The new Bulgarian constitution was – for a large part – drawn up along lines set by former party–leader Petar Dertliev. On economic issues the party favors mass privatization and protection of people's small savings.

United Labour Block (ULB) Party leader: Krastyu Petkov.

KNSB trade union chairman Krastyu Petkov formed the United Labour Block, after his last term as chairman ended in 1997, just after the elections of that year. It presented itself as a bridge builder between the other left wing forces in the country. Officially it is not a union party, but thanks to Petkov's leadership its main constituency is union members. The ULB is part of the leftist Coalition for Bulgaria.

Other Political Parties National Movement Simeon II (NMSII) Party leader: Simeon Saxe–Coburg Gotha. Website: www.ndsv.bg

The NMSII has its roots in 2001 but did not register as a party until the 6th of April 2002. The movement was founded by former King Simeon II and proposed to bring about change to Bulgaria's economic and political outlook »within 800 days. In the 2001 elections it won out of nowhere and took the lead in forming a new government. Simeon Saxe–Coburg, the former king in exile who lived almost his whole life in Spain, became the prime minister of Bulgaria. The popularity of the party quickly declined, which can be mainly attributed to the government's failure to meet unrealistic expectations and lack of good quality ministers, as well as new divisions within the party itself. In the parliamentary elections of April 2005 it ended up second after the Coalition for Bulgaria, thereby becoming the first biggest single political party after the elections, gathering 21, 9%. NMSII has profiled as a liberal party and became a member of the European Liberal Democrat Party (ELDR) and of the Liberal International (LI). Bulgaria became a member of NATO and signed Accession Treaty with the EU during the NMSII rule.

Union of Democratic Forces (UDF) Party leader: Petar Stoyanov www.sds.bg

UDF was created at the time the communist regime collapsed (1989) as a platform movement uniting 15 different formerly dissident political groups. The UDF was not transformed into a single party until February 1997. Ideologically, the party is Christian democrat and is also an associated member of the European People's Party (EPP). The UDF participated in the 2005 elections in a coalition with two other rightist formations – Gergyovden and Democratic Party. Together, they got 8,4% of the vote. After the big loss in the parliamentary elections of June 2005, former president Petar Stoyanov (1997 – 2001) nominated himself for party chairman and was elected during the UDD conference of 30 September 2005.

Democrats for Strong Bulgaria (DSB) Party leader: Ivan Kostov www.dsb.bg

After Ivan Kostov and his followers left the Union of Democratic Forces, the group around him established a new right–wing party named Democrats for Strong Bulgaria, in May 2004. Centered on its leader it had 28 members in parliament until 2005, when they received 17 MPs. At the constituent meeting Kostov stressed upon the desire to have a country with strong democracy, competent state institutions, a stable government and wealthy and open–minded society. Over 1.300 people were registered as party founders. Even more than the UDF, the DSB focuses on anti–communism. Its main opponents are the BSP and the ruling coalition parties NMSII and MRF.

Union of Free Democrats (SSD) Party leader: Stefan Sofianski Website: www.ssd.bg

SSD is one of the smaller rightist parties in Bulgaria. It was founded in December 2001 as a split off of the Union of Democratic Forces. Its main goals are reaching economic prosperity, political stability, joining the EU and NATO. Its founder Stefan Sofiyanski, was a prime minister in 1997 in the interim government. The SSD picked up 6 percent of the seats in the 2003 local elections. For the 2005 elections, it runs in a coalition with People's Union and VMRO.

Bulgarian Agrarian National Union – People's Union (PU) Party leader: Anastasia Mozer

The BANU has its roots in 1899. Since then it has been in government as well as been banned and splits occurred. At the end of 1989 different wings of the union were restored, however it took until 1992 to unite the different agrarian wings under the name of BANU. Since 1992, chair of the party has been Mrs. Anastasia Mozer. Her leadership was rejected by the wing of Mr. Petko Iliev, which took the name. Mrs. Mozer's wing had to register the party with a new name – Bulgarian Agrarian National Union – People's Union. Both agrarian wings took part in the center–right coalition United Democratic Forces (UDF). In March 2004 the PU officially split from the UDF and registered a new parliamentary group together with the small Democratic Party.

Movement for Rights and Freedoms (DPS) Party–leader: Ahmed Dogan Website: www.dps.bg

MRF was founded shortly after the communist regime fell in 1989. The party is predominantly of Ethnic Turks but it tries to attract Bulgarian ethnic votes as well. The MRF had become the pivot on which the Berov–cabinet hinged and indispensable for a workable government in the early 90's. In 1992 it switched from the UDF to the BSP as informal coalition partner. For the 2001 parliamentary elections MRF formed a coalition with two small parties, the Liberal Union and Euroroma. The MRF did unexpectedly well, receiving 7,45 percent of the votes. The party was together with the Simeon II National Movement in government. It was not until 2005 however that the MRF showed its power. With 13,7%, it became the third party in parliament. It was because of the MRF that a cabinet could be formed – a tripartite coalition of BSP, NMSII and MRF.

Internal Macedonian Revolutionary Organization (VMRO) Party leader: Krasimir Karakachanov Website: www.vmro.bg

The VMRO is the descendant of an anti–Ottoman group founded in 1893, and formed part of the UDF until 1999. The party is small, though it has strong support in a few regions and a good position in local government. VMRO is a nationalistic party that focuses on »national interest«, issues such as the integrity of the Bulgarian state, the rights of Bulgarian minorities abroad. etc, in the 2005 elections, it participated in a coalition with People's Union and the Union of Free Democrats. The coalition received 13 seats, of which 5 for the VMRO.

Source: Bulgaria Update 05 May 2006

6. Bulgarian Presidential Election 2006

– The 2006 presidential election was held on 22 Oct.2006. The run off took place on 29 Oct.2006 as the electoral campaign spanned between 19 Sept. –20 Oct. At the election Georgi Parvanov won his second term as President of Bulgaria.

– Some of the right–wing parties were disunited at the time but still chose to support a common candidate Nedelcho Beronov.

– In the first round, incumbent Georgi Parvanov came in first with 64% of the vote, ahead of ultra nationalist leader Volen Siderov with 21,5% whom he had to face in a runoff, as Bulgarian law requires a turnout of 50% for a president to be elected in the first round. The voter turnout in the first round was 42.51%

The second round saw a decisive Parvanov victory of around 75.9% as opposed to Siderov's 24.1%, Thus Parvanov became the first person to be democratically re–elected as President of Bulgaria. The turnout was 41.21%.

Results
First round

#	President	Vice President	Nominated by	Number of votes	Per cent
1	Nedelcho Beronov	Yuiana Nikolova	Initiative committee	271,078	9.753%
2	Gen.Lyben Petrov	Neli Topalova	Initiative committee	13,854	0.498%
3	Georgi Parvanov	Gen.Angel Marin	**Initiative committee**	**1,780,119**	**64.047%**
4	Grigor Velev	Yordan Mutafchiev	Union of Bulgarian Nationalists »Whole Bulgaria«	19,857	0.714%
5	Petar Beron	Stela Bankova	Initiative committee	21,812	0.785%
6	Volen Siderov	Pavel Shopov	Attack	**597,175**	**21.486%**
7	Georgi Markov	Maria Ivanova	Order, Lawfulness, Justice	75,478	2.716%

Second round

	President	Vice President	Nominated by	Number of votes	Per cent
8	Georgi Parvanov	Gen.Angel Marin	**Initiative committee**	**2,050,488**	**75.948%**
9	Volen Siderov	Pavel Shopov	Attack	649,387	24.052%

Source: Centralna ibiratelna komisija, (Numbers indicate number of registered voting bulletins of candidates)

7. First European Parliament elections 2007

On May 20, 2007 the first European Parliamentary elections took lace in Bulgaria. The country has now 18 MEPs (previously appointed by the Bulgarian national parliament). The top two parties all scored 5 seats each: Citizens for European Development of Bulgaria and European Socialist Platform, followed by the Movement of Rights and Freedoms with four, Ataka with three and National Movement Simeon II (NDSV) with one.

It was considered likely that the results of the elections would cause a major political crisis in Bulgaria, due to the expected weak results of the National Movement Simeon II. Controversially, the eligible voters were limited to citizens of Bulgaria and the EU within their permanent and current address within the Union and minimum of 60 days of the last three months before the elections spent within its borders. Because of this requirement, 232,800 people were rendered ineligible to vote, 185, 000 of which were Turkish Bulgarian immigrants to Turkey.

According the official results announced on May 21, 2007 by the Central Electoral Commission, the winner of the elections was Citizens for European Development of Bulgaria, followed by a small margin by the Bulgarian Socialist Party and the Movements for Rights and Freedoms, with distance between the third and the first being less than 1,5%. The voter turnout was 298,6 %.

Summary of the 20 May 2007 Bulgarian delegation in the European Parliament election results

Parties	**EP Party**	**Votes**	**%**	**Seats**	+/–
Citizens for European Development of Bulgaria	EPP	420,001	21.68%	5	
European Socialist Platform	PESS	414,786	21.41%	5	
Movement for Rights and Freedoms	ELDR	392,650	20.26%	4	
National Union Attack	ITS	275,237	14.20%	3	
National Movement Simeon II	ELDR	121,398	6.27%	1	
Union of Democratic Forces	EPP	91,871	4.74%	0	
Democrats for Strong Bulgaria	EPP	84,350	4.35%	0	
Source: Izbori2007.eu					

8. IDEA Framework of comparative study of Stand of Democracies *

(List of Search Questions)

1. Citizenship, Law and Rights

1.1 Nationhood and citizenship

Overarching question: Is there public agreement on a common citizenship without discrimination?

How inclusive is the political nation and state citizenship of all who live within the territory?
How far are cultural differences acknowledged, and how well are minorities protected?
How much consensus is there on state boundaries and constitutional arrangements?
How far do constitutional and political arrangements enable major societal divisions to be moderated or reconciled?
How impartial and inclusive are the procedures for amending the constitution?
What measures, if any, are being taken to remedy publicly identified problems in this field, and what degree of political priority and public support do they have?

1.2 The rule of law and access to justice

Overarching question: Are state and society consistently subject to the law?

How far is the rule of law operative throughout the territory?
To what extent are all public officials subject to the rule of law and to transparent rules in the performance of their functions?
How independent are the courts and the judiciary from the executive, and how free are they from all kinds of interference?
How equal and secure is the access of citizens to justice, to due process and to redress in the event of misadministration?
How far do the criminal justice and penal systems observe due rules of impartial and equitable treatment in their operations?
How much confidence do people have in the legal system to deliver fair and effective justice?

What measures, if any, are being taken to remedy publicly identified problems in this field, and what degree of political priority and public support do they have?

1.3 Civil and political rights

Overarching question: Are civil and political rights equally guaranteed for all?

How free are all people from physical violation of their person, and from fear of it?

How effective and equal is the protection of the freedoms of movement, expression, association and assembly?

How secure is the freedom for all to practice their own religion, language or culture?

How free from harassment and intimidation are individuals and groups working to improve human rights?

What measures, if any, are being taken to remedy publicly identified problems in this field, and what degree of political priority and public support do they have?

1.4 Economic and social rights

Overarching question: Are economic and social rights equally guaranteed for all?

How far is access to work or social security available to all, without discrimination?

How effectively are the basic necessities of life guaranteed, including adequate food, shelter and clean water?

To what extent is the health of the population protected, in all spheres and stages of life?

How extensive and inclusive is the right to education, including education in the rights and responsibilities of citizenship?

How free are trade unions and other work–related associations to organize and represent their members' interests?

How rigorous and transparent are the rules on corporate governance, and how effectively are corporations regulated in the public interest?

What measures, if any, are being taken to remedy publicly identified problems in this field, and what degree of political priority and public support do they have?

2. Representative and Accountable Government

2.1 Free and Fair elections

Overarching question: Do elections give the people control over governments and their policies?

How far is appointment to governmental and legislative office determined by popular competitive election, and how frequently do elections lead to change in the governing parties or personnel?

How inclusive and accessible for all citizens are the registration and voting procedures, how independent are they of government and party control, and how free from intimidation and abuse?

How fair are the procedures for the registration of candidates and parties, and how far is there fair access for them to the media and other means of communication with the voters?

How effective a range of choice does the electoral and party system allow the voters, how equally do their votes count, and how closely does the composition of the legislature and the selection of the executive reflect the choices they make?

How far does the legislature reflect the social composition of the electorate?

What proportion of the electorate votes, and how far are the election results accepted by all political forces in the country and outside?

What measures, if any, are being taken to remedy publicly identified problems in this field, and what degree of political priority and public support do they have?

2.2 Democratic role of political parties

Overarching question: Does the party system assist the working of democracy?

How freely are parties able to form and recruit members, engage with the public and campaign for office?

How effective is the party system in forming and sustaining governments in office?

How free are opposition or non–governing parties to organize within the legislature, and how effectively do they contribute to government accountability?

How fair and effective are the rules governing party discipline in the legislature?

How far are party's effective membership organizations, and how far are members able to influence party policy and candidate selection?

How far does the system of party financing prevent the subordination of parties to special interests?

To what extent do parties cross ethnic, religious and linguistic divisions?

What measures, if any, are being taken to remedy publicly identified problems in this field, and what degree of political priority and public support do they have?

2.3 Government effectiveness and accountability

Overarching question: Is government accountable to the people and their representatives?

How far is the elected government able to influence or control those matters that are important to the lives of its people, and how well is it informed, organized and resourced to do so?

How much public confidence is there in the effectiveness of government and its political leadership?

How effective and open to scrutiny is the control exercised by elected leaders and their ministers over their administrative staff and other executive agencies?

How extensive and effective are the powers of the legislature to initiate, scrutinize and amend legislation?

How extensive and effective are the powers of the legislature to scrutinize the executive and hold it to account?

How rigorous are the procedures for approval and supervision of taxation and public expenditure?

How comprehensive and effective is legislation giving citizens the right of access to government information?

What measures, if any, are being taken to remedy publicly identified problems in this field, and what degree of political priority and public support do they have?

2.4 Civilian control of the military and police

Overarching question: Are the military and police forces under civilian control?

How effective is civilian control over the armed forces, and how free is political life from military involvement?

How publicly accountable are the police and security services for their activities?

How far does the composition of the army, police and security services reflect the social composition of society at large?

How free is the country from the operation of paramilitary units, private armies, and warlordism and criminal mafias?

What measures, if any, are being taken to remedy publicly identified problems in this field, and what degree of political priority and public support do they have?

2.5 Minimizing corruption

Overarching question: Are public officials free from corruption?

How effective is the separation of public office from the personal business and family interests of office holders?

How effective are the arrangements for protecting office holders and the public from involvement in bribery?

How far do the rules and procedures for financing elections, candidates and elected representatives prevent their subordination to sectional interests?

How far is the influence of powerful corporations and business interests over public policy kept in check, and how free are they from involvement in corruption, including overseas?

How much confidence do people have that public officials and public services are free from corruption?

What measures, if any, are being taken to remedy publicly identified problems in this field, and what degree of political priority and public support do they have?

3. Civil society and popular participation

3.1 The media in a democratic society

Overarching question: Do the media operate in a way that sustains democratic values?

How independent are the media from government, how pluralistic is their ownership, and how free are they from subordination to foreign governments or multinational companies?

How representative are the media of different opinions and how accessible are they to different sections of society?

How effective are the media and other independent bodies in investigating government and powerful corporations?

How free are journalists from restrictive laws, harassment and intimidation?

How free are private citizens from intrusion and harassment by the media?

What measures, if any, are being taken to remedy publicly identified problems in this field, and what degree of political priority and public support do they have?

3.2 Political participation

Overarching question: Is there full citizen participation in public life?

How extensive is the range of voluntary associations, citizen groups, social movements etc. and how independent are they from government?

How extensive is citizen participation in voluntary associations and self–management organizations, and in other voluntary public activity?

How far do women participate in political life and public office at all levels?

How equal is access for all social groups to public office, and how fairly are they represented within it?

What measures, if any, are being taken to remedy publicly identified problems in this field, and what degree of political priority and public support do they have?

3.3 Government responsiveness

Overarching question: Is government responsive to the concerns of its citizens?

How open and systematic are the procedures for public consultation on government policy and legislation, and how equal is the access for relevant interests to government?

How accessible are elected representatives to their constituents?

How accessible and reliable are public services for those who need them, and how systematic is consultation with users over service delivery?

How much confidence do people have in the ability of government to solve the main problems confronting society, and in their own ability to influence it?

What measures, if any, are being taken to remedy publicly identified problems in this field, and what degree of political priority and public support do they have?

3.4 Decentralization

Overarching question: Are decisions taken at the level of government, which is most appropriate for the people affected?

How independent are the sub–central tiers of government from the center, and how far do they have the powers and resources to carry out their responsibilities?

How far are these levels of government subject to free and fair electoral authorization, and to the criteria of openness, accountability and responsiveness in their operation?

How extensive is the co–operation of government at the most local level with relevant partners, associations and communities in the formation and implementation of policy, and in service provision?

What measures, if any, are being taken to remedy publicly identified problems in this field, and what degree of priority and public support do they have?

4. Democracy Beyond the State

4.1 International dimensions of democracy

Overarching question: Are the country's external relations conducted in accordance with democratic norms, and is it itself free from external subordination?

How free is the governance of the country from subordination to external agencies, economic, cultural or political?

How far are government relations with international organizations based on principles of partnership and transparency?

How far does the government support UN human rights treaties and respect international law?

How far does the government respect its international obligations in its treatment of refugees and asylum seekers, and how free from arbitrary discrimination is its immigration policy?

How consistent is the government in its support for human rights and democracy abroad?

What measures, if any, are being taken to remedy publicly identified problems in this field, and what degree of political priority and public support do they have?

* Source, IDEA Stand of Democracy, University of Essex, 2006

9. Milestones of Bulgarian accession in EC:

– Bulgaria (along with Romania) is part of the second stage of the EU's fifth enlargement. It has joined the union on January 1, 2007.

– This date was set at the Thessalonica Summit in 2003 and confirmed at Brussels on June 18, 2004.

– The country reports of October 2004 also affirmed the date of accession. Bulgaria (and Romania) signed their Treaty of Accession on April 25, 2005 at Luxembourg Neumunster Abbey.

– Within the framework of integration meetings held between the EU member states and Bulgaria, an ›Association Committee‹ was held on 22 June 2004. It confirmed overall good progress for the preparation of accession.

– It highlighted however the need for further reform of Bulgaria's judicial structures, as well more effective fight against corruption and organized crime.

– The 26 September 2006 of the European Commission confirmed the date of accession, announcing that Bulgaria (and Romania) would meet no direct restrictions. Progress in the above mentioned areas however would be strictly monitored.

– Bulgaria entered the EU as full member on Jan.1, 2007.

– First European Parliament elections took place on May 20, 2007.

Index